Literary Lives

Founding Editor: **Richard Dutton**, Professor of English, Lancaster University

This series offers stimulating accounts of the literary careers of the most admired and influential English-language authors. Volumes follow the outline of the writers' working lives, not in the spirit of traditional biography, but aiming to trace the professional, publishing and social contexts which shaped their writing.

Cedric C. Brown JOHN MILTON	*Tony Sharpe* WALLACE STEVENS
Peter Davison GEORGE ORWELL	*Joseph McMinn* JONATHAN SWIFT
Linda Wagner-Martin SYLVIA PLATH	*Leonée Ormond* ALFRED TENNYSON
Felicity Rosslyn ALEXANDER POPE	*Peter Shillingsburg* WILLIAM MAKEPEACE THACKERAY
Ira B. Nadel EZRA POUND	*David Wykes* EVELYN WAUGH
Richard Dutton WILLIAM SHAKESPEARE	*Caroline Franklin* MARY WOLLSTONECRAFT
John Williams MARY SHELLEY	*John Mepham* VIRGINIA WOOLF
Michael O'Neill PERCY BYSSHE SHELLEY	*John Williams* WILLIAM WORDSWORTH
Gary Waller EDMUND SPENSER	*Alasdair D. F. Macrae* W. B. YEATS

Literary Lives
Series Standing Order ISBN 0–333–71486–5 hardcover
Series Standing Order ISBN 0–333–80334–5 paperback
(outside North America only)

You can receive future titles in this series as they are published by placing a standing order. Please contact your bookseller or, in case of difficulty, write to us at the address below with your name and address, the title of the series and one of the ISBNs quoted above.

Customer Services Department, Macmillan Distribution Ltd, Houndmills, Basingstoke, Hampshire RG21 6XS, England

Portraits of

Willm Blake

at the ages of 28 & 69 years.

Born November 20th 1757.   Died August 12. 1827

Ætat. 69.

William Blake: A Literary Life

John Beer

First published in 2005 by
PALGRAVE MACMILLAN
Houndmills, Basingstoke, Hampshire RG21 6XS and
175 Fifth Avenue, New York, N.Y. 10010
Companies and representatives throughout the world.

PALGRAVE MACMILLAN is the global academic imprint of the Palgrave Macmillan division of St. Martin's Press, LLC and of Palgrave Macmillan Ltd. Macmillan® is a registered trademark in the United States, United Kingdom and other countries. Palgrave is a registered trademark in the European Union and other countries.

ISBN-13: 978–1–4039–3954–8
ISBN-10: 1–4039–3954–3

This book is printed on paper suitable for recycling and made from fully managed and sustained forest sources.

A catalogue record for this book is available from the British Library.

Library of Congress Cataloging-in-Publication Data

Beer, John B.
    William Blake : a literary life / John Beer.
        p. cm.
    Includes bibliographical references and index.
    ISBN 1–4039–3954–3 (cloth)
        1. Blake, William, 1757–1827. 2. Poets, English – 18th century –
    Biography. 3. Poets, English – 19th century – Biography. 4. Artists – Great
    Britain – Biography. I. Title.

PR4146.B34 2005
821'.7—dc22   2005043355
[B]

10   9   8   7   6   5   4
14 13 12 11 10 09 08 07 06

Printed and bound in Great Britain by
Antony Rowe Ltd, Chippenham and Eastbourne

Contents

List of Figures

Preface

Much recent work on Blake has been devoted to examination of the techniques of his visual art, especially those in which he believed himself innovative. Readers with an interest in this side of his work will find it profitable to turn to recent works such as Michael Phillips's *William Blake: The Creation of the Songs*, Joseph Viscomi's *Blake and the Art of the Book* and Peter Ackroyd's *Blake*, and (especially for the purposes of form and iconography) to consider the work of scholars such as Anne Mellor and W. J. T. Mitchell. They should also, if possible, visit the room at Tate Britain devoted to him, where a generous collection of his work is accompanied by explanations of his use of materials and related exhibits. My chief concern here is with Blake's literary life – which is of course by no means irrelevant to his visual designs, since his art nearly always involved, whether explicitly or not, a verbal text of some kind. He was above all a *literary* artist; in other words, which helps to explain why historians of art sometimes find it difficult to fit him into categories that are based on the evolution of changing designs and techniques.

In transcribing quotations from Blake's writing, I have tended to accept the text of the *Complete Poetry and Prose*, edited by D. V. Erdman, with commentary by H. Bloom, as produced in the revised edition (Berkeley and Los Angeles, 1982) (E) and, in an electronic edition, by Morris Eaves, Robert Essick and Joseph Viscomi (Charlottesville, Virginia, 2001). These follow Blake's original punctuation. For the convenience of some English readers, however, I also refer to Keynes's 1957 Nonesuch edition of the *Complete Writings* (K) which was taken over for the Oxford Standard Authors series (1966–), the pagination remaining the same. Keynes normally changed the punctuation where he thought an improvement in clarity would result.

Sources for many of the biographical statements will be found in the magisterial works of G. E. Bentley, Jr: *Blake Records* (Oxford, 1969), the *Supplement* to this (Oxford, 1988) and his biography of Blake, *The Stranger from Paradise* (New Haven and London, 2001). The task of the biographer of Blake in gaining reliable materials has been immeasurably lightened in recent years by his work in assembling all the known records of his life and production, followed by the additional account in his comprehensive biography.

I owe a particular recent debt also to David Worrall, who told me about the recent work by Keri Davies and M. K. Schuchard on Blake's Moravian connections, and to Dr Davies himself, who generously sent me a copy of his thesis to read in advance of the publication in 2004 of their article. In addition, the recent work of Robert W. Rix on Blake's interest in animal magnetism and similar matters has provided some valuable further information.

I must warmly thank the staff of the Yale Center for British Art who have been very helpful in enabling me to acquire copies of the illustrations needed. I should also express renewed gratitude to scholars such as the late Sir Geoffrey Keynes, the late Edward Thompson, the late David Erdman, Morton Paley and Michael Phillips, who have all given me considerable assistance and encouragement in my Blake studies over the years.

J. B. B.

Abbreviations

Place of publication is London unless otherwise indicated.

BQ   *Blake: An Illustrated Quarterly* (formerly *Blake Newsletter*) (Albuquerque, New Mexico)

BR   G. E. Bentley, Jr, ed., *Blake Records* (Oxford, 1969)

BRS   *Supplement* to the above (Oxford, 1988)

BSP   G. E. Bentley Jr, *The Stranger from Paradise: A Biography of William Blake* (New Haven and London, 2001)

CL   Coleridge, *Collected Letters*, ed. E. L. Griggs (6 vols., Oxford, 1956–71)

E   *The Poetry and Prose of William Blake* ed. D. V. Erdman and H. Bloom with commentary by H. Bloom (1965) following Blake's original punctuation. Newly revised edition including complete letters, University of California Press, Berkeley and Los Angeles, 1982

G   (1863) Alexander Gilchrist, *Life of William Blake, 'Pictor Ignotus'* (London and Cambridge, 1863)

G   (1942) Alexander Gilchrist, *Life of William Blake*, ed. Ruthven Todd (London and New York, 1942)

HW   *The Complete Works of William Hazlitt*, ed. P. P. Howe (21 vols., 1930–4)

K   Blake, *Complete Writings*, with variant readings. ed. G. Keynes, 1957; reprinted with additions and corrections in the Oxford Standard Authors series (Oxford, 1966)

LL   (Marrs) Edwin J. Marrs, Jr, *The Letters of Charles and Mary Lamb 1796–1817* (all published) (3 vols., Ithaca and London, 1975–8)

PTE   Morton D. Paley, *The Traveller in the Evening: the Last Works of William Blake* (Oxford, 2003)

TWB   E. P. Thompson, *Witness against the Beast: William Blake and the Moral Law* (New York, 1974)

W Prel (1799)   The 1799 text in *The Prelude: 1799, 1805, 1850*, ed. Wordsworth, Abrams and Gill (New York, 1979)

W Prel (1805)   The 1805 text in *The Prelude: 1799, 1805, 1850* above.

WPW   Wordsworth, *Poetical Works*, ed. Ernest de Selincourt and Helen Darbishire (5 vols., Oxford, 1940–9)

1
Rescuing the Human Spirit

During the late eighteenth century signs of an intellectual disturbance began to show themselves in English culture, signified at first by little more than a few tremors, experienced within what was otherwise a firmly stable edifice established by exercise of logical reasoning. The work of Isaac Newton had been seen as having set the design of the universe into a mathematically ascertainable pattern, while John Locke had endeavoured to follow this up by seeking an equivalent ordering for the human mind, built up by organizing the sense-impressions with which the external world provided it so as to match Newton's arrangement.

Within this achieved security two areas of tension and questioning had come to be recognized – even though they offered no immediately threatening challenge. The first was the need to reconcile this new world of logical and scientific reasoning with the authority of the Bible. Since the chronology of the Old Testament had not yet been seriously challenged, even if any historical record concerning humanity's origins seemed lost in the impenetrable mists of the past, it was a rational course to continue receiving the biblical narrative as a sufficiently acceptable account of the emergence of human beings and their moral nature.

Secondly, it seemed necessary to extend Locke's account of the mind by attending to the full nature of the sensibility involved. For some human beings, it seemed, the orderings of reason did not offer a sufficient account of the matter; indeed, the idea that nothing existed beyond them could well give individuals a sense of their own failings and lead to states of depression: while at one end of the behavioural spectrum this might prompt a rejection of reason and even a lapse into insanity, those less afflicted by the depressing implications of the world presented might still feel a need to supplement the world of reasoning

1

by invoking areas of sensibility beyond – looking particularly to modes of feeling. Hence the growing tendency to propitiate the tender affections, for example, whether through concentration on loving human relationships or through bypassing them and devoting one's interest to animals.

The kinds of problem that might arise from this settlement included those that sprang from a need to exercise the restraints demanded by religious belief. The difficulties this could raise for an intelligent writer can be seen by looking at the careers of men such as Samuel Johnson and William Cowper. Johnson always gives the sense of a man in whom reason – modified as necessary by what he could claim to be 'common sense' – acted as a constant guide. Yet having been brought up in what at the time was accepted as orthodox Christian faith, he could suffer acute anxiety at his own breaches of the moral code and fear the verdict of a Last Judgment in which his own career would be weighed and found to be wanting, For the most part he could subdue such fears beneath the demands of everyday social life, but Boswell's *Life* displays the way in which they could emerge from time to time, escaping his rational guard, as when he argued against Dr Adams that where individuals were concerned the infinite goodness of God had to be limited:

> JOHNSON: … and as I cannot be sure that I have fulfilled the conditions on which salvation is granted, I am afraid I may be one of those who shall be damned. (looking dismally)
> DR ADAMS: What do you mean by damned!
> JOHNSON (passionately and loudly): Sent to Hell, Sir, and punished everlastingly.[1]

Johnson could fear the pains of judgment while still keeping his fears, however imperfectly, under the watchful guard of his rationality; but a more sensitive person might not be able to sustain such control. In the next generation, William Cowper allowed his religious hopes to be undermined by forceful figures such as John Newton until his reason itself gave way, leaving him for the last years of his life despairing and unhinged.

Three men in particular sensed the strains now being felt: William Wordsworth, Samuel Taylor Coleridge and William Blake – the last-named being perhaps the most ambitious of all. Wordsworth and Coleridge, in their different ways, saw it as their task to find a new way of recreating the Miltonic achievement for their time and take the English language further towards a contemporary epic mode. One could not proceed very far along that path, however, without discerning a greater need – formulated later by James Joyce as Stephen Dedalus's ambition to 'encounter ... the reality of experience and to forge in the smithy of my soul the uncreated conscience of my race'.[2] The growing requirement, in other words, was to engage with the circumstances of one's time at such a profound level as to recognize the internal contradictions of a culture in danger of becoming severed from its Christian roots. The melancholy examples of men such as Johnson and Cowper prompted young intellectuals to search for a better way of being human, while trying to safeguard the ultimate values which the traditional culture might be seen as defending.

William Blake, who was born on 28 November 1757 as the son of a successful London hosier, had an instinctively questioning and potentially rebellious nature which was to make him the most challenging of the three. The London in which he grew up was still far from assuming its later size, consisting still, basically, of two areas – Westminster and the City – which had recently been drawn together, and which stood in a developing relationship to various villages that were being drawn, however gradually, into its sway. The countryside was still close at hand, with agricultural labourers working in nearby fields and farms that could be reached easily from the town. When Blake walked through the streets, similarly, the buildings that surrounded him were still usually the first that had ever stood on the spots that they occupied, reinforcing their impression of permanence. Such factors help to nourish a sense of the century as a time of elegant furniture and well-proportioned buildings in the midst of highly cultivated landscapes, of moderation and decency in the home, but also of uproarious life and broad humour in the streets: the age of Thomas Gainsborough and Alexander Pope alongside that of William Hogarth and Henry Fielding.

Mention of the last two is a reminder that there was another side to the picture, however. Poverty was rife in town and country, with little to cushion the deprived against starvation and death, while disease could strike at all levels in society, cutting down the children of the well-to-do as well as of the poor. The law took its course, often oppressively and mercilessly, creating a sense of imprisonment that was widespread in the age, and beyond. When Jean-Jacques Rousseau began his famous work with the words 'Man is born free, and is everywhere in chains', the sentiment could be greeted by a sense of liberated relief. Yet the whole culture, particularly in a large city, seemed imbued with an opposite sense. Justice was summary and brutal in its punishments: its victims might find themselves either committed to the gallows at Tyburn, where their executions would be watched by enormous crowds, or flung into jail. Eighteenth-century prisons were notoriously grim: it was a time when even the modest reforms instigated by John Howard were only just beginning, and criminals could hope for little remission. The most notorious prison of the age, the Bastille in Paris, moved Cowper (a poet not given to very radical sentiments) to declare that there was not an Englishman who would not be delighted if it were to be torn down.

It was not only the harshness of physical incarceration that fostered this atmosphere of oppressive enclosure. Locke's view of the human mind, identified above as the dominating philosophy of the time, likened the understanding, as we shall see, to 'a closet, wholly shut from light, with only some little opening left'. The image of the mind itself was thus transformed into something dangerously resembling a prison cell. Guilt-ridden elements in the religious teaching of the time, similarly, would make any sensitive listener think of the body as a containing power, imprisoning the will, which tried to overcome its urges. Pope, a central spokesman for the contemporary intellectual view, could write:

> Most Souls, 'tis true, but peep out once an age,
> Dull sullen pris'ners in the body's cage ...[3]

Isaac Watts, the hymn-writer, similarly, could count it a blessing that

> Shortly this Prison of my Clay
> Must be dissolv'd and fall.[4]

Human beings could be haunted by a sense that they suffered from an imprisonment extending beyond the political and the physical. Years later, William Hazlitt, recalling the impact of Coleridge, could still say, 'my heart, shut up in the prison-house of this rude clay, has never found, nor will it ever find, a heart to speak to', going on to claim that Coleridge had at least liberated his understanding into expression.[5] The sense of oppression reflected the popular religious conception of a God who, while favouring those who kept his commandments, would not show pity to those who resolutely disobeyed them.

For Blake reflections such as this were intensified by an imaginative power that all too easily found fuel for nightmares. He once said that he could look at a knot in a piece of wood until he felt frightened by it.[6] Yet this capacity for fear was matched by an equally strong power of ecstatic vision that could transform the world into a place of joy and beauty.

He evidently enjoyed the power of eidetic vision, a condition in which human perception projects images so powerfully that the perceiver cannot easily tell the difference between them and images in the physical world. Although such a power is found from time to time among children, it seldom persists beyond the age of twelve; in Blake it lasted all his life. In old age he would often sketch visionary heads 'from the life', sitting at his table and looking at his subjects as if they were actually in the room.

Blake's strong visionary powers were further nurtured and chastened by his religious upbringing. Keri Davies's work on Blake's forebears has added to the richness of the picture by enquiring into the beliefs of his mother, originally Catherine Wright, and establishing that she came from Walkeringham, a small village in Nottinghamshire. Born in 1725, she married Thomas Armitage, a hosier, at the London Mayfair chapel on 14 December 1746, and with him was received into a Moravian congregation in Fetter Lane in London. They had a child, also named Thomas, who died in infancy. After her husband died of consumption in 1751 she left the congregation and six years later married James Blake, William's father, again in the Mayfair chapel. If James was not a fellow Moravian, the effect of the new marriage was to join her with someone of a different persuasion – though not necessarily a different denomination: the Moravians, as episcopal, were in communion with the Church of England, while not discouraged from regarding themselves as dissenters. Nancy Bogen's suggestion some years ago that the Blakes might have attended the Fetter Lane chapel while not ceasing to be Anglicans is thus fortified: 'It was possible to be at the time both of and not of the Anglican Church.'[7]

The members were notable for strong outpourings of emotion: John Wesley, an important adherent before he became one of the founders of Methodism, dated his conversion to an evening of 24 May 1738, when at a meeting among them in Aldersgate Street he felt his heart 'strangely warmed'. Such manifestations no doubt had some effect on William Blake also: the issue of a possible resemblance between Moravian hymns and some of Blake's early poetry was in fact raised some years ago.[8*] The indications are, however, that while his mother aligned herself with her first husband she found total commitment difficult. A letter from her to the brethren is extant (presumably following the example of Thomas, who had written similarly), in which she recorded that the Saviour had been pleased to make her 'Suck his wounds and hug the Cross more then Ever'. Her letter was equally open and honest, however ('I have very littell to say of my self for I am a pore crature and full of wants') and she confessed, 'I do not Love our Dear Saviour half enough' – trusting nevertheless that it would be his will to bring her 'among his hapy flock in closer connection'.[9] Her description of herself as a 'pore crature' is particularly interesting in view of her son's use of the similar locution in *An Island in the Moon*: 'to be sure, we are all poor creatures'.[10]

Her letter also bears witness to the strong part played by feeling in the Moravian hymns, as in their extravagant devotion to the detail of Christ's sufferings. It is hard to imagine that her son enjoyed their more mawkish expressions or that he took over much more than their general tone of humane feeling and philosophy of love: a devotion to Christ's blood and wounds is notably absent from his own work. Imagery in Moravian hymnody such as that of lion and lamb looks forward to his more sophisticated use of such child-like imagery in the *Songs of Innocence*, but his comments on phrases such as the 'lambkins and chickens of Christ' might well have been scathing.

It is hard to judge further the religious leanings of the Blake family in which William grew up, since we cannot even be sure of James Blake's attitude to Moravianism.[11*] There is some evidence that he joined the Baptists, at least for a time,[12*] while the children, including William, were for the most part baptized in the Grinling Gibbons font at the Anglican St. James's church in Piccadilly – in line again, perhaps, with the Moravian position that made it possible for their followers to be at one and the same time Anglican and 'dissenting'; but, as Bentley argues, the best way of describing Blake's own religious position as he grew up would probably be to speak rather of 'Enthusiasm', a term to be associated less with a particular religious persuasion than with a widely ranging religious attitude, and by no means untrue to a Moravianism which, as Davies points out, was less a sect than a spirituality. One advantage of considering him in this context is that 'enthusiasts' of the time could well feel themselves justified in culti-vating extremes which might lead others to label them as mad – a category which they felt they could accept with equanimity. In a letter of 26 November 1800, Blake wrote of himself as an 'Enthusiastic, hope-fostered visionary',[13] and shortly before this William Hayley said that he could not even write the word without recalling him.[14] A few years later he would write to a correspondent, 'Dear Sir, excuse my enthusi-asm or rather madness, for I am really drunk with intellectual vision whenever I take a pencil or graver into my hand, even as I used to be in my youth.'[15] To use the word of him avoids the need to identify his beliefs too narrowly.

His own early 'enthusiasms', meanwhile, were even more devoted to literature and philosophy than to art, his memory of them being summarized in a letter to Flaxman of 1800:

> Now my lot in the Heavens is this; Milton lovd me in childhood & shewd me his face
> Ezra came with Isaiah the Prophet, but Shakespeare in riper years gave me his hand
> Paracelsus & Behmen appeard to me. terrors appeard in the Heavens above.[16]

That Blake should have been drawn to Milton and Isaiah is hardly surprising, given the strong visionary element in the writings of both, but the prominence of Ezra at so early a point is more puzzling – until one recalls the stress in his writings on the return from captivity in Babylon and his efforts to set in motion the building of the Temple. Ezra's visions of the glory of the Lord and the building of the Heavenly City were destined to bear fruit in Blake's later work. From the first, however, such dreams – like those of the Old Testament prophets – alternated with others of fear and destruction. Indeed, the letter just quoted continues with an account of the major terrors that visited his youth:

> ... a mighty & awful change threatend the Earth.
> The American War began. All its dark horrors passed before my face
> Across the Atlantic to France. Then the French Revolution commenc'd in thick clouds,
> And My Angels have told me that seeing such visions I could not subsist on the Earth,
> But by my conjunction with Flaxman who knows to forgive Nervous Fear.[17]

Other imaginative terrors could beset such a sensitive child, If while attending dissenting chapel services he found himself confronted by the hymns and writings of Isaac Watts,[18*] the impression left on him would seem to have been deep. It has already been observed by scholars that some of the *Songs of Innocence and of Experience* read like satirical versions of, or answers to, verses in Watts's *Divine and Moral Songs for Children*, such as one that portrays the smugness of a child walking among poor people and invited to give thanks for his own superior condition.[19] What has been less noticed is the degree to which the God whom Watts paints in his hymns is a recognizable version of the 'Cruel Being' whom Blake grew to dislike. This was the God who had penetrated to a deep substratum of fear in men such as Johnson and Cowper. The fact that Watts was not a very subtle poet should not blind us to the impact that the descriptions of divine justice which he felt to be authorized by the orthodoxy of his time would have had on an imagination so vivid as Blake's. It is easy to picture him as a child turning Watts's pages and finding himself terrified by the moral universe conveyed there, a universe in which men who are misguided enough to pursue their pleasures heedlessly find themselves awaited by a day of judgment. One of the hymns begins:

> Adore and tremble, for our GOD
> Is a Consuming Fire.
> His jealous Eyes his Wrath inflame
> And raise his Vengeance higher.[20]

This figure, which takes literally the words of the Bible by assigning to him the human quality of jealousy, is a prototype of the figure of 'starry jealousy' that Blake was to depict as his controlling deity Urizen. Another of Watts's portraits comes even closer to the cold power stored in Blake's figure:

> God has a Thousand Terrors in his Name,
> A thousand Armies at Command,
> Waiting the signal of his Hand,
> And Magazines of Frost, and Magazines of Flame.
> Dress thee in Steel to meet his Wrath,
> His sharp Artillery of the North
> Shall pierce thee to the Soul, and shake thy mortal Frame.[21]

Imagery such as this, along with that of a God with 'Stores of Lightning', seems to have stayed in Blake's mind when he later depicted Urizen in *The Four Zoas* as basing himself in the north, or in *America* described how

> ... his jealous wings wav'd over the deep;
> Weeping in dismal howling woe he dark descended howling
> Around the smitten bands, clothed in tears & trembling
>   shudd'ring cold.
> His stored snows he poured forth, and his icy magazines
> He open'd on the deep, and on the Atlantic sea white shiv'ring
> Leprous his limbs, all over white, and hoary was his visage.[22]

In Blake's writing Urizen would be a cold deity, working through snow, ice and cold plagues. Fire and lightning, on the other hand, would be reserved for his opponent Orc, the uprising spirit of an energy that was not being allowed to find humanized form. There are other places in which Watts's images look forward to Blake's writings, particularly when he is betraying his horror at the workings of such a God:

> Long e'er the lofty Skies were spread,
> *Jehovah* fill'd his Throne;
> Or Adam form'd, or Angels made,
> The Maker liv'd alone[23]

Watts also painted a vivid picture of God making the human body, heart, brains, and lungs, in turn, and writing out his promise of redemption for men:

> ... His Hand has writ the sacred Word
>   With an immortal Pen.
>
> Engrav'd as in eternal Brass
>   The mighty Promise shines ...[24]

Translating this language into its visual imagery, Blake could have gained strong hints towards his depiction of Urizen as one who turned aside from the light, colour and harmony of Eternity to brood in solitude, 'A self-contemplating shadow, | In enormous labours occupied,' and who wrote out his laws with an 'iron pen'. When he is eventually made to report on his activities, it is in the words:

> Lo! I unfold my darkness, and on
> This rock place with strong band the Book
> Of eternal brass, written in my solitude.[25]

  The man who grew up from such a haunted imaginative childhood was one who might have found some difficulty in fitting into any human society, but whose nature rebelled particularly against the one that surrounded him. His unusually strong imaginative powers rendered the darker side of eighteenth-century life more oppressive to him than to most of his fellows. When he was only four years old, he told his wife, God 'put his head to the window' and set him screaming. All his life he was beset by images of prisons. Depictions of human beings in gloomy, confined places appear throughout his designs, and he several times illustrated Dante's account of Count Ugolino and his sons in the Tower of Hunger.[26] At least one direct experience of a contemporary prison, as we shall see, was afforded him by the 1780 the anti-Catholic Gordon Riots; in his later life, also, he was himself to run the risk of imprisonment when he fell under suspicion of treason. Yet he was also aware that imprisonment did not stop with buildings: the men and women he saw as he walked the streets of London had to him the air of captives, held by invisible bonds. Rousseau's vivid account of man as being 'born free' but as 'everywhere in chains' only deepened the mystery. Could it be that the chains envisaged by Rousseau were manufactured not by 'society' but by human beings themselves?

In considering the blend of nightmare and potential ecstatic vision in his mind it becomes evident that he must also have been touched at a profound level in childhood by visionary writing such as that of Bunyan in *The Pilgrim's Progress*. Although it would not be until within a decade of his death that he would produce a series of designs devoted to it, he had already named the writing in the book as one of his criteria for imaginative vision.[27] When as a child he saw a tree full of angels, spangling every bough, or on another occasion saw angelic figures walking among haymakers working in the nearby fields, one suspects that this was a boy whose reading had included Bunyan's accounts of 'the Shining Ones'. When, similarly, he broke in on an account by a traveller describing the splendours of a foreign city with the words 'Do you call that splendid? I should call a city splendid in which the houses were of gold, the pavement of silver, the gates ornamented with precious stones', he was surely bearing witness to an idea of the heavenly city in Revelation that had been further nourished by Bunyan's description of the Celestial City which 'shone like the sun; the streets also were paved with gold'.[28] On the first of these occasions he just escaped a thrashing from his father for telling a lie, being saved only by intercession from his mother, who was evidently more sympathetic to the power of eidetic vision. In his father's demand for adherence to literal truthfulness and impatience with fantasy the spirit of the age declared itself once again.

The London in which he was growing up was dominated, meanwhile, by the concept of expansion, caught as it was in transition between the mercantile city that it had been in the past and the industrialized metropolis that it was shortly to become: buildings of one kind and another were increasingly advancing across the countryside, swallowing villages into continuous suburbs. Blake evidently spent a good deal of time walking, but left few clues concerning his favourite routes. His vision among the haymakers[29] was said to have taken place at Peckham Rye: his biographer Gilchrist pictured him crossing Westminster Bridge to pass Blackheath, or Dulwich and the Norwood hills, and on 'through the antique rustic town of Croydon, type once of the compact, clean, cheerful Surrey towns of old days, to the fertile verdant meads of Walton-upon-Thames; much of the way by lane and footpath'.[30] What authority Gilchrist had for this route is not clear, though he goes on to claim that these scenes 'stored his mind with lifelong pastoral images'. In his lyrics for *Jerusalem*, on the other hand, the London landscape evoked lay in a different direction, looking north:

> The fields from Islington to Marybone
> To Primrose Hill and Saint Johns Wood
>   Were builded over with pillars of gold,
> And there Jerusalems pillars stood.
>
>   Her Little-ones ran on the fields
> The Lamb of God among them seen
>   And fair Jerusalem his Bride:
> Among the little meadows green.
>
>   Pancrass & Kentish-town repose
> Among her golden pillars high:
>   Among her golden arches which
> Shine upon the starry sky.
>
>   The Jews-harp-house & the Green Man;
> The Ponds where Boys to bathe delight:
>   The fields of Cows by Willans farm
> Shine in Jerusalems pleasant sight.[31]

Drawing on the landscape implied in these lines, Peter Ackroyd has mapped a walk Blake might have taken in his youth, striking up Tottenham Court Road and towards Hampstead and taking in the view from Islington to Marylebone as he did so. Willan's Farm, along with others, was in the area now occupied by Regent's Park. On the way, Ackroyd points out, he would have passed through decrepit and run-down areas, 'fetid ditches and piles of stinking refuse, smoking brick kilns and hog pens, ugly pipes belonging to the New River Company that were propped up at the height of some six or seven feet and beneath which grew abundant water-cress'.[32] Considering similar evidence, Stanley Gardner warned against reading the *Jerusalem* lines as representing a nostalgic portrait drawn from Blake's youth. The indications are, however, that in both his youth and old age there were still enough green landscapes in the region to justify his picture. Gardner is no doubt correct to draw from the subsequent question

> What are those golden Builders doing
> Near mournful ever-weeping Paddington
> Standing above that mighty Ruin
> Where Satan the first victory won

and the following references to 'Tyburn' and 'London Stone' some reference to John Nash and the terraces that were being constructed in Blake's lifetime, culminating in Regent Street (near which Tyburn formerly stood). But it has to be assumed (as Gardner also seems to have done) that this is a form of romantic irony, the projection of the building of Blake's Jerusalem being a sublime visionary counterpart to the material constructions which Nash was undertaking. Blake's tirade against high places north of the Thames should not be forgotten ('When I was young, Hampstead, Highgate, Hornsea, Muswell Hill & even Islington & all places North of London always laid me up the day after & sometimes two or three days').[33]* And in support of Gilchrist's concentration on his having been mostly aware of South London, it may be pointed out that places in Surrey figure particularly in the later Prophetic Books in pastoral contexts – whether it is the 'wild thyme from Wimbletons green & impurpled Hills'[34] or his invocation of the scene

> From the Hills of Camberwell & Wimbledon: from the Valleys
> Of Walton & Esher: from Stone-henge & from Maldens Cove ...[35]

Together, these suggest – at least marginally – a more sensuous immediacy, while his marshalling of the London northern heights – as when

> Hampstead Highgate Finchley Hendon Muswell Hill rage loud[36]

– is more often made in terms of the sublime. There is no firm distinction, however; he is quite capable, for instance, of writing lines describing how Los's emanation

> Like a faint rainbow waved before him in the awful gloom
> Of London City on the Thames from Surrey Hills to Highgate ...[37]

– thus reordering the polarity of his London map.

Within the streets of this London there was much to appeal to someone of an inquiring mind. While the Established Church maintained its ascendancy, the century-old existence of toleration kept alive many strains of independent thought, including those of religious sects. The Moravians themselves, through the work of John Wesley, helped spawn the Methodist movement as a vehicle of renewal for the Church of England which would eventually assume a character of its own. The line of dissent extended to cover many other forms of independent thinking, ranging from the Non-juring group in the Church of England to the protests of Quakerism and taking in groups as diverse as the Freemasons, the Sandemanians, the Muggletonians and the Hutchinsonians, climaxing, as the century drew to a close, with the rise of various Apocalyptic prophets such as Richard Brothers and Joanna Southcote. The arrival of Swedenborgianism in the 1780s promised a new assimilation of scientific thinking to religious beliefs, complementing the strong rationalism of many that had led to acceptance of 'Natural Religion' by the incorporation of a visionary and prophetic element.

So far as English culture more generally was concerned, the effect of imprisonment seemed to be emphasized by the impoverished state of the arts – in comparison with their flourishing condition in a period such as, say, the Elizabethan. At the same time there were signs of change. A new kind of poetry had begun to be heard from writers such as James Macpherson and Thomas Chatterton. In both cases their practice had been deeply compromised by suspicion of their claims to have discovered ancient works, which apparently masked a facility in forgery: for practitioners of the old school this was enough to discredit them. Followers of the new nationalisms, on the other hand, were anxious to believe in the genuineness of what was being offered, while younger writers, less stirred by the passions of the two sides, might simply be excited by the irregularity of the forms used and by the thought that they could be seen as springing from the direct expression of human emotions rather than the following of worn-out rules. Blake, whose early versification was strongly affected, retained throughout his career a belief in the Ossian presented by Macpherson.[38] He was also aware of other stirrings that might challenge the stranglehold of pure reason. A notable symptom was the cultivation of popular religious feeling encouraged by the Methodists: the later reference to 'Whitefield & Westley',[39] which signals his approval, suggests a tribute to the force of their enthusiasm rather than assent to their theology.

His ardent delight in all the arts was shown not only by his progress in drawing and engraving but in the writing of poems also, which he accompanied on the harp to airs of his own composing. So impressed was the company at the home of the Reverend Anthony Mathew, where he sometimes performed, that he was encouraged to publish a collection of his poems, which had evidently having won favour for their note of inspiration:

> Much about this time, Blake wrote many ... songs, to which he also composed tunes. these he would occasionally sing to his friends; and though, according to his confession, he was entirely unacquainted with the science of music, his ear was so good, that his tunes were sometimes most singularly beautiful, and were noted down by musical professors.[40]

Yet there was also a side to his nature that resisted adulation, particularly when it might impinge on his independence. He did not take easily to patronage at any time of his life; at the Mathews' he was after a time discouraged from continuing his attendance because, it was said, of his 'unbending deportment'.[41]

The available evidence suggests that the latter trait included a strain not only of independence but also of a notable reserve. As far as popular culture is concerned, there is little sense that he entered sympathetically into the raucous life of the streets – even if he did not quite experience it, either, as the scene of unmanageable confusion that impressed the young Wordsworth at the time of Bartholomew Fair, when

> All moveables of wonder, from all parts,
> Are here – albinos, painted Indians, dwarfs,
> The horse of knowledge, and the learned pig,
> The stone-eater, the man that swallows fire,
> Giants, ventriloquists, the invisible girl,
> The bust that speaks and moves its goggling eyes,
> The wax-work, clock-work, all the marvellous craft
> Of modern Merlins, wild beasts, puppet-shows,
> All out-of-the-way, far-fetched, perverted things
> All freaks of Nature, all Promethean thoughts
> Of man, his dullness, madness, and their feats
> All jumbled up together to compose
> This parliament of monsters. Tents and booths
> Meanwhile – as if the whole were one vast mill –
> Are vomiting, receiving, on all sides,
> Men, women, three-years' children, babes in arms ...

For Wordsworth this London created a 'blank confusion' which was a 'true epitome' of the City herself.[42] Not everyone was so bewildered. It was also the London which, according to Johnson, contained 'all that life can afford'[43] and where Charles Lamb claimed that he would 'often shed tears in the motley Strand from fullness of joy at so much Life'.[44] Blake's vision of the place, meanwhile, was more penetrating, prompting him, while he rejoiced in its inherent sense of life, to be admonished by awareness of the fear to which such a vulnerable community was open. With little in the way of an efficient police force, the response to violence was likely to be both peremptory and implacable. With efficient communications not available, 'risings' of the London mob, constructed as they might be from causes consisting of little but rumour, could be unpredictable and alarming. In such a case the only resource that the Lord Mayor would find available was to call out the militia, who might in turn feel themselves licensed to use extreme force – as was the case in 1780 after the horrific outburst of violence in the Gordon Riots. On this occasion, as Gilchrist describes, Blake at one point found himself carried along helplessly by the mob:

> In this outburst of anarchy, Blake long remembered an involuntary participation of his own. On the third day, Tuesday, 6th of June, 'the Mass-houses' having already been demolished – one, in Blake's near neighbourhood, Warwick Street, Golden Square and various private houses also, the rioters, flushed with gin and victory, were turning their attention to grander schemes of devastation. That evening, the artist happened to be walking in a route chosen by one of the mobs at large, whose course lay from Justice Hyde's house near Leicester Fields, for the destruction of which less than an hour had sufficed, through Long Acre, past the quiet house of Blake's old master, engraver Basire, in Great Queen Street, Lincoln's Inn Fields, and down Holborn, bound for Newgate. Suddenly, he encountered the advancing wave of triumphant Blackguardism, and was forced (for from such a great surging mob there is no disentanglement) to go along in the very front rank, and witness the storm and burning of the fortress-like prison, and release of its three hundred inmates.[45]

In some cases the soldiers refused to fire on people whom they regarded as fellow citizens. This did not stop the aftermath and response from being equally violent, however: large numbers of the rioters, some of them no more than boys, were subsequently hanged at Tyburn. Remembering such events, it is not surprising that Blake carried for the rest of his life a hatred of mob violence, which would reach a climax in times of war.

2
Traces of Tradition?

During his childhood Blake's independence of mind had been bolstered by the fact that he did not receive a conventional education (another possible sign of influence from the Moravians, who were against exposing children to formal schooling). Instead, he was sent to Henry Pars's Drawing School, where, in the spirit of the age, he was taught above all things to copy correctly.

His visionary nature may have champed at such restraints, but it was also curbed by a sense of the practical. By the time that he left Pars's instruction his gifts as a visual artist were already so impressive that the most obvious course would have been for him to be to go to some well-known artist and be taught under his own roof, but this would have been a notable drain on the resources of a family with four children – and even then would not have guaranteed him a secure living. According to Frederick Tatham,[1] William himself argued against a course of action that would be unfair to his siblings and proposed to be trained as an engraver, which would offer a surer future and the acquisition of a readily marketable skill.

The man first approached was William Wynne Ryland, but this plan was abandoned when, after visiting the studio with this father, Blake remarked that he did not like Ryland's face: 'It looks as if he will live to be hanged.' (In the face of all likelihood, this turned out to be the case when Ryland was later sentenced to death for forgery.) He was then apprenticed to James Basire, in whose house he lived for seven years. Basire belonged to a school of engraving that was often praised for its cultivation of 'firm and correct outline'. After a time, however, Blake fell out with some of the other apprentices and Basire, evidently having noticed the nature of his talents, and having been commissioned to engrave some of the monuments in Westminster Abbey, sent him to spend some time drawing them. The hours spent working alone there fed his historical imagination still further, awakening a taste for the Gothic; he also claimed to have had visionary experiences there, including one of 'Christ and the Apostles'. Meanwhile he worked on a design of his own which he inscribed 'JOSEPH of Arimathea among The Rocks of Albion' – later adding to a proof of an early state the words 'Engraved when I was a beginner at Basires from a drawing by Salviati after Michael Angelo'.

After leaving Basire, Blake studied for a while at the recently formed Royal Academy, then awaiting its new buildings. What he had by now learned no doubt assisted the artistic taste that he displayed in his own work, where he proved consistent in his admiration for good outline, while unwilling to acknowledge virtue in the work of those who followed different techniques. This led to sharp strictures on the current state of the visual arts, from which even Moser, his Swiss-born teacher at the Royal Academy, was not exempt:

> I was once looking over the Prints from Rafael & Michael Angelo in the Library of of the Royal Academy Moser came to me & said You should not Study these old Hard Stiff & Dry Unfinishd Works of Art, Stay a little & I will shew you what you should Study. He then went & took down Le Bruns & Rubens's Galleries How I did secretly rage. I also spoke my Mind. ... I said to Moser, 'These things that you call Finishd are not Even Begun how can they then, be Finishd? The Man who does not know The Beginning, never can know the End of Art.[2]

There are few sidelights on this period of his study, the most dramatic being provided by the records of a trip he made to Upnor on the Medway – probably in September 1780 – in the company of Thomas Stothard and his former fellow apprentice, James Parker. We should probably not have heard about this, even, were it not for the fact that they moored opposite Chatham Docks, where warships often assembled, and found themselves apprehended by some soldiers on suspicion of being French spies who had been sent to gather information on preparations for the current war. Their explanation that they were simply making landscape sketches was not accepted and they were placed under arrest, to be guarded by a sentinel until their story could be verified by someone at the Academy. Once this had happened they 'spent a merry hour with the commanding officer', though Parker declared that he 'would go out no more on such perilous expeditions'.[3]

1 Illustration to Thomas Gray's 'Epitaph on Mrs Clarke', Yale Center for British Art, Paul Mellon Collection

This event also suggests the extent to which Blake was willing to pursue naturalism in his art even while cultivating clarity of outline. For good examples of this persisting duality of aim one might cite some of his designs illustrating poems, such as that for Gray's 'Epitaph on Mrs Clarke' (Figure 1).[4] Eventually, the vehemence of his attitudes on the subject would lead to cutting comments on contemporaries such as Joshua Reynolds himself, as in his angry annotation to the opening of Reynolds's *Works*:

> Having spent the Vigour of my Youth & Genius under the Opression of Sr Joshua & his Gang of Cunning Hired Knaves Without Employment & as much as could possibly be Without Bread, The Reader must Expect to Read in all my Remarks on these Books Nothing but Indignation & Resentment While Sr Joshua was rolling in Riches Barry was Poor & Unemployd except by his own Energy Mortimer was calld a Madman & only Portrait Painting applauded & rewarded by the Rich & Great. Reynolds & Gainsborough Blotted & Blurred one against the other & Divided all the English World between them Fuseli Indignant almost hid himself – I am hid.[5]

Despite the forthright anger of this vein of criticism it could also transpose itself into a general positive championing of Imagination as against Nature, which would remain a constant feature of his doctrines. Yet it should not be supposed that Blake was contemptuous of Nature. For the precise nature of his convictions one may turn to a letter of 1802, in which he acknowledges the need for remaining true to it when one is turning from landscape to portraiture:

> & now I must intreat you to Excuse faults for Portrait Painting is the direct contrary to Designing & Historical Painting in every respect – If you have not Nature before you for Every Touch you cannot Paint Portrait. & if you have Nature before you at all you cannot Paint History it was Michall Angelos opinion & is Mine[6]

His first book of poems, *Poetical Sketches*, published in 1783, contained a lament for the current state of the arts that pressed further the need for nature to be transfused by the imagination – for which the Muses were appropriate symbolic guardians:

> Whether on Ida's shady brow,
>   Or in the chambers of the East,
> The chambers of the sun, that now
>   From antient melody have ceas'd;
>
> Whether in Heav'n ye wander fair,
>   Or the green corners of the earth,
> Or the blue regions of the air,
>   Where the melodious winds have birth;
>
> Whether on chrystal rocks ye rove,
>   Beneath the bosom of the sea
> Wand'ring in many a coral grove,
>   Fair Nine, forsaking Poetry!
>
> How have you left the antient love
>   That bards of old enjoy'd in you!
> The languid strings do scarcely move!
>   The sound is forc'd, the notes are few![7]

This is by no means the only note to be struck in *Poetical Sketches*, however. The alternation between visionary ardour and firm independence that has already been noted in his early dealings corresponds to a feature of Blake's personality that shows itself repeatedly. Not only was he subject to contrary moods, he seems to have cultivated them actively, believing (in the words of what was apparently his advice to others) that 'Truth is always in the extremes – keep them'. The maxim, however unwelcome to a century that valued the 'golden mean' and sought to dissuade people from extremes of any kind, was one to which he firmly adhered. Even in these early lyrics Blake could proceed by evoking contrary states of mind: two consecutive poems, for example, each entitled 'Song', give opposing versions of a village love. The first describes the pleasures of going to visit his beloved ('Each village seems the haunt of holy feet') and concludes:

> But that sweet village where my black.ey'd maid
> Closes her eyes in sleep beneath night's shade:
> Whene'er I enter, more than mortal fire
> Burns in my soul, and does my song inspire.

The second song, by contrast, describes the torments of jealousy. His voicing of fear lest some other youth should walk with his love concludes

> O should she e'er prove false, his limbs I'd tear,
> And throw all pity on the burning air;
> I'd curse bright fortune for my mixed lot,
> And then I'd die in peace, and be forgot.[8]

Blake's ability to see the same situation from varying points of view, recognizing that in different moods all the lights of a scene could change, would come into its own in his later writing, notably in the *Songs of Innocence and of Experience*. Already in *Poetical Sketches*, however, there was much that looked to the future, including an image of winter ('O Winter! bar thine adamantine doors') which had the lineaments of his cold deity Urizen, while a characteristic image of imprisonment was wrought unexpectedly into what might appear at first sight to be a pleasant little love poem:

> How sweet I roam'd from field to field,
>   And tasted all the summer's pride,
> 'Till I the prince of love beheld,
>   Who in the sunny beams did glide!
>
> He shew'd me lilies for my hair,
>   And blushing roses for my brow;
> He led me through his gardens fair,
>   Where all his golden pleasures grow.

With sweet May dews my wings were wet,
  And Phoebus fir'd my vocal rage;
He caught me in his silken net,
  And shut me in his golden cage.

He loves to sit and hear me sing,
  Then, laughing, sports and plays with me;
Then stretches out my golden wing,
  And mocks my loss of liberty.[9]

In spite of the resonances of the final word, there is little sign that Blake had proceeded far along the road to freedom, beyond an early conviction that its true home was in England. In the *Poetical Sketches* he showed little or no sign of dissent from the political views regarded as orthodox in the England of his time. Even in the dramatic piece 'King Edward the Fourth' and 'A War Song to Englishmen', which proclaimed the need to fight valiantly for Albion's liberty and future prosperity, there are no signals to suggest that they were intended to be read in any way ironically. This seems to imply that his mind was busier elsewhere, however, not that he was slavishly following a traditional path of patriotism.

Was there, indeed, any body of traditional thought in his mind against which he could have judged contemporary events – particularly when the nature of social thinking at this time was such that political and religious elements could not easily be disentangled? It is time to examine this question.

E. P. Thompson, who worked for many years on relevant historical documents, explored a perception that if Blake belonged to any tradition, it was that of the dissenters who had been most active at the time of the English Civil War – the Ranters, Levellers, Fifth Monarchy Men, and so on. He was particularly struck by the content of A. L. Morton's book *The Everlasting Gospel*, in which it was argued that Blake's use of this phrase for the title of a long poem of his own indicated his acquaintance with a number of earlier writers for whom it was a commonplace. Various clues led him to suppose also that Blake had been particularly affected by the doctrines of Ludowick Muggleton; he even toyed with the idea that one or more members of his family might have belonged to the sect, which was notoriously secretive about its proceedings. G. E. Bentley has pointed out that the need for members of the sect to meet in public houses to avoid prosecution would square interestingly with the assertion in 'The Little Vagabond' that an ale-house was preferable to a church.[10]

In the work that Thompson produced, which, though naturally dominated by the details of the thesis with which he had set out, was notable for depth and thoroughness, he was able to show possible sources of various of Blake's preoccupations and favourite phrases. Concentrating on the seventeenth-century dissenters who had formed the groups mentioned above, he found himself involved with the questions that had bothered them most – notably the argument whether Christians were saved by faith or by works. As far as that issue was concerned there can be little doubt that since the advocacy of good works as a means of salvation usually prompted attacks on the 'legalism' of those who believed in them, Blake would have been more likely to come down on the side of 'faith'. And since asserting the latter led such dissenters to be charged in their turn with antinomianism Thompson is prompted to set him in their succession. It is possible, for example, to look, as he does, at the 1798 annotation in which Blake affirms that if the 'Abomination' of reading the Bible without taking into account 'Conscience or the Word of God Universal' is removed, 'every man can converse with God & be a King & Priest in his own house',[11] and relate it to Theophilus Evans's millenarian statement that once man regains the perfection of Adam, the Law will be 'writ in every Man's heart, so that … every Man should be Priest unto himself':[12] the language seems remarkably similar. Yet Blake's own version of Enthusiasm moves well beyond matters of biblical interpretation: in a letter written shortly before his death he would look forward to his forthcoming release into 'The Mind in which every one is King & Priest in his own House'.[13] One can accept the existence of a base for his beliefs in earlier dissenting religion, in other words, only if one also takes into account the extent to which his antinomianism acquired a life of its own, whereby what earlier dissenters thought of as 'faith' became in his eyes transfigured into Imagination. Eventually, that Imagination would become more recognizably Christian, but not before he had passed through stages in which he made striking statements that would have been unacceptable to the orthodox.

While there can be no doubt of Blake's antinomianism, it is perhaps misleading to link him too closely with the growth of an urban working class or with the development of radical groups at the time. The attempt to link him with the Muggletonian sect, championed by Thompson, has come under fire as a result of close examination of the genealogical evidence.[14*] Instead, we have seen reason to promote the term 'enthusiasts' – a word which, as we have seen, Blake was happy to apply to himself.[15] One advantage of considering him in this context would be that 'enthusiasts' felt themselves justified in cultivating extremes which might lead others to label them as mad – a tendency that would square with the taste for thinking dialectically which has already been noted in his work. To use this term in speaking of him, therefore, is not only to avoid identifying him with a particular sect, but to suggest further the range of his mental processes.

The fact is – and both Thompson and Jon Mee recognize this – that Blake's antinomianism was in important respects paradoxical. The dissenters with whom he is being aligned were inveighing against a particular rule of Law associated with the Old Testament, and this was responsible for attacks on them as literally 'antinomian'. He himself went further, however. None of the associated figures that have been unearthed so far by scholars doubted what were regarded in contemporary terms as the ultimate bases for Christian belief. The accuracy of the biblical record remained for the most part unquestioned, as did the traditional terms in which the opposition between good and evil was conceived. Blake, it seems, was alone, at least in England, in exploring the need for a possible transposition of values, deposing the hegemony of angels, and in return playing with the prospect of exalting the devils as exponents of a morality based on energy.

How far Blake expected his ideas to be taken completely seriously is hard to determine. Allowance must certainly be made for his sense of irony. The very fact that *The Marriage of Heaven and Hell* was cast in precisely those terms suggests that he was allowing for a possible equality of value between the two sides. What he was questioning rather was the assumption that angels deserved an enhanced status on account of a superior rationality such as Newton's. If Newton was indeed now regarded unreservedly as a 'mighty angel' his status needed to be challenged.

On one point Blake would have agreed firmly with the antinomians: their conviction that no special learning was required to understand the teachings of Christianity. Whatever his differences, he would have felt with them that there was indeed an 'Everlasting Gospel', available to all. Equally, he was suspicious of any kind of authority basing itself on 'law', which made his opposition more wide-ranging, He did not, of course, object on principle to 'order', but his instinctive sympathy with rebellious spirits took his feeling for Christianity to an antinomianism well beyond that of most fellow-believers. His own pronouncements for a time reflected this – as when he wrote how

Jesus (a man of sorrows) reciev'd
... A Gospel from wretched Theotormon.[16]

In any case, this failure to find limits for his antinomianism has been a source of unease to those who have wanted to claim him for a particular cause. He always refused to be pinned down in this way. Writing after the Second World War, Kathleen Raine was intrigued to discover links between his writings and the Perennial Philosophy as rediscovered by Aldous Huxley and to notice that at the time when Blake was writing, Thomas Taylor, 'the English pagan', was reviving interest in Platonism and Neoplatonism with his series of translations from Plato, Plotinus and others. It also came to be known that the two men knew one another and that Taylor gave Blake some lessons in mathematics – which did not, however, proceed very far. He

> got as far as the 5th propos[n] wch proves that any two angles at the base of an isosceles triangle must be equal. Taylor was going through the demonstration, but was interrupted by Blake, exclaiming, 'ah never mind that – what's the use of going to prove it, why I see with my eyes that it is so, & do not require any proof to make it clearer.'[17]

Kathleen Raine was able to find many points of contact between Blake and the Platonic tradition, and there can be little doubt that he sometimes seized on such words and images when they were needed for his work; he could also be critical of Plato, however, whom he saw not only as a supporter of Vision ('The Ancients did not mean to Impose when they affirmd their belief in Vision & Revelation Plato was in Earnest ...'[18]) but also – particularly after the end of the 1790s – as a lawgiver and the author of a philosophy falling short of Christian revelation. 'Plato did not bring Life & Immortality to light Jesus only did this', he wrote in the pages of Berkeley, adding a little later, 'God is not a Mathematical Diagram'.[19] His inscriptions for 'Laocoön' in the 1820s included the accusation: 'The Gods of Greece & Egypt were Mathematical Diagrams – See Plato's Works.'[20]

Plotinus, meanwhile, was recognized only obliquely, as we shall see. A key to Blake's view of his admirer Thomas Taylor may be looked for in the fact that he was apparently caricatured in *An Island in the Moon* as Sipsop the Pythagorean – a suggestion that Blake found him and his writings somewhat vapid, lacking in the incisive energy that he looked for in a thinker.

Such reservations would not have militated against the central perception which he had seized upon – that of the need to see the infinite element in all things. On the contrary, he began work on writings which would in a variety of ways explore its implications. Given the wayward manner in which his ideas moved, however, there is a third tradition against which they should also be considered, that of Gnosticism. Morton Paley, who has looked at the range of traditions, esoteric and exoteric, against which Blake's thinking might be considered, has drawn attention to the particular relevance of this one, which has also been investigated at some length by Andrew Welburn.[21] It is quite clear that Blake was fascinated throughout life by the conception of a secret knowledge which could liberate those fortunate enough to recognize it; yet as Welburn points out, it is hard to discover sources that we can be sure he used. His interest in old folios, particularly in old engravings, might have led him anywhere, but no specific sources are named by him, apart from Boehme, Paracelsus and Swedenborg. It seems that the content of what was to be discovered in the Gnostic writings fascinated him less than the fact of such esoteric knowledges existing at all. Nor would he have followed Gnostic teaching to the extent of disregarding the material existence of Jesus. Yet in many respects we are closer here to a tradition for Blake than in either of the other patterns discussed. In the discussion whether we are justified by works or by faith he would, after all, have been most likely to opt for *knowledge* – though he might well have asserted that the true knowledge he valued was less available to the painstaking intellectual searcher than to the innocent child.

In any case, however, the search for a 'tradition' seems in itself misguided. Just as what we should be looking for is less influence than confluence, so it is necessary to recognize that we are dealing with a man who is ultimately setting himself against traditions. When he senses himself coming up against one, his instinct is to divert it, question it or stand it on its head.

Being stood on its head is something that can also happen to one's view of the world as the result of an unusual experience. One such, which claimed Blake's primary attention in these years, came as a concomitant to the death of his brother Robert in 1787, when he claimed to have seen the released spirit ascending through the ceiling, 'clapping its hands for joy'. Having watched by the bedside day and night for the previous fortnight he then fell into an unbroken sleep for three days and three nights.[22] It is not uncommon for an experience of this kind to leave a momentous impression on the person involved – even to change his or her entire view of the world. In Blake's case the event was to be reflected in one or two designs, such as the vignette in 'The Gates of Paradise' showing an elderly man rising from his death-bed (Figure 2). Whatever the further effects, there are certainly from this time signs of a change in his attitudes. A few small engraved groups of

2   'Fear and Hope are—Vision', from *The Gates of Paradise*

sayings produced at about this time are eloquent of what was happening. They can easily be passed over if treated in the single, long-page tabulation that serves to render them in most of the published versions, but in the originals each aphorism is given an entire small page, with its own illustration, resulting in an increased impressiveness of effect.

The third set of these designs, entitled 'ALL RELIGIONS are ONE', maintains that the human faculty which can deal with the lack inherent in all rationally bound discourse, responding instead to the infinity inherent in all things, is the Poetic Genius; it also shows itself (as in the Old and New Testaments, for instance) in prophecy. This human truth Blake sees as the unifying quality in all religion.

The first two sets, before it, are each given the same title: 'THERE is NO Natural Religion'. One is devoted to the point that human beings are imprisoned into attitudes of despair by their assumption that no experiences are available to them beyond those furnished by the evidence of the five senses. The other explores the evidence that perception is not bounded by the organs devoted to it, the opposite being suggested by the existence of human desire, which opens out into infinity. The very fact that desire itself is infinite opens the eyes of human beings to the very existence of that dimension to human existence: for Blake, infinity is not simply (as is often assumed) a matter of endlessness in space or time but of a *quality*, inherent in certain kinds of behaviour: if one wanted to know what it is, one would be better employed in gazing into a spring of water, for example, and asking what is the essential nature of its being fountainous. The point involved was to be made perfectly in the opening of his 'Auguries of Innocence':

> To see a World in a Grain of Sand
> And a Heaven in a Wild Flower
> Hold Infinity in the palm of your hand
> And Eternity in an hour[23]

It was while still under the spell of the new vision induced by the vision at Robert's death that Blake also embarked on the little series of designs which he called 'The GATES of PARADISE' in 1793 and published in association with Joseph Johnson. These designs (reproduced in many editions of Blake's writings) carried the dedication 'For Children', each being accompanied by an inscription. For the frontispiece it was 'What is Man', then 'I found him beneath a Tree', 'Water', 'Earth', 'Air' and 'Fire', followed by a series of comments showing the trials awaiting human beings and presenting them with a series of images of the life that they may expect if they remain content to be imprisoned by their five senses and the four elements, and by the consequent human disorders that will urge them to hold on to pleasures rather than simply enjoy them, as when they chase to capture a butterfly, or cry for the moon ('I want! I want!') – or even attack a helpless parent. In this dismal scene the only pleasure to be looked for is that denoted by the hope of immortality that Blake claimed to have experienced himself at the death of his brother: a design showing a figure rising from his death-bed carries the words, mentioned above, 'Fear & Hope are – Vision'. This is followed by a series of more hopeful designs, indicated with the words 'The traveller hasteth in the Evening' (Figure 22, p. 205), 'Death's Door' and 'I have said to the Worm, Thou art my mother & my sister'. The implication of the designs as a whole is that once one considers the agonies of mortal existence, as opposed to the delights of Eternity that can be glimpsed in experiences of Vision, the experience of death may be awaited without fear and seen simply as the passing through a gateway, with the graveyard worm not consumer but friend – even a relation. The entry into 'Death's Door' then suggests the pleasure of a traveller finally reaching his destination by nightfall'. The captives of their senses are thus brought into the true universe that has always been there and available had they only realized it, enabling them to pass beyond the grave into a paradisal state and a sense of unity with all life.

It is doubtful whether anyone who had not had the designs explained by the artist would have found in them a source of hope. In themselves they seem cast in a uniformly pessimistic mould. Yet Blake must have hoped for an audience that would pierce the carapace of gloom and glimpse beyond it the implication of delight. The substance of the series – while certainly unlikely to appeal directly to any children who happened to pick it up – was in fact well in line with the graveyard philosophy of many contemporary English poets who, as an encyclopaedia entry puts it,

> wrote primarily about human mortality. Often set in a graveyard, their poems mused on the vicissitudes of life, the solitude of death and the grave, and the anguish of bereavement. Their air of pensive gloom presaged the melancholy of the romantic movement.[24]

Blake, who was brought up in the shadow of this school – and would indeed later produce illustrations for writers commonly associated with it such as Gray, Young or Blair – would not have wanted to terrify children into compliance with contemporary moral codes but rather to offer them a means of release. It is unlikely that any child ever in fact grasped that point with the readiness that he may have hoped for.[25*] But in thus affirming that it was children who, if anyone did, held 'the keys of paradise', he was performing a radical act: he was quietly indicating the fragility, in his view, of all 'traditions' that had been constructed solely on adult experience.

3
Through Satire to Innocence

So far as Blake's intellectual life as a young man can be traced (the evidence is mostly indirect) he read intensely in certain books: not only the favourite English poets mentioned above but works of imaginative philosophy such as the writings of Plato and the Neoplatonists, and of occult writers such as Paracelsus and Jakob Boehme.[1] The Bible and Milton, his especial favourites, he read by the light of his own intuition, valuing their passages of imaginative vision or fiery prophecy; but he could also be seized by more prosaic possibilities, as when he played on the concept of a literally 'jealous God'.

His feeling for works of strong imagination made him impatient at the dominating thought of his time, which despite its progress in the sciences struck him as often uninspired and even trifling. In his 1787 squib *An Island in the Moon* he presents a group of cultured individuals each wrapped in the limitations of his or her own pursuits, and does not shrink from gross burlesque. Joseph Priestley, for example, a man notable for the range of his intellectual interests, was probably the inspiration behind the character Inflammable Gas. Such caricatures could not, of course, altogether belittle the originals, some of whom were leading thinkers of the time, discussing issues and making discoveries that carried important implications. Blake's satire seems, rather, to poke fun at what is seen as an ultimate ineffectuality, an unwillingness to think with true freedom. Their island may be pleasant enough, but it remains essentially a place of confinement.

Even Mrs Nannicantipot is not quite as absurd as her name makes her sound; her 'Song' displays something of the direct feeling that Blake felt to be missing from the fashionable poetry of the age:

> When the tongues of children are heard on the green
> And laughing is heard on the hill

My heart is at rest within my breast
And every thing else is still

Then come home my children the sun is gone down
And the dews of night arise
Come Come leave off play & let us away
Till morning appears in the skies

No No let us play for it is yet day
And we cannot go to sleep
Besides in the Sky the little birds fly
And the meadows are coverd with Sheep

Well Well go & play till the light fades away
And then go home to bed
The little ones leaped & shouted & laughd
And all the hills echoed.[2]

This, together with the pieces before and after, was to provide one of the most haunting lyrics of the *Songs of Innocence*. And if a cynical reader were to point out that while the children's voices might seem innocent enough at a distance, they would sound very different at a nearer approach, it could be pointed out that Blake knew this very well also: another piece shortly afterwards gives us the real voice of such a child:

O I say you Joe
Throw us the ball
Ive a good mind to go
And leave you all
I never saw saw such a bowler
To bowl the ball in a tansey
And to clean it with my handkercher
Without saying a word

That Bills a foolish fellow
He has given me a black eye
He does not know how to handle a bat
Any more than a dog or a cat
He has knockd down the wicket
And broke the stumps
And runs without shoes to save his pumps[3]

The various lyrics and speeches in *An Island in the Moon* exhibit Blake trying his hand at various effects. More than anything that he achieved afterwards they suggest a young writer testing the limits of what might be done – in terms not only of verse, but also of taste. Although an amusing piece of satire, it has an unfinished quality that seems at the same time to betray an uneasiness. Indeed, later critics have found some difficulty in deciding how much is real satire. When Obtuse Angle sings his song in favour of Sutton the philanthropist, 'looking on the corner of the ceiling', we are entitled to infer from his name, his gesture and the banal quality of the verse that his praise has more than a touch of irony, and that in spite of Sutton's well-doing its mercenary nature is being indicated, covering a lack of real feeling for those he has helped, so that to prefer him to 'Sir Isaac Newton, or Locke, or Doctor South or Sherlock upon Death (the last a treatise rather than an actual human being)' is not totally to dissociate him from them. The subject of the lyric then produced by Steelyard the Lawgiver, with its more rollick-ing rhythm and its nostalgic praise of 'Good English hospitality' and the time when it 'did not fail' seems satiric only at the edges. It is as if Blake's love of the autonomous prohibits him from pressing his satire too far, since to rejoice in the individuality of every human being is a way of guarding against the uniformity that Urizen would seek to impose. If that individuality takes the form of enjoying what is there to be enjoyed while not inquiring too closely into the deprivations suffered elsewhere by the 'hungry poor' who were given 'good beef & ale' in the supposed benefits of the old time, should the Lawgiver be taken to task?

This may also have stirred further unease. Was there really any point in satirizing his contemporaries in this way? Was it not more important to find a bold line of his own that might lead the way to a more genuine art? Some such reasoning would seem to lie behind the change from the inspired pastiches of *Poetical Sketches* and the probing satires of *An Island in the Moon* to the clearer, more incisive line of subsequent work. From now on, he would show himself truer to a cultivation of the extremes by choosing a particular line at any one time and pursuing it with energy and determination – even if he would also feel free to strike out in a quite new, perhaps contrary, direction just afterwards.

He was questioning the limits not only of conventional sensibility and poetic verse but also of the very commercial methods by which literature was produced. A separate page at the end of *An Island* shows his character Quid (closely identifiable with himself, surely) setting out a programme for a new kind of art – and incidentally hoping to make his own fortune in the process:

> ... Illuminating the Manuscript – Ay said she that would be excellent. Then said he I would have all the writing Engraved instead of Printed & at every other leaf a high finishd print all in three Volumes folio, & sell them a hundred pounds a piece. they would Print off two thousand then said she whoever will not have them will be ignorant fools & will not deserve to live Dont you think I have something of the Goats face says he. Very like a Goats face – she answered – I think your face said he is like that noble beast the Tyger – Oh I was at Mrs Sicknakens & I was speaking of my abilities but their nasty hearts poor devils are eat up with envy – they envy me my abilities & all the Women envy your abilities   my dear   they hate people who are of higher abil[it]ies than their nasty filthy [Souls] Selves but do you outface them & then Strangers will see you have an opinion – now I think we should do as much good as we can when we are at Mr Femality's do yo[u] snap & take me up – and I will fall into such a passion Ill hollow and stamp & frighten all the People there & show them what truth is – at this Instant Obtuse Angle came in Oh I am glad you are come said quid[4]

Despite the touch of self-satirizing in these lines they point to Blake's enjoyment of experimentation in his visual art and look forward to the mode of printing that he was eventually to adopt. Yet the variety of his experiments, together with his apparent self-identification as Quid the Cynic, suggest once again an uneasiness, a desire to find a more straightforward means of expression.

By 1787, moreover, he was in an unusual state of mind. The death of his brother, and the accompanying experience described earlier, had led him to believe more firmly in the existence of a spiritual world surrounding and infusing the world of nature: not to be identified with it – but not to be ignored, either. This was no simple 'spiritualism' of the kind that would become popular in the middle of the nineteenth century. So far as one can reconstruct his thinking during these years, he was moved by the discovery that the human psyche was not a simple entity, but changed according to one's physical state. When one exercised oneself in energy one was not the same as when occupied in rational study; when surrounded by affection, especially sexual love, one again became a different person. It is necessary to grasp this triple (and possibly multiple) set of distinctions if one is to understand significant features of his work, since it gave him an uncommon view of the world and even an unusual vocabulary.

Further discriminations are also necessary. When at this time he speaks of science and reason, Blake is thinking of the state of nature as it presents itself when contemplated and studied passively; when he speaks of wisdom, intellect and the 'spiritual', on the other hand, he thinks primarily of the mind and imagination in their energized state; and when he speaks of love and innocence, he has in mind the state of affection as activated by the other two as well. (In later years the distinctions are less clear, but are still touched by this early ferment of thought.) From such distinctions he developed his idea of the man of spirit as a 'mental traveller', who, walking through the world of experience or labouring at his creative work, develops his real 'intellect', and in doing so discovers true wisdom. (Representations of this figure in his work range from the traveller hasting in the evening in *The Gates of Paradise* (Figure 22, p. 205) to his apparent self-identification with Chaucer's Plowman in his *Canterbury Tales* design (Figure 21, p. 205)). His own ideal of the passive state, similarly, submits him not to the world of sense perception but to the inner illuminations of innocent vision, mediated by affection.

As he developed these ideas, Blake was assisted by a number of contemporary developments. In 1787, Thomas Taylor published a pamphlet entitled *Concerning the Beautiful*, a short translation from Plotinus that was to be harbinger of his many further translations from Platonic and Neoplatonist writers. In that pamphlet a number of unusual words occur with a charge of particular meaning: 'non-entity', 'indefinite', the study of 'particulars'. Likewise Taylor distinguishes between the 'corporeal eye' and the 'intellectual eye' – a distinction that Blake was to take over in his own way. For him the 'intellectual eye' is the natural reward of the energetic human being who is at once a maker and a mental traveller.

The inclusion of 'Sipsop the Pythagorean' as one of the characters in *An Island in the Moon* may indeed reflect Blake's impatience at Taylor's enthusiasm for a philosopher such as Plotinus, who regarded matter as being 'neither soul nor intellect, nor life, nor form, nor reason nor bound, but a certain indefiniteness'; this left the way open for a man such as himself to assert the true activity for the artist to lie, by contrast, in the creation of definite outlines and living forms. From this time forward, one of his most distinctive features as an artist and poet – his love of the distinct and vibrant image, visual or verbal – emerges, leading to the decisive line and dramatic directness of statement that characterize some of his best work.

Meanwhile, the element in him that was caught up by imagination and vision found a source of stimulus in the work of John Flaxman.

Among other things Flaxman was a Swedenborgian, providing Blake with a direct link to the recently established New Jerusalem Church. To anyone who was oppressed by a sense of gloomy imprisonment in the teachings of the eighteenth-century dissenting sects, the writings of Swedenborg opened new windows by reasserting the power of visionary knowledge and insisting on a reading of the Bible according to its 'Internal sense'. Nature was to be seen not as the intricately wrought machine of eighteenth-century rationalism, but as a world in which were to be traced correspondences with the nature of a God who was most himself when most human in his activities.

Leaving behind his early religious background, Blake was for a time deeply drawn to teachings that ran in such close parallel with his own visionary leanings. When in 1789 an invitation was issued to 'all the readers of the Theological Works of the Hon. Emmanuel Swedenborg, who are desirous of rejecting, and separating themselves from the Old Church ... and of fully embracing the Heavenly Doctrines of the New Jerusalem', he and his wife were among those who subscribed to all the propositions set out, which included not only specific doctrines, but agreement concerning which books of the Bible should be treated as canonical.[5] He was to become disillusioned concerning the sect, and about Swedenborg himself, but not before he had been profoundly influenced by a cast of mind that encouraged symbolic thinking in various directions.

The influence of Swedenborg's ideas can be found here and there in the *Songs of Innocence* – published, as it happens, in the same year. In exploring the new world that opened for him after the death of his brother, Blake seems to have subdued the more satirical and sardonic side of his personality to an art that was the medium of direct, light-filled vision. In particular, he drew on a belief that the time when the imaginative powers are at their most intense is in childhood.

Swedenborgian provenance has also been claimed, however, for certain other poems in the *Songs of Innocence*:

> To Mercy Pity Peace and Love,
> All pray in their distress:
> And to these virtues of delight
> Return their thankfulness.
>
> For Mercy Pity Peace and Love,
> Is God our father dear:
> And Mercy Pity Peace and Love,
> Is Man his child and care.

For Mercy has a human heart
Pity a human face:
And Love, the human form divine,
And Peace, the human dress.

Then every man of every clime,
That prays in his distress,
Prays to the human form divine
Love Mercy Pity Peace.

And all must love the human form,
In heathen, turk or jew.
Where Mercy, Love & Pity dwell
There God is dwelling too.

These familiar verses were claimed by F. W. Bateson to constitute 'a thoroughly Swedenborgian poem'.[6] As E. P. Thompson subsequently pointed out, however, this was a point with which many Swedenborgians would have been bound to disagree: they would have differed crucially concerning the nature of 'Divine Humanity'. Blake himself may originally have misunderstood the Swedenborgians' position, believing that when they used the phrase they meant something corresponding to his own conviction that 'Thou art a man, God is no more ...'. During this time, however, there were strong voices among the sect urging them on the contrary to approach more closely to orthodox Christianity. In particular, Blake probably came across the Reverend Joseph Proud, a convert who joined the New Jerusalem Church after many years as a Baptist minister. Examination of Proud's songs shows that when he used the idea of Divine Humanity it was very much with emphasis on the word 'Divine': he was still accepting, in other words, God's utter supremacy. Blake, in contrast, was making a different argument, hoping to find in Swedenborgianism a religion where humanity would be treated as divine.

For such reasons Thompson questioned the frequently made assumption that Blake was for a time a convinced Swedenborgian, arguing that such a claim needed to be treated with caution. If true, it entailed a change of his mind by the time he wrote *The Marriage of Heaven and Hell* a year or two later, where he protested that having shown the folly of churches and exposed hypocrites, Swedenborg had come to think himself 'the single one on earth that ever broke a net'. He continued:

Now hear a plain fact: Swedenborg has not written one new truth: now hear another: he has written all the old falsehoods.[7]

From this account of Blake's development it will also be seen that the idea – still sometimes to be found in criticism – that the succession from *Songs of Innocence* to *Songs of Experience* in 1794 corresponded to a dramatic change in Blake's view of the world as he passed from the innocence of youth to the bitterness of maturity will hardly bear serious examination. It ignores, among other things, not only the fact that Blake was more than thirty when he put together the *Songs of Innocence*, but that in the previous *Island in the Moon* he had already apparently written himself into the part played by the cynical Quid. The case seems, rather, to be the one suggested earlier: that Blake came increasingly to derive enjoyment from pressing a particular point of view to its extreme. If its contrary then emerged in response, that too could be allowed its own voice – even if it called for the shaping of a new way of writing. As already mentioned, texts that had first appeared in *An Island in the Moon* could reappear in some of the *Songs of Innocence*: 'The Little Boy Lost' and 'Nurse's Song', for example; in their new setting, however, they would no longer be subdued to the general tone of amusement, but were free to transmit their vision in a purer form. No doubt there were shifts in Blake's attitudes, corresponding to the dominant tone of the work he was producing at any given time, but his personality cannot be contained within any single one of them. As with many creative artists, he had the gift of concentrating himself in a particular point of view for a time while leaving much in reserve, ready to generate further changes once those were ready to emerge.

So far as the *Songs of Innocence* are concerned, an important guide to their achievement can be found in the work of Heather Glen, who has considered their relation to many of the existing analogues in contemporary life and literature that surrounded their production. In particular, she shows how much in the rhetoric of the verses demands a response from the reader that differs from the linear approach associated with a normal reading. The uses of rhyme, alliteration and repetition assist in the creation of a world of its own for the collection, a world circular, spherical and reflecting – encapsulated, indeed, in the title-phrase of the poem 'The Ecchoing Green' – where words and images respond to one another, creating a universe of sustaining reflection with things echoing and mirroring one another in a manner like that which parents and carers instinctively draw upon (or learn to construct) for the reassurance of young children. Although this usually runs counter to the play of ironies and ambiguities that readers value in the wit of finely worked poetry, it can sometimes achieve a similar effect by way of supplementation and increased intensity, including an echoing of previous and already familiar literature. A good example can be found in the concluding second and third stanzas of the first 'Holy Thursday', which replace the moral and sententious reactions often to be found in descriptions of this well-known contemporary pageant:

> O what a multitude they seemd, these flowers of London town
> Seated in companies they sit with radiance all their own
> The hum of multitudes were there but multitudes of lambs
> Thousands of little girls & boys raising their innocent hands
>
> Then like a mighty wind they raise to heaven the voice of song
> Or like harmonious thunderings the seats of heaven among
> Beneath them sit the aged men the guardians of the poor
> Then cherish pity lest you drive an angel from your door

The lines create a crescendo of reinforcement, the most prominent motif being offered by a verse of Revelation:

> And I heard as it were the voice of a great multitude, and as the voice of many waters, and as the voice of mighty thunderings ...[8]

This unusual example, by sustained pressure, will awaken in a well-read reader further echoes of the great choruses of praise punctuating that final biblical text.

By the time that he put together *Songs of Innocence*, Blake was indeed deeply read in many authors and points of view. The indications are that in the wake of his early enthusiasms, he had embarked on a long study of the significance of human nature in the light of his own experiences, turning particularly to authors (particularly some flourishing much earlier) who had explored the relationship between nature and the imagination. The fruits of his thought can be found, before the *Songs*, in the little collections of aphorisms already touched on: 'THERE is NO Natural Religion' and 'ALL RELIGIONS are ONE', in which he launched his first open attacks on contemporary intellectual attitudes. For many eighteenth-century philosophers, following in the wake of Bacon, Locke and Newton, the human body seemed to be a highly appropriate instrument for dealing with nature. If the five senses were finely attuned to all that it had to offer, the task of the intellectual was simply to investigate the relationships between man and nature until they were brought into harmony. Blake could not agree. For him the idea that there was nothing in the universe that could not be perceived by the five senses was a prime source of the contemporary sense of imprisonment. He would have agreed with Andrew Baxter, who argued that 'the body, in its present constitution, limits and confines the perceptions of the soul, but no way effects them'.[9] Even Locke had suggested that there might be other faculties locked up in man for want of an organ by which they could be perceived, creating the situation in which the understanding was a 'closet, wholly shut from light, with only some little opening left, to let in external visible resemblances, or ideas of things without'.[10]

Blake took from both Locke and Baxter the point that if we had only three senses, we would not have the means to know of the other sense experiences that we in fact possess, and used it in the first 'THERE is NO Natural Religion', which concluded with the reflection: 'If it were not for the Poetic or Prophetic character the Philosophic & Experimental would soon be at the ratio of all things, & stand still, unable to do other than repeat the same dull round over again.' For him such a vision of science was nightmarish, since the necessary limits to knowledge that it implied must abandon human beings to the dull fate of continually contemplating repeated rounds of the same limited mechanism.

This experience of depression from sameness was shared by other Romantic observers at the time. Goethe and his friends, it is said, felt as if

> they were walking among countless moving spools and looms in a great factory where the bewilderment produced by the machinery, the incomprehensibility of the complicated interlocking process, and the consideration of all that goes into the production of a piece of cloth, caused them to grow disgusted with the very coats they had on.[11]

At such times the Enlightenment could seem more like a darkening – or at the very least a dulling into unrelieved monotony of what should have been bright. In Blake's view, on the other hand, the 'Poetic or Prophetic character' liberated them by invoking a vision that transcended the sum of sense-experiences. They no longer need feel themselves trapped within the confines of their own physical bodies, but could learn a sense of true freedom. That sense is implicit in the vision that informs *Songs of Innocence*.

Events seemed to be on the side of a more positive, optimistic view. A few months after the meeting that established the Swedenborgian New Church, the French Revolution broke out, an event that, following so soon after the American War of Independence, appeared to mark a decisive movement forward in human affairs. For a time Blake was a fervent supporter and is said to have worn the emblem of the revolutionaries openly in the streets of London. The sense that a new era was opening in human affairs, already prophesied in the writings of Swedenborg, must for a time have been compelling. At this time he was also producing engravings for Joseph Johnson, publisher of books by a number of forward-looking writers that included Price, Priestley, Fuseli, Godwin, Paine and Mary Wollstonecraft. Blake, who is said to have met some of these figures at Johnson's weekly dinners, would have heard much talk of new ideas, not only in politics but also in social affairs.

Primary among his responses were the *Songs of Innocence*, which from one point of view can also be regarded as a reaction to the disquiet sensed above in the production of *An Island*. The wit of that collection, tinged by the bitterness of discovering how little his visionary world was shared by his contemporaries, was now relieved by a more positive evaluation of innocence. In the light of his new enterprise it was not enough to assign 'When the tongues of children' to the foolish Mrs Nannicantipont; moreover, such a song deserved a prominence of its own. His renewed version would begin 'When the voices of children' and, with a few other changed lyrics, be afforded a higher standing.

This new note of assertiveness has on the whole been welcomed by subsequent critics, even though one problem with its extreme simplicity is that it leaves the critic with less to do. When complexity does arise, on the other hand, it is sometimes difficult to deal with, as with the controversy that has surrounded 'The Chimney-Sweeper'. The speaker of this poem, himself a sweeper, tells how one of his fellows, who had to be comforted when his head was shaved, had a dream in which the sweepers, all locked in black coffins, were set free by an angel to 'wash in a river and shine in the Sun':

> Then naked & white, all their bags left behind,
> They rise upon clouds, and sport in the wind.
> And the Angel told Tom if he'd be a good boy,
> He'd have God for his father & never want joy.
>
> And so Tom awoke and we rose in the dark
> And got with our bags & our brushes to work.
> Tho' the morning was cold, Tom was happy & warm,
> So if all do their duty, they need not fear harm.

Those who have registered the anger of Blake's later poetry find the apparently reactionary message of these last lines hard to understand. Can this really be the same poet who was to write another version of

'The Chimney-Sweeper' in his following collection and who must have known the stark conditions in which the 'climbing boys' of the time struggled for their existence?[12] How could both versions sit side by side in the same brain?

In order to consider this question further it will be necessary to turn to the collection in which he expressed more fully the disillusioned bitterness that had come to alternate with his affirmations of innocent vision. Before that, however, his marriage, and the relation of that to his own developing ideas of love and sexual experience, needs to be considered.

4
Love, Marriage and Sexual Lore

Throughout his career William Blake enjoyed the supporting presence of his faithful wife, Catherine. According to Gilchrist, their relationship began shortly after a period of depression following his rejection by another young woman.[1] One of his early biographers, Frederick Tatham, gave a more elaborate account of their first encounter:

> He became ill & went to Kew near Richmond for a change of air & renovation of health & spirits & as far as is possible to know lodged at the House of a market Gardener whose name was Boutcher. The Boutchers appear to have been a respectable & industrious family. He was relating to the daughter, a Girl named Catherine, the lamentable story of Polly Wood, his implacable Lass, upon which Catherine expressed her deep sympathy, it is supposed in such a tender & affectionate manner, that it quite won him, he immediately said with the suddenness peculiar to him 'Do you pity me?' 'Yes, indeed I do' answered she 'Then I love you' said he again. Such was their courtship. He was impressed with her tenderness of mind & her answer indicated her previous feeling for him. For she has often said that upon her mother asking her who among her acquaintances she could fancy for a Husband, she replied that she had not yet seen the man & she has further been heard to say that when she first came into the Room in which Blake sat she instantly recognized (like Britomart in Merlins wondrous glass) her future partner, & was so near fainting that she left his presence until she had recovered. After this interview, Blake left the House having recruited his health & spirits, & having determined to take Catherine Boutcher to Wife. He returned to his Lodgings, & worked incessantly that he might be able to accomplish this End at the same time resolving that he would not

41

see her until he succeeded. This interval which she felt dolefully long was one whole year, at the expiration of which with the approbation & consent of his parents he married this Interesting beautiful & affectionate Girl. Nimble with joy & warm with the glow of youth, this bride was presented to her noble bridegroom. The morning of their married life was bright as the noon of their devoted love, The noon as clear as the serene Evening of their mutual equanimity. Although not handsome he must have had a noble countenance, full of expression & animation, his hair was of a yellow brown, & curled with the utmost crispness & luxuriance. His locks instead of falling down stood up like a curling flame, and looked at a distance like radiations, which with his fiery Eye & expansive forehead, his dignified & cheerful physiognomy must have made his appearance truly prepossessing. After his Marriage he took lodgings in Green St Leicester Square.[2]

For any further sense of the Blakes' married life one is again reliant largely on traditions recorded by the biographers, but occasionally further light breaks through from hints that he himself left. In the Notebook there is a sketch of a couple in their bedroom accompanied by the telling couplet

> When a Man has Married a Wife
>   he finds out whether
> Her knees & elbows are only
>   glued together

Blake evidently had a strong interest in sexual behaviour, but it is hard to know much about the general state of his own marriage from anything he himself said on the subject. It is necessary to fall back on another biographical account – again from Gilchrist[3] and referring this time to his brother Robert, for an absorbing sidelight:

One day, a dispute arose between Robert and Mrs. Blake. She, in the heat of discussion, used words to him, his brother (though a husband too) thought unwarrantable. A silent witness thus far, he could now bear it no longer, but with characteristic impetuosity – when stirred – rose and said to her: 'Kneel down and beg Robert's pardon directly, or you never see my face again!' A heavy threat, uttered in tones which, from Blake, unmistakably showed it was meant. She, poor thing! 'thought it very hard,' as she would afterwards tell, to beg her brother-in-law's pardon when she was not in fault! But being a duteous, devoted wife, though by nature nowise tame or dull of spirit, she did kneel down and meekly murmur: 'Robert, I beg your pardon, I am in the wrong.' 'Young woman, you lie!' abruptly retorted he: 'I am in the wrong!'[4]

As a young man Blake had a fiery temperament, which could flare into anger if he thought human beings were being misused. Surviving stories tell of indignant interventions against an employer who punished a lad by having a log tied to his foot and against a man he saw beating a woman in the street.[5]

His own domestic life was more peaceful, however, and as he and Robert set up shop to sell prints the marriage seemed to go smoothly. Prints had long been an absorbing interest: in his boyhood, according to Malkin, he had attracted the attention of an auctioneer who, noticing his keen interest, sometimes saw to it that particular lots could be knocked down swiftly so that they could go to his 'little connoisseur'.[6] Now he also supported the household by devoting himself to teaching – which might on occasion include acts of pure charity:

A young man passed his House daily whose avocations seemed to lead him backward & forward to some place of study, carrying a Portfolio under his Arm. He looked interesting & eager, but sickly.

After some time Blake sent Mrs Blake to call the young man in; he came & he told them, that he was studying the Arts. Blake from this took a high interest in him & gave him every instruction possible, but alas! ... the young man shortly after fell sick, & was laid upon his bed, his illness was long & his sufferings were great during which time, Mrs Blake or Blake never omitted visiting him daily & administering medicine, money, or Wine & every other requisite until death relieved their adopted of all earthly care & pain. Every attention, every parental tenderness, was exhibited by the charitable pair.[7]

Frederick Tatham, who reported this, has also left an interesting account of Blake's prowess as a teacher during the 1790s:

he taught Drawing & was engaged for that purpose by some families of high rank; which by the bye he could not have found very profitable, for after his lesson he got into conversation with his pupils, & was found so entertaining & pleasant, possessing such novel thoughts & such eccentric notions, together with such jocose hilarity & amiable demeanour, that he frequently found himself asked to stay dinner, & spend the Evening in the same interesting & lively manner, in which he had consumed the morning. Thus he stopped whole days from his work at home, but nevertheless he continued teaching, until a remarkable effort & kind flirt of fortune, brought this mode of livelihood to an inevitable close. He was recommended & nearly obtained an Appointment to teach Drawing to the Royal Family. Blake stood aghast; not indeed from any republican humours, not from any disaffection to his superiors, but because he would have been drawn into a class of Society, superior to his previous pursuits & habits; he would have been expected to have lived in comparative respectability, not to say splendour, a mode of life, as he thought, derogatory to the simplicity of his designs & deportment ...

His friends ridiculed & blamed him by turns but Blake found an Excuse by resigning all his other pupils, & continued to suffice himself upon his frugality ...[8]

A rather different picture of Blake in the 1790s here emerges from that which might be derived from the *Songs* or the early Prophetic Books. This is a figure recognizable from *An Island in the Moon*, independent and on the whole debonair: it would be interesting to have more exact details of the initiative. A possible date would be 1783: in April 1784, Flaxman wrote that a Cornish gentleman named Hawkins was trying to raise a subscription In the hope that Blake could be sent to finish his studies in Rome,[9] though the plan evidently came to nothing. Whatever the exact chronology, however, the anecdotes just recorded suggests that the Blakes were settling into a contented London life.

Blake's intellectual development was nevertheless complicated in the 1790s by the turmoil of the time, and this inevitably included the raising of questions concerning sexual behaviour. As has been pointed out already, his work for Joseph Johnson brought him into contact with various associated radical thinkers. He would probably not have agreed with all that he heard from them (Peter Ackroyd points out, for example, that Paine's dismissal of Isaiah as 'one continual incoherent rant' would hardly have appealed to one who claimed him as an early benevolent influence and who fantasized him as a dining companion in *The Marriage of Heaven and Hell*[10]), but he certainly had some contact with Mary Wollstonecraft, for whose *Original Stories from Real Life* he produced some illustrations, and must have known of her strong attraction to Fuseli, despite his failure to reciprocate her feelings. The views which she was to express in her *Vindication of the Rights of Woman*, and which were in any case in the air following the French Revolution, may well have acted as a strong stimulus shortly afterwards for his *Visions of the Daughters of Albion*, a poetical work notable for its unprecedented openness about the state of relations between the sexes at the time, with Albion's daughters and sons shown to be suffering the pains of ungratified desire:

> The moment of desire! The moment of desire! The virgin
> That pines for man; shall awaken her womb to enormous joys
> In the secret shadows of her chamber; the youth shut up from
> The lustful joy shall forget to generate & create an amorous image
> In the shadows of his curtains and in the folds of his silent pillow.[11]

Oothoon, the heroine of this poem, is depicted as selflessly generous. The action of the poem begins when her rape by the lustful tyrant Bromion is followed immediately by his branding her a harlot and rejecting her, telling her lover Theotormon to look after the child that will arrive in nine months' time. But if Bromion is a hypocrite, Theotormon is religiously lethargic, rapt in the self-consumings of his gloomy meditations. While Oothoon praises the joys of desire, she also reproaches the 'Father of Jealousy' whose 'cold floods of abstraction' and 'forests of solitude' she senses as the landscape and presence behind her lover's 'secret tears' and dark abstention.

> With what sense does the parson claim the labour of the farmer?
> What are his nets & gins & traps & how does he surround him
> With cold floods of abstraction, and with forests of solitude,
> To build him castles and high spires. where kings & priests may dwell.
> Till she who burns with youth. and knows no fixed lot; is bound
> In spells of law to one she loaths: and must she drag the chain
> Of life, in weary lust! must chilling murderous thoughts. obscure
> The clear heaven of her eternal spring? to bear the wintry rage
> Of a harsh terror driv'n to madness, bound to hold a rod
> Over her shrinking shoulders all the day; & all the night
> To turn the wheel of false desire: and longings that wake her womb
> To the abhorred birth of cherubs in the human form
> That live a pestilence & die a meteor & are no more.
> Till the child dwell with one he hates and do the deed he loaths
> And the impure scourge force his seed into its unripe birth
> E'er yet his eyelids can behold the arrows of the day.[12]

How did assertions such as this (prophetic in their lore of sexual deprivation) square with Blake's own relationships? The story that bears most directly on the question is the one that tells how Blake at one point thought that married men should be allowed to have concubines and how he was dissuaded from the idea by Catherine's tears.[13]* This story, which may be apocryphal, is sometimes recounted in connection with a lyric, 'William Bond', that may or may not be related to the matter: it tells of a man who returns home from church in a deep depression and confides in 'Mary Green', who tries to nurse him and replies that if he loves another woman better he can take her and she will act as her servant. William accepts the offer,

> For thou art Melancholy Pale
> And on thy Head is the cold Moons shine
> But she is ruddy & bright as day
> And the sun beams dazzle from her eyne

At this Mary collapses and almost dies, but then wakes to find herself in William Bond's bed. The next stanza (presumably voicing his subsequent reaction) runs:

> I thought Love lived in the hot sun shine
> But O he lives in the Moony light
> I thought to find Love in the heat of day
> But sweet Love is the Comforter of Night

Whatever the relevance or otherwise of this matter, most evidence points to William and Catherine as having been unusually happy in their relations. Hayley wrote:

Heaven has bestowed on this extraordinary Mortal perhaps the only female on Earth, who could have suited him exactly. They have been married more than 17 years & are as fond of each other, as if their Honey Moon were still shining – They live in a neat little cottage, which they both regard as the most delightful residence ever inhabited by a mortal; they have no servant – the good woman not only does all the work of the House, but she even makes the greatest part of her Husbands dress, & assists him in his art – she draws, she engraves, & sings delightfully & is so truly the Half of her good Man, that they seem animated by one Soul, & that a soul of indefatigable Industry & Benevolence – it sometimes hurries them both to labour rather too much …[14]

Catherine Blake suffered from various ailments, particularly when they lived for a time in a Sussex cottage, but as to their sexual relations, one assumes that his endorsement of those human beings who had 'The lineaments of Gratified Desire' included her in the company – particularly when one recalls his gleeful reminiscence of a day in August 1807 when he and Catherine practised the *sortes* and she stumbled on a piece from Aphra Behn:

> My Wife was told by a Spirit to look for her fortune by opening by chance a book which she had in her hand it was Bysshes Art of Poetry. She opend the following

> I saw 'em kindle with desire
> While with soft sighs they blew the fire
> Saw the approaches of their joy
> He growing more fierce & she less coy
> Saw how they mingled melting rays
> Exchanging Love a thousand ways
> Kind was the force on every side ⎫
> Her new desire she could not hide ⎬
> Nor would the shepherd be denied ⎭
> The blessed minute he pursued
> Till she transported in his arms
> Yields to the Conqueror all her charms
> His panting breast to hers now Joind
> They feast on raptures unconfind
> Vast & luxuriant such as prove
> The immortality of Love
> For who but a Divinity ⎫
> Could mingle souls to that degree ⎬
> And melt them into Extasy ⎭
> Now like the Phoenix both expire ⎫
> While from the ashes of their fire ⎬
> Spring up a new & soft desire ⎭
> Like charmers thrice they did invoke
> The God & thrice new Vigor took

Blake then recalls how he was so well pleased with her luck that he followed suit, opening at a passage from Dryden's *Virgil* which described the rooted steadfastness of an oak tree.[15]

One of his few other recorded statements on the subject was his annotation to Lavater's account in his *Aphorisms on Man* of 'four wonders': 'a great woman not imperious, a fair woman not vain, a woman of common talents not jealous, an accomplished woman, who scorns to shine'. Blake wrote:

> let the men do their duty & the women will be such wonders, the female lives from the light of the male. see a mans female dependants you know the man.[16]

At the time when he wrote this (perhaps soon after the publication of Lavater's book in 1789), Blake evidently adhered to the view of the relationship between the sexes indicated in Milton's line 'Hee for God only, shee for God in him'.[17] Man was for intellect, woman for tender grace. Yet it is no doubt misleading to assume that his doctrine of the sexes and their relationship was a fixed one: it is equally likely that he took his views on the subject from the circumstances of the moment.

Certain orderings remained constant, nevertheless. He was as firm in his delight in the pleasures of sexual love as he was insistent on their subordinate place in the order of human activity. Discussing Milton with Crabb Robinson in 1825, according to the latter,

> he wished me to shew the falsehood of his doctrine that the pleasures of sex arose from the fall – The fall could not produce any pleasure ...[18]

In so far as he had a scheme of things, in fact, it seems to have been closely bound up with his sense of differing levels of vision, the sexual belonging to the 'threefold'. This he also thought of as the state of 'Beulah', a term which he presumably arrived at by combining its appearance in Isaiah, where it was equated with 'married',[19] and that in Bunyan's *The Pilgrim's Progress*, where the pilgrims enter the country of Beulah after passing through the Enchanted Ground:

> Here they were within sight of the City they were going to, also here met them some of the inhabitants thereof; for in this land the Shining Ones commonly walked, because it was upon the borders of Heaven. In this land also the contract between the Bride and Bridegroom was renewed; yea, here, *as the bridegroom rejoiceth over the bride, so did their God rejoice over them.*
> ... and, drawing nearer to the City, they had yet a more perfect view thereof. It was built of Pearls and Precious Stones, also the Street

thereof was paved with Gold: so that by reason of the natural glory of the City, and the reflection of the Sun-beams upon it, *Christian* with desire fell sick ...[20]*

In sexual matters Blake's doctrine corresponded to that in his quatrain 'Eternity':

> He who binds to himself a joy
> Does the winged life destroy
> But he who kisses the joy as it flies
> Lives in eternity's sun rise[21]

Sexual pleasure was to be enjoyed in the moment of its visitation, but attempts to retain it or make it permanent would be akin to hoping for lasting possession of fourfold vision. The point is made even more vehemently in *Milton*, where the impossibility of human beings fully seeing the heavenly city Golgonooza is stated explicitly:

> For Golgonooza cannot be seen till having passed the Polypus
> It is viewed on all sides round by a Four-fold Vision
> Or till you become Mortal & Vegetable in Sexuality
> Then you behold its mighty Spires & Domes of ivory & gold

As a momentary revelation, the fourfold vision of the artist can give him a sight of the heavenly city, which is also glimpsed – if only momentarily – in sexual activity; but neither level of vision is to be confused with eternal access: this can be attained only by passing out of the mortal body altogether, through death.

Awareness of this injunction throws light on much else that Blake has to say about the body. In the 1790s, as he devised the book *Europe*, he offered a searching description of the nature of the Fall that he believed to have led to the imprisoned condition of human brings in his time, 'when the five senses whelm'd I In deluge o'er the earth-born man':

> then turn'd the fluxile eyes
> Into two stationary orbs, concentrating all things.
> The ever-varying spiral ascents to the heavens of heavens
> Were bended downwards, and the nostrils golden gates shut
> Turn'd outward, barr'd and petrify'd against the infinite.[22]

This attempt to portray a fall caused by limiting the number of senses firmly to five could then be extended to the world that resulted. The infinite in humanity which caused human beings to relate to one another, not being cultivated as such, became fearful; the serpent that should emblematize this eternity was in consequence recoiled from as an object of horror.

When he turned to devise an alternative myth, as will shortly be described, he produced some brilliant speculations on a means of creating the human body that would involve limiting its powers. Blake produced more than one such account, according to whether the agent of this creation was to be thought of as 'Urizen', turning away from the Eternals, or 'Los', striving to continue his making in the midst of chaos. In point of fact, however, the two are sometimes presented as if their work is being produced by two forces of a not dissimilar power: in *The Book of Urizen*, after the 'second age', as Los/Urizen labours, his nervous brain shoots branches

> On high into two little orbs
> And fixed in two little caves
> Hiding carefully from the wind,
> His Eyes beheld the deep,
> And a third Age passed over
> And a state of dismal woe.
> The pangs of hope began,
> In heavy pain striving, struggling.

There were problems involved, however, in an attempt to produce this kind of 'prophetic' writing on a larger scale. Witty as it might be to aim at writing a creation story that parodied Genesis by envisaging the making of this world as a process of shrinking and limitation, questions inevitably remained. What, then, was the ideal which this world failed to match? And was it possible to represent it satisfactorily? The process of the *Book of Urizen* inevitably resulted in a dour atmosphere of painful suffering as the 'Eternals' faced the fact of human ills – whatever the process that had produced the reality with which we are all familiar. One would imagine however, that if Blake thought that things might have been otherwise, he would have created figures corresponding to those other possibilities. Yet there is very little attempt to delineate such alternatives.

Tristanne Connolly, who has carried out a far-ranging and detailed discussion of Blake's thinking on the subject of the body,[23] confesses herself somewhat baffled by this issue, since if one were to try to realize the kind of human form that would answer to all the desirable features inherent in his vision (fluxile, expansive eyes, ears that would be 'ever-varying spiral ascents to the heavens of heavens', nostrils serving as 'golden gates'), one would be faced not with an ideal human being but with a monstrosity. But of course it is a part of Blake's philosophy that, given our human condition, we cannot only never know, but never even *visualize* a humanity corresponding to the ideal characteristics he postulates.

Meanwhile the mortal body could still impress him by its limitations when he or his wife fell ill.[24*] Catherine continued nevertheless to be his 'Shadow of Delight' – as he called her twice in *Milton*[25] – a term which is probably related to his sense of the ideal state of being in 'Vala' as that of a Spirit whose female emanation was a Garden of Delight ('thou & I in undivided Essence walkd about | Imbodied. Thou my Garden of delight & I the spirit in the garden').[26] Their relationship, though admirable for its time, could hardly be a model for the future, however. Although Blake deserves to be celebrated as a great humanist, he was not equally a prophet of feminism. It would be truer to say that he took his cue from the Miltonic formula already mentioned: 'Hee for God only, Shee for God in him'. His own 'Let the men do their duty & the women will be such wonders' might be thought of as a variation on that theme; although he certainly showed great insight into feminine views, the signs are that in social terms he was affected by the prejudices of his contemporaries; and the fact that Catherine had not received any formal education would have left her with little chance of holding her own in any intellectual debate on the issue. The one point that the biographers seem to agree on, nevertheless, is her extraordinary devotion to her husband. One account relates that she had the same literal belief in his visions as John Varley and that

> when he ... would tell his friends that King Alfred, or any great historical personage, had sat to him, Mrs. Blake would look at her husband with an awe-struck countenance, and then at his listener to confirm the fact. Not only was she wont to echo what he said, to talk as he talked, on religion and other matters – this may be accounted for by the fact that he had educated her; but she, too, learned to have visions; – to see processions of figures wending along the river, in broad daylight; and would give a start when they disappeared in the water.[27]

Such accounts do not necessarily mean that she was entirely meek in her nature, of course; simply that in their marriage she was content to accept his leadership. What she seems to have responded to above all, particularly in earlier years, was the extraordinary energy that was the distinctive quality of his thinking and art, while also fuelling the sardonicism that could at times give his view of human experience an unusual intensity.

5
Finding a Voice for Experience

Any optimism that Blake might have imbibed from the effervescence of thinking and writing by himself and others that was prompted by news of the French Revolution was shortly to be dealt a devastating blow. His enthusiasm is said to have come to an abrupt end at the time of the September massacres in 1792, when he tore off his revolutionary cockade and never wore it again.

It is to this event, the disappointing sequel – at least in political terms – to the intellectual ferment that had been brewing over the previous few years, that the increasing bitterness of his writings around 1793 may be due. Blake could not renege on the excitement and enthusiasm he had felt during the previous years; he was forced to admit, on the other hand, that his fellow-citizens showed few signs of allowing themselves to be possessed by new ideals in the shaping of their society. On the contrary, since they remained largely under the control of those who wished to manipulate them, the future looked bleak. Early in 1795 his friend George Cumberland wrote of fears that England would soon be living under an absolute government or be plunged into a civil war. Neither prospect would be inviting to Blake: either would intensify the imprisonment from which his fellows seemed powerless to escape.

The most notable link between public events and his private life that Blake made during the subsequent period was in his letter to Flaxman of September 1800, where, as will be recalled, he mentioned the 'dark horrors' of the American War and continued,

> ... Then the French Revolution commenc'd in thick clouds
> And My Angels have told me that seeing such visions I could not
>   subsist on the Earth,
> But by my conjunction with Flaxman, who knows to forgive
> Nervous Fear.[1]

Despite his disenchantment, the events in France had in certain respects affected his attitude to the world permanently. As we have seen, the man who published the *Poetical Sketches* in 1778 had shown little or no sign of dissent from the political views regarded as orthodox in the England of his time. Towards the end of the century, however, events had been taking place that were likely to imprint themselves lastingly on his memory: apart from the Gordon Riots, when his involuntary position at the front of the mob had enabled him to see at first hand the storming of Newgate jail and the release of hundreds of prisoners, he must have been affected by the burning in March 1791 of the Albion Flour Mills near Blackfriars Bridge. The destruction of these huge, steam-powered mills, which had opened only a few years before and already achieved considerable fame as a tourist attraction, had a momentous impact in the city: Horace Walpole recorded that, apart from the hundred thousand pounds' worth of damage caused, the Palace Yard and part of St James's Park were left covered with half-burnt grains. It was to be recalled some years later by Coleridge, who had then been still at school. Although Blake left no record, it is inconceivable that he did not know of it – nor, indeed, that he could have failed to make a connection with his own, already invoked, figure of Albion.[2*] Given such public events about him, it is not surprising that their impact should have been reflected in notes of an intensified realism.

Perhaps, also, the effect of painting Innocence in such vivid colours was to invoke – almost automatically, in so spirited a man – a complementary sense of ways in which children responded to the forces of oppression from their earliest years by subtly growing into practices of deceit and submitting themselves to secret, self-enclosed pleasures. And as the idea grew of following the *Songs of Innocence* with a contrasting *Songs of Experience*, based on this alternative, more cynical vision, Blake's movement towards such a collection must have gained impetus from his disillusioned reaction to the current political situation. With the two concepts brought together to form a fuller sequence, moreover, their linking helped to fulfil Blake's insistence that contraries needed to be in tension with one another. 'Innocence dwells with Wisdom,' he wrote, 'but never with Ignorance'; and again, 'Unorganizd Innocence, All Impossibility'.[3]

In the preceding years, around 1794, his poetic and literary powers were at their peak. The quality of his writing at this time becomes all the clearer when one looks at the notebook drafts and sees the processes by which he reached his final versions: the ruthless parings and bendings into place are undeniably improvements. In 'The Tyger', for instance, the early draft ran (with various deletions en route):

> And what shoulder & what art
> Could twist the sinews of thy heart?
> And when thy heart began to beat
> What dread hands & what dread feet
>
> Could fetch it from the furnace deep
> And the horrid ribs dare steep
> In the well of sanguine woe
>
> In what clay & in what mould
> Were thy eyes of fury rolld[4]

By the time of the final version the second of these draft stanzas is omitted, so that the last line of the first one turns into the more indefinite, yet more immediately vivid, question:

> What dread hand? & what dread feet?[5*]

The spare, questioning voice is much closer to what readers have valued most in this poem. By its very construction it appeals directly to the workings of the subconscious, evoking collocations of images that can work closely with one another towards an effect of awe coupled with attraction that would have been the envy of any Gothic literary writer.

Blake's revisions do not always work simply by way of dramatic contraction. An instructive example of another kind may be found in the first version of the notebook poem that begins 'I heard an Angel singing'. In this early draft the angel's theme, 'Mercy Pity & Peace I Is the worlds release', is followed at the third stanza by another voice:

> I heard a Devil curse
> Over the heath & the furze
> Mercy could be no more
> If there was nobody poor
>
> And pity no more could be
> If all were as happy as we
> Thus he sang the sun went down
> And the heavens gave a frown
>
> And down pourd the heavy rain
> Over the new reapd grain,
> And Mercy & Pity & Peace descended
> The Farmers were ruind & harvest was ended.[6]

The swift and sardonic conclusion of the last stanza was later deleted; and when he came to draw on the draft for 'The Human Abstract', he took nothing but the four lines of the Devil's song, which formed, with slight changes, the opening stanzas of his new poem. He moved from this piece of sophistic logic to set up further examples ('mutual fear brings Peace', for instance). The result of the process was then made to emerge in the growth of a Tree of Mystery, nurtured by cruelty with the aid of humility. He concluded:

> The Gods of the Earth and Sea,
> Sought thro' Nature to find this Tree
> But their search was all in vain:
> There grows one in the Human Brain[7]

This brilliant use of the eighteenth-century image of the Upas Tree (the tree that in contemporary mythology was said to poison the atmosphere for miles around[8]) exemplifies a characteristic working of Blake's mind. When faced with the effects and processes of social injustice, his first impulse was to speak out in indignation, sullen resentment or simple sardonic statement; in the longer term, he looked for deeper causes. If his society allowed itself to build great mills in which human beings were imprisoned most of the day, that must be because they already had dark satanic mills in their own minds, screening from them the incongruity and inhumanity involved. If they swallowed the spurious logic of contemporary spokesmen in favour of the status quo, similarly, it must be because their minds were so overshadowed by self-imprisonment: as a result they could not detect false reasonings that they would be only too swift to spot in a matter that affected their own material interests.

It is a germane feature of Blake's own mental honesty, as with his desire to rouse his fellows to think for themselves, that he does not attempt a refutation of the writers with whom he disagrees. If there is a positive energy or illumination to which he can respond, he will respect that, while subtly subverting those elements he believes false. A good example is to be found in his dealings with Swedenborg, who interpolated into his writings passages that he called 'Memorable Relations'. One of these, as Kathleen Raine pointed out, throws direct light on the chimney sweep of *Songs of Innocence*: 'There are also Spirits among those from the Earth Jupiter, whom they call Sweepers of Chimneys, because they appear in like Garments, and likewise with sooty Faces ...'[9] Swedenborg is informed that these figures will later, when they form part of the Grand Man, or Heaven, 'constitute the province of the

Seminal Vessels'. This implication that the chimney sweep is a symbol of sexual activity can draw also on popular traditions, such as that of the chimney sweep kissing the bride to give her good luck. Heather Glen refers to a number of such instances.[10] But for Blake the chief importance of the symbolism might well lie in the suggestion that a reason for tolerating the practice of forcing boys to climb chimneys to sweep them as part of the social system was that sexual activity itself was thought of as secret and dirty. He would also have approved of Swedenborg's further assertion that it was the burning intensity of the sweeper's desire to be in heaven that led to his being called upon to cast off his clothes with a promise of new and shining raiment – a detail that resembles the dream of Tom Dacre in his first 'Chimney Sweeper' poem.

But although Blake could draw directly on Swedenborg's visions, he must have found his 'Memorable Relations' in general long and rambling, just as he came to discern in Swedenborg's philosophy, for all its imaginative promise, little more than another way of presenting conventional teachings. So in *The Marriage of Heaven and Hell* he would produce several 'Memorable Fancies' in conscious satire.

Although the satirical intent is clear in some of these poems, many of his most typical poems contain an element that resists interpretation. It is a feature all the more unexpected when the directness of the language carries the reader along in assent. Only when one tries to make out and paraphrase the sense of what has just been read may it be discovered that the poem is less simple than it at first appeared. A good example of this is one of his most simple lyrics, 'The Fly', which has several times been the subject of excited hermeneutical discourse. It begins:

> Little Fly
> Thy summer's play,
> My thoughtless hand
> Has brush'd away.
>
> Am not I
> A fly like thee?
> Or art not thou
> A man like me?
>
> For I dance
> And drink, & sing;
> Till some blind hand
> Shall brush my wing.

The poem has some clear antecedents in eighteenth-century poetry, notably in the closing lines of Gray's 'Ode on the Spring':

> Methinks I hear in accents low
> The sportive kind reply:
> Poor moralist! and what art thou?
> A solitary fly!
> Thy joys no glittering female meets,
> No hive hast thou of hoarded sweets,
> No painted plumage to display:
> On hasty wings thy youth is flown;
> Thy sun is set, thy spring is gone –
> We frolick, while 'tis May.[11]

Whereas Gray's point is simple enough, however, Blake's 'Fly' involves a strange shift of subject so that the poem does not end as we might have expected. In the conclusion we discover that we can be happy whether we live or die – which might suggest, logically, that after all it does not matter very much whether or not we treat flies kindly. Yet there is a clear moral, connected with the lines in *King Lear*: 'As flies to wanton boys, are we to the gods; | They kill us for their sport.'[12] We should not like to be treated in the way that boys treat flies, and this might be thought a good reason for being kind to insects. There is also an implication that those who show cruelty to living things are more likely to be cruel to their fellow human beings. To encourage kindness to animals and insects is to encourage habits of mind that may benefit human society generally.

All this is in the vein of late eighteenth-century humanitarianism; there is little to criticize – apart, perhaps, from a veiled anthropocentrism. But Blake's interest in such closed systems of semi-moral approbation is limited. Their basis is ultimately an enlightened self-concern that has more to do with interest than with light. And behind this scene of moral instruction there remains a disturbing further implication from the *Lear* quotation: however we treat flies, or each other, we must eventually die in circumstances over which we shall have no control. Across the questions of kindness to others or not there falls the shadow of a recognition that nature certainly entertains no such feeling for human beings.

The main problem with the poem is, however, that the second half does not cohere properly with the first, an impression which is exacerbated when one looks at the drafts out of which it grew. It originally began with the words 'Woe alas my guilty hand I Brushd across thy summer joy ...' It then modulated to read 'Little fly I Thy summers play, I My thoughtless hand I Has brush'd away.'[13] In the second and third stanzas of the finished poem he proceeds, in good eighteenth-century fashion, to identify his own fate with that of the fly. The fourth and the final ones, however, are marked by a new turn:

> If thought is life
> And strength & breath:
> And the want
> Of thought is death;
>
> Then am I
> A happy fly,
> If I live,
> Or if I die.

This shift (accurately signalled in the illuminated version by the appearance of branches and a tendril discreetly cutting off the last two stanzas from the rest) gives the effect of a strange conjuring, whereby we find ourselves, at the end of the poem, in the unexpected place of having passed through a subterranean transformation of meaning that cannot easily be unravelled into ordered sense, but that has changed the terms of the discussion from the question of kindness to that of life and its significance. For if the want of thought is death, and if this brings a happiness similar to that of the dead fly, its human destroyer seems to be excused from responsibility or guilt. The attitude is strangely quietist and accepting.

The poem, however, is defying a kind of logic that in Blake's eyes belongs to the same sphere of death. The business of the speaker is to choose the kind of thinking which is to be identified with life, strength and breath – after which he or she will no longer be thoughtless enough to brush away a harmless fly. This mode of being has its own logic.

There is a similar back-loaded syntax in the well-known 'Proverb of Hell' which reads: 'Sooner murder an infant in its cradle than nurse unacted desires.'[14] This has attracted criticism from some critics, who take it as an injunction to follow one's desires however inhuman and cruelly murderous they may prove. But here again the logic needs to be read backwards rather than forwards. Acted desires are being compared to infants reared in proper freedom. It will be impossible for such desires to be inhuman or murderous, because they will by their very nature be the expression of a freedom which is fully human, embodying a full vision of human potentiality. It is *unacted* desires that are likely to fester, and which will then resemble children whose development has been thwarted by ill usage. Once again the stress on the positive in Blake's thinking has to be fully grasped before the nature of his logic can be appreciated.

Having said this, one must still acknowledge the fact that the *Songs of Experience* – particularly when compared to those of *Innocence* – are largely cast in a negative mode. Just as Tolstoy remarked that while happy families are all alike, unhappy ones find many ways of being different, so the harmonic quality in Innocence contrasts with the very diverse achievements displayed in observing the ways of Experience. Heather Glen discriminates between the two states neatly in her sentence 'Where the Experienced speaker registers sameness yet division, the Innocent celebrates mutuality in diversity'; she also shows how several particular examples, as mental puzzles, like those already examined in 'The Fly', which stimulate the reader's mental activity, give place to the inaction of 'Ah! Sun-flower', a poem expressing again and again nothing more than a lazy desire for unattainable realms, the static effects of this condition being beautifully encapsulated in the second stanza where, as she points out, the four lines are unusual in that each contains a verb, yet the poem as a whole has no central main verb of action to carry the characters forward.

Equally complex is the effect of a poem such as 'A Poison Tree', the original intent being indicated, as she points out, by the fact that on the evidence of the Notebook the first quatrain,

> I was angry with my friend;
> I told my wrath, my wrath did end.
> I was angry with my foe:
> I told it not, my wrath did grow.

was intended originally to stand separately, bearing the title 'Christian Forbearance'. The subsequent development, by which the festering wrath is figured as an apple, its growth lovingly tended, and eventually, under cover of darkness, likely to produce a murderous revenge gratifying to the speaker, complicates the effect of the poem. What was at first an admonition in favour of plain dealing has become a little psychodrama of its own in which events have moved well beyond the protagonist's conceiving. The point is spelt out further in 'The Human Abstract', where the devilish false reasoning of 'Pity would be no more I If we did not make somebody poor' is traced to its root in the assertion that the

Upas Tree is not to be looked for anywhere in the natural world: 'There grows one in the Human Brain'.

The modern reader coming to these poems for the first time will soon pick up the underlying bitterness, but is likely to be seized even more immediately by the extraordinary directness of the writing. This is all the more striking if one reads Blake's verses alongside others that were being written in his time. 'London', one of his best poems, begins:

> I wander thro' each charter'd street,
> Near where the charter'd Thames does flow.
> And mark in every face I meet
> Marks of weakness, marks of woe.[15]

This has been compared[16] with one of Isaac Watts's hymns for children, which begins:

> Whene'er I take my Walks abroad,
> How many Poor I see
> What shall I render to my God
> For all his gifts to me?[17]

Despite an obvious similarity, the difference between the two verses is revealed immediately as that between formally 'taking a walk' and informally 'wandering'. Watts's stanza consists primarily of an observation and a question, the first dominated by the second. We hardly have time to glimpse the poor before the speaker is counting his blessings in not being of their number. Blake, by contrast, makes a single factual statement. We have the immediate impression of a man walking the streets, reflecting on the civilization about him, peering intently into the faces of all whom he meets to see what is to be read there, and disturbed to find primarily two bleak qualities: weakness and woe.

The purposes of the two poets are, of course, different. Watts is writing a hymn for children: like all hymn writers his first aim is to lead those who sing it into suitable sentiments that all can share. He regards himself as the spokesman for a society of shared beliefs. Blake is a lonelier figure, offering to speak for no one but himself. His is an adult poem: we are not sure whether even the speaker of the poem knows of a more positive vision – or whether he too may not bear the marks of weakness and woe.

The directness of 'London' carries on into its remaining stanzas:

> In every cry of every Man,
> In every Infants cry of fear,
> In every voice: in every ban,
> The mind-forg'd manacles I hear[18]

One of Blake's greatest poems, this has the quality, which shapes his most characteristic utterances, of describing the world as if one were looking at it for the first time. There is nothing naive about the vision, moreover; we need only turn back to the first stanza to see complex effects at work. 'And mark in every face I meet | Marks of weakness, marks of woe': there is something awkward in the repetition of the word 'mark'. The observer 'marks', but what he marks are 'marks'. Yet the awkwardness is in no way inept: by that dulling repetition Blake reinforces the effect of being dragged into an imprisoned world, where nothing radiates from the faces he sees: he marks them, but they do not seem to mark him in return. The arrow of his perception finds its mark, but finds itself fixed there, no longer at liberty.[19]

The word 'charter'd', repeated in the second line, also draws the reader's attention by its suggestion of irony. The word was originally associated with liberty. Magna Carta, signed by King John in 1215, was traditionally one of the foundations of British liberty, and one of many such charters over the centuries. But these charters were freedoms granted to particular classes of people: they automatically involved a loss of liberty for others who did not belong; and by Blake's time it was hard to walk around London without feeling that the whole city had been parcelled out among different groups in this way, leaving no freedom for the individual human beings who were excluded. 'It is a perversion of terms to say that a charter gives rights,' wrote Thomas Paine in *The Rights of Man*; 'it operates by a contrary effect – that of taking rights away.'[20] Even the Thames, which might be thought by definition to be free, was so given over to the uses of commerce as to lose all identity except as a trade route. One of Shakespeare's characters describes the air as a 'chartered libertine'; used in connection with the Thames, the word would read more like 'shackled' – looking forward to the 'mind-forg'd manacles' of the second stanza. The poetic compression which first brings together the words 'mind-forged' and 'manacles', then makes the manacles what is heard in the cries about him, is masterly.

A rare glimpse into the process of his composition is afforded by the existence of a notebook fragment which formed one of the building-blocks for the finished lyrics. It was presented as 'An ancient Proverb' and – including deletions – runs:

> Remove away that blackning church
> Remove away that marriage hearse
> Remove away that ~~place~~ man of blood
> '~~Twill~~ Youll quite remove the ancient curse

The most striking elements in this were then taken into the still more finished concluding stanzas of his lyric:

> How the Chimney-sweeper's cry
> Every blackning Church appalls;
> And the hapless Soldiers sigh
> Runs in blood down Palace walls
>
> But most thro' midnight streets I hear
> How the youthful Harlots curse
> Blasts the new born Infants tear,
> And blights with plagues the Marriage hearse

The verse here is not only complex in its effects, but unusually straightforward. There is a sense of accumulating power, gathering strength from the dramatic use of certain words, such as 'appalls' (which draws into itself the sense of 'pall'), and culminating in the 'Marriage hearse' of the ending. And the lines are once again packed with meaning. It has been pointed out that the 'newborn infant's tear' may well carry a reference to the effects of venereal disease – which in turn may be condemning to death not only the newborn babe that inherits it, but also those victims who attempt to escape into lawful wedlock and who in the process transform a human bed into a hearse. In this way Blake's poetic language can not only produce a triumph of compressed meaning, but in doing so reinforce the underlying emotions into greater intensity.

If one now turns to other poems in the *Songs of Experience*, Blake's use of such wordplay can be traced into further refinement. His poetry can at times work with ambiguity, stimulating a kind of reflection that so far from resulting in very exact pinpointing of meaning, leaves the mind itself at play. A good example can be found in the 'Introduction' that opens the collection:

> Hear the voice of the Bard!
> Who Present, Past, & Future sees
> Whose ears have heard,
> The Holy Word,
> That walk'd among the ancient trees.
>
> Calling the lapsed Soul
> And weeping in the evening dew;
> That might controll,
> The starry pole;
> And fallen fallen light renew!
>
> O Earth O Earth return!
> Arise from out the dewy grass;
> Night is worn,
> And the morn
> Rises from the slumberous mass,
>
> Turn away no more:
> Why wilt thou turn away
> The starry floor
> The watry shore
> Is giv'n thee till the break of day.

The wealth of ambiguities involved in this text make it difficult to hold it in the mind as a clear entity. F. R. Leavis summarized the problems of the second stanza long ago:

> In spite of the semi-colon at the end of the second line we find ourselves asking whether it is the Holy Word or the Bard that is calling the 'lapsed soul'. There is clearly a reference to the Voice of God in the garden calling Adam, but is it God who is weeping in the evening dew? And is it God that might control the starry pole? – though it could hardly be the Soul (an interpretation permitted by punctuation and syntax) that might? and surely 'fallen light' is Lucifer?

And so he continues with his queries, only to conclude,

> Interpretation is not a matter of deciding, here and there, which of two or more possible readings gives the right sense. Blake by his own poetic means, which essentially disdains the virtues of prose, is defining his own peculiar intuition of evil, disharmony and a general fall.

I have elsewhere looked further into Leavis's critique and suggested that there are one or two literary references which, once spotted, help to clarify Blake's meaning more distinctly here,[21] but the main thrust of his argument is hard to resist. To seek for precise meaning as one would look for it in a passage of prose is to close one's eyes to resonances and alternative meanings that render a full reading more profitable.

Edward Larrissy has shown how this point is particularly true of one or two words that Blake uses forcefully, since once one sees what he is doing, ambiguity becomes a form of metamorphosis – as if one can turn a word inside out, or look at it alternately from the inside or the outside. Heather Glen's demonstration of this in relation to 'mark' has already been mentioned. Larrissy illustrates a similar effect with the word 'bound', which at different times seems to be used both negatively and positively.[22] In 'THERE is NO Natural Religion,' Blake writes. 'Man's perceptions are not bounded by organs of perception' and 'The bounded is loathed by its possessor'; but in *The Book of Los* he declares, 'Truth has bounds Error none'. In fact, however, two kinds of negativity are involved, the difference being between, on the one hand, an organization undertaken by processes of limiting, which will always deliver one into a universe that is dead; and on the other, the danger that if one avoids invoking even this kind of energy one may be precipitated into the abyss.

There is, however, a third possibility, a resort to the employment of energies in the service of life, where dead boundaries are transformed into vivid bounding forms – which is apparently what Blake had in mind when he came to write his Descriptive Catalogue. There, so far from treating the idea of bounds with contempt, he wrote:

> The great and golden rule of art, as well as of life, is this: That the more distinct, sharp, and wiry the bounding line, the more perfect the work of art; and the less keen and sharp, the greater is the evidence of weak imitation, plagiarism, and bungling ... The want of this determinate and bounding form evidences the want of idea in the artist's mind, and the pretence of the plagiary in all its branches ... What is it that builds a house and plants a garden, but the definite and determinate? What is it that distinguishes honesty from knavery, but the hard and wiry line of rectitude and certainty in the actions and intentions. Leave out this line and you leave out life itself ...

It is of the very nature of life, in other words, to express itself in bounding forms; and it is only the absence of life that causes Urizenic figures to stave off their fear of the abyss by relying on restrictive mathematical ones.

How did all this relate to the Experience of which he was writing in his *Songs*? The poems written in his notebook a short time before, many of which were to find a place in that collection, are redolent of his mood at this time. Among other things Blake was haunted by a sense of human failure and restriction, particularly in sexual relations, of potentialities of fulfilment that were thwarted, almost inexplicably, among his fellows:

> Thou hast a lap full of seed,
> And this is a fine country.
> Why dost thou not cast thy seed
> And live in it merrily

The reply is hopeless:

> Shall I cast it on the sand
> And turn it into fruitful land
> For on no other ground
> Can I sow my seed
> Without tearing up
> Some stinking weed[23]

Yet Blake could not believe that human beings fully assented to this situation: 'What is it men in women do require?' he asked in 'Several Questions Answered', and went on to answer his own question: 'The lineaments of Gratified Desire'. He then put the same question and the same answer in relation to women's need from men. His thoughts on the matter often look forward to those associated with Freud:

> Abstinence sows sand all over
> The ruddy limbs & flaming hair
> But Desire Gratified
> Plants fruits of life & beauty there

A similar point is found in another fragment in the same notebook:

> In a wife I would desire
> What in whores is always found
> The lineaments of Gratified desire[24]

In contrast to this vision of a free and happy gratification of sexual desire, Blake detected everywhere about him the secret indulgence of lust devoid of pleasure. The very chapels in which abstinence was preached were caricatures of the bodily organ of sexual desire that had been made secret, and their adherents reaped a cruel crop:

> I saw a chapel all of gold
> That none did dare to enter in
> And many weeping stood without
> Weeping, mourning, worshipping
>
> I saw a serpent rise between
> The white pillars of the door
> And he forcd & forcd & forcd,
> Down the golden hinges tore
>
> And along the pavement sweet
> Set with pearls & rubies bright
> All his slimy length he drew
> Till upon the altar white
>
> Vomiting his poison out
> On the bread & on the wine
> So I turnd into a sty
> And laid me down among the swine[25]

Blake did not include this, or some of his other bitter poems, in *Songs of Experience*. Since it was still intended, evidently, as a book that might be read by children, he perhaps wished to omit poems that presented too dispiriting a view of the world that awaited them. Among the poems he did publish, however, a similar trend is to be traced: a despair when he looked about him in society, coupled with a belief that the ultimate truth behind things was not what his fellows might suppose it to be as they listened to the complacent preachings in their chapels and followed the discussions of contemporary scientists and philosophers.

This may help to explain his attitude for those readers who feel that the ending to the 'Chimney Sweeper' poem of *Innocence* must be fraught with conscious irony (though without signal of ironic intent) or else that Blake must have undergone an extreme political change of mind in the interval between writing his two collections. Since Blake never claimed that 'the Contrary States of the Human Soul' would be shown to be mutually consistent, the best way of solving the puzzle of the attitudes displayed in poems of the two collections may in fact be to charge them back to the contrary states of his own soul: the visionary and the inhabitant of experience. The visionary found it wonderful to think of a climbing boy taking total consolation from the thought of his obedience being rewarded in a paradisal state, whereas the Blake of experience could regard such a thought only as a source of indignation.

The difficulty that the two Blakes sometimes found in trying to inhabit the same body is best shown at the end of the poem just quoted:

> So I turnd into a sty
> And laid me down among the swine.

A self-disgust of this kind could indeed seem the most appropriate reaction to the corruption of innocence hinted at in this defiling of a holy place. If there were to be any hope for the human beings demeaned in such a setting it must lie in a different cultivation of the energies underlying their existence.

6
The Challenge of Energy

Even while the events in France were unfolding, Blake's life was affected
by a new acquaintance, who proved a more turbulent influence. Some
of his early enthusiasm for Swedenborgianism evidently derived from
the fact that his friend John Flaxman was associated with the sect.
Flaxman, a gentle and humane man, was to remain a friend for most of
Blake's life and seems always to have appealed to his more visionary
side. For several years from 1787, however, Flaxman was in Rome, where
he had gone with his family to improve his knowledge of sculpture, and
during this time Blake got to know another artistic contemporary, Henry
Fuseli. Unlike Flaxman, who had been brought up in England and learnt
his trade in the workshop of his father, providing casts for sculptors,
Fuseli had been born in Switzerland, and initially trained for the
Zwinglian ministry. After protesting against the activities of a corrupt
magistrate, however, he left the church and travelled to London, where
for some time he worked as a translator and so came across the writings
of Rousseau, imbibing particularly his arguments against the 'moral util-
ity' of the arts. Having then decided to become a painter he too spent
time in Italy, exploring his passion for Michelangelo. Although he was
to incur criticisms of his painting technique, the style he developed
impressed many by its expressive and passionate qualities. As far as
Blake's development was concerned, he provided a fine counterpart to
the more docile Flaxman: what the latter had offered in the cultivating
of visionary faculties, Fuseli could complement by the example of his
extraordinary artistic energy. Particularly devoted to Shakespeare and
Milton, he produced some striking designs for *Paradise Lost*. Blake, who
respected and shared his aspiration to raise the profile of English art,
became devoted to his rough honesty and was quite untroubled by the
fact that polite society tended to shun him. (His swearing gave such

particular offence that Flaxman asked Blake how he reacted to it. Blake replied that he simply swore again, whereupon Fuseli would say in astonishment 'Vy Blake you are swearing' – but would leave off himself.[1]) He evidently found such openness refreshing, appreciating the attitude of a man who, like himself, could accept his position as an outsider in polite English society, while preserving a firm independence of mind. His later epigram is well known:

> The only Man that eer I knew
> Who did not make me almost spew
> Was Fuseli he was both Turk & Jew
> And so dear Christian Friends how do you do[2]

The importance of the engagement with Fuseli was evidently due partly to his flamboyant behaviour and vehemence of expression. Though himself a quieter man in demeanour, Blake would have been attracted by such positive qualities in a man who must often have seemed to him to have 'all the fury of a spiritual existence', and at whose side Flaxman would inevitably seem passive. It is difficult to trace their interaction in detail: according to Anthony Blunt, 'it is futile to argue the question of priority', since 'there were certain motives and images that were, one might almost say, the common property of the whole group to which Blake, Fuseli, Flaxman, Romney and Stothard belonged'.[3] Anne Mellor, accepting this, finds it sufficient to note that Fuseli's style and influence 'did much to encourage Blake's own predilection for strong linear rhythms and expressively attenuated figures'.[4] She also indicates a number of designs which raise the question of mutual influence. The larger question that arises, however, concerns the effect of the two men on one another at a more general intellectual level. It is very noticeable that the time of their greatest contact corresponds with Blake's transition towards a greater emphasis on the role of energy in human activity. It was now that he produced critical annotations of some of Swedenborg's writings, including his comment 'Good & Evil are here both Good & the two contraries married', moving thus towards his creation of *The Marriage of Heaven and Hell*, with its rewriting of *Paradise Lost* to magnify the role of Satan's energetic defiance of God, and his view of it as expressing a revolt against the philosophy which makes God the equivalent of Destiny and his son a figure trapped by the five senses. It is hard to resist the conclusion that it was his encounter with Fuseli's energetic pursuit of a dynamic art that prompted these new insights, stimulating among other things his movement towards a collection of poems based on an alternative to the *Songs of Innocence*.

His impulse towards a more cynical vision no doubt also gained impetus from the current political situation. Looking at the apparently hopeless outcome for those who had delighted in the events of 1789 and the relapse towards re-establishment of the previous status quo, Blake was at first moved to indignation and even abuse, giving to the anonymous god who seemed to be in control of events, the originator of the rule of law in his own society, the belittling name of 'Nobodaddy'. His favourite form of attack remained the pithy rhyme or epigram:

> Why art thou silent & invisible,
> Father of jealousy
> Why dost thou hide thyself in clouds
> From every searching Eye
>
> Why darkness & obscurity
> In all thy words & laws,
> That none dare eat the fruit but from
> The wily serpent's jaws
> Or is it because Secresy
> gains females loud applause[5]

Elsewhere Nobodaddy enters some of Blake's more powerful political poems, as when he attacks the French monarch's tyranny in the poem that begins 'Let the Brothels of Paris be opened':

> Then old Nobodaddy aloft
> Farted & belchd & coughd
> And said I love hanging & drawing & quartering
> Every bit as well as war & slaughtering[6]

These lines were followed by three more, subsequently deleted:

> Damn praying & singing
> Unless they will bring in
> The blood of ten thousand by fighting or swinging

The next stanza now read:

> Then he swore a great & solemn Oath
> To kill the people I am loth
> But If they rebel they must go to hell
> They shall have a Priest & a passing bell

This picture of a divine ruler who could not content himself with condemning human beings to death but must have them damned to all eternity as well expresses Blake's extreme feelings at the time. The most successful means of combating it that he discovered, however, was that of a satire playing on the comic instinct.*The Marriage of Heaven and Hell* was undertaken firmly in this vein. His device of satirizing Swedenborg's 'Memorable Relations' by introducing 'Memorable Fancies' of his own has already been mentioned; the second of these is of a particularly quizzical kind, beginning:

> The Prophets Isaiah and Ezekiel dined with me, and I asked them how they dared so roundly to assert. that God spake to them; and whether they did not think at the time, that they would be misunderstood, & so be the cause of imposition.
>
> Isaiah answer'd: 'I saw no God, nor heard any, in a finite organical perception; but my senses discover'd the infinite in every thing, and as I was then perswaded, & remain confirm'd; that the voice of honest indignation is the voice of God, I cared not for consequences, but wrote.
>
> Then I asked: Does a firm perswasion that a thing is so, make it so?
>
> He replied. All poets believe that it does, & in ages of imagination this firm perswasion removed mountains; but many are not capable of a firm perswasion of any thing.[7]

This narrative should be borne in mind when one is reading some of the anecdotes told about Blake himself, since it bears on his own satiric practice. Even while Blake is asking whether Isaiah and Ezekiel thought they might be misunderstood when they said that God spoke to them, he knows perfectly well that he is in danger of being misunderstood for saying that Isaiah and Ezekiel dined with him. The defence they offer is also his own: the poet can be effective through the statement of firmly held convictions, which will also, if asserted powerfully enough, carry conviction back into his own mind.

In this little treatise the one conviction that dominates throughout is the one that had also been uppermost in Blake's mind in recent years: that of the need to perceive the infinite in all things. Here it is the Devil who insists on a question that raises the whole possibility. Chatterton, with different suppositions in mind, had asked:

> How dydd I knowe that every darte
> That cutt the airy waye,
> Might not fynd passage to my harte
> And close my eyes for aie?[8]

Blake's Devil, putting a similar question, poses a different possibility:

> When I came home; on the abyss of the five senses, where a flat sided steep frowns over the present world. I saw a mighty Devil folded in black clouds, hovering on the sides of the rock, with corroding fires he wrote the following sentence now percieved by the minds of men, & read by them on earth.

> How do you know but ev'ry Bird that cuts the airy way,
> Is an immense world of delight, clos'd by your senses five?

Apart from his central assertion of a need to cleanse human perception, Blake's own convictions turn out to be, paradoxically, dual, his boldest statements of them stressing, as with the *Songs*, the necessity for dialectic:

> Without Contraries is no progression. Attraction and Repulsion, Reason and Energy, Love and Hate, are necessary to Human existence.
> From these contraries spring what the religious call Good & Evil. Good is the passive that obeys Reason Evil is the active springing from Energy.
> Good is Heaven. Evil is Hell.

After this, 'The Voice of the Devil' is heard again, voicing his version of what is 'contrary':

> All Bibles or sacred codes. have been the causes of the following Errors.
> 1. That Man has two real existing principles Viz: a Body & a Soul.
> 2. That Energy, calld Evil, is alone from the Body, & that Reason, calld Good, is alone from the Soul.
> 3. That God will torment Man in Eternity for following his Energies.

> But the following Contraries to these are True
> 1. Man has no Body distinct from his Soul for that calld Body is a portion of Soul discernd by the five Senses. the chief inlets of Soul in this age
> 2. Energy is the only life and is from the Body and Reason is The bound or outward circumference of Energy.
> 3. Energy is Eternal Delight

The Marriage of Heaven and Hell provides the best example of Blake's dramatic facility – a power that emerges at times in *Songs of Experience* also. 'The Voice of the Devil' need not be taken as Blake's own in more

3 Detail from *The Book of Urizen*, plate 3, Courtesy of Library of Congress, Washington

than a limited sense, of course, since his assertions fall within the larger postulated dialectic. A reader with an ear for self-contradictions will soon detect as much, in any case. To say that 'everything that lives is holy' is one thing; but when we read elsewhere in the book that 'As the caterpiller chooses the fairest leaves to lay her eggs on, so the priest lays his curse on the fairest joys', we may legitimately ask whether the life of a caterpillar is not, after all, holy also. Blake's purpose in *The Marriage* is not to proclaim the holiness of life or the gospel of energy as such, but rather to allow room for voices not commonly heard in his society: to look at the world through the eyes of a human being exalted by the exercise of energy, for example, and to ask whether the resulting picture is not more attractive than the view projected by the eye of a containing and self-contained reason.

In one sense the enterprise was successful almost beyond his expectations. His wit found room for full play in his little sketches of life in Hell, and his assertion that the reason Milton 'wrote in fetters when he wrote of Angels & God, and at liberty when of Devils & Hell, is because he was a true Poet and of the Devil's party without knowing it' turned out to be true of himself in ways that he would hardly have acknowledged.

Indeed, as he begins to enumerate 'The Proverbs of Hell', they turn into a rhapsodic poetry on their own account:

> The pride of the peacock is the glory of God.
> The lust of the goat is the bounty of God.
> The wrath of the lion is the wisdom of God.
> The nakedness of woman is the work of God.
> Excess of sorrow laughs. Excess of joy weeps.
> The roaring of lions, the howling of wolves, the raging of the stormy sea, and the destructive sword, are portions of eternity, too great for the eye of man.

The change of line length at the end is one that no lyric poet of his time could readily have tolerated, yet, as in some of his early extended poems, it works triumphantly, looking forward to the large rhythmic shifts of later writers.

Although much in *The Marriage of Heaven and Hell* is to be ascribed to Blake's dramatic invention, there are places where it is possible to misread him because of failures of communication that he probably did not foresee. If it is the price he pays for not having submitted to a formal education, it is a small one, in view of his liberation from the constraints imposed by overly formal grammar and syntax; it needs to be recognized, nevertheless.[9] Possibilities of self-contradiction are bound to exist in such a homespun philosophy, similarly, and Blake was sometimes conscious of them. Reading once about a meanness of mind that he disliked, he wrote in the margin, 'To hell till he behaves better!' then added hastily, 'Mark that I do not believe there is such a thing litterally. but hell is the being shut up in the possession of corporeal desires which shortly weary the man. *All life is holy.*'[10] He is not calling for a transvaluation of values, in other words, but for recognition of a dialectic between different views of the world – a dialectic that may in turn point back to a hidden power that would harmonize what are now warring elements. When he asserts that the Devil's version of events is that the Messiah, not himself, fell, he is not saying that the Devil is right, but simply pointing to the impoverishment of reason once it is deprived of connection with energy. His book is not called 'The Supremacy of Hell', but *The Marriage of Heaven and Hell*; and it is that marriage, in the form of reconciliation between reason and energy within a larger human vision, that he seeks to promote.

Although his indignation against the effects of social and religious oppression found natural vent in the language of satire and contempt, his prophetic writing began to take a broader sweep and concentrate on a more political survey of the world, in which he saw events in his own time as being under the ultimate sway of the supremely conservative being whom he had now named Urizen.

Jon Mee has drawn attention to another aspect of the contemporary context in which the thinking of the Prophetic Books was initially embedded. In his *Lectures* of 1787, Robert Lowth had written that the obscurity of prophecy could serve a good rhetorical purpose: 'It whets the understanding, excites an appetite for knowledge, keeps alive the attention, and exercises the genius by the labour of the investigation.'[11] As Mee points out, this relates interestingly to Blake's 'The wisest of the Ancients considerd what is not too Explicit as the fittest for Instruction, because it rouzes the faculties to act'.[12] It also leads quite naturally to his other great dictum on the subject:

> Prophets in the modern sense of the word have never existed. Jonah was no prophet in the modern sense for his prophecy of Nineveh failed. Every honest man is a Prophet he utters his opinion both of private & public matters /Thus/ If you go on So / the result is So / He never says, such a thing Shall happen let you do what you will. a Prophet is a Seer not an Arbitrary Dictator ...[13]

Even while he was working through his more humanitarian poems, then, Blake was increasingly preoccupied by intellectual issues. His belief that it was necessary to explore the political implications of what was happening in the contemporary world went hand in hand with his efforts to work towards the cleansing of human perception until human beings could see the infinite in all things.

Although his first essay in a new mode, the poem 'The French Revolution', was never to be completed, the surviving section makes it clear that Blake had embarked on a manner of writing political history in poetry which would not be tied to reliance on strict documentary record. Instead, he would produce a semi-historical account which could equally relate to the events in *Paradise Lost* – particularly the debates in Hell in Book Two. The method he devised involved, among other things, a series of speeches from the nobles involved that were characterized by an enlarged rhetoric. This is never better displayed than in the speech on events by the supposed 'aged Duke of Burgundy' – a fictional character, since the historical line of Burgundy had died out by this time, but a use-ful figure for poetic purposes since his figuring could thus join the imagery of the wine associated with the Burgundy region to that of the blood of revolutionary conflict. The Duke could be a mouthpiece for a Urizenic view of the word which fears the implications of a humane revolution that might, for example, produce preference of a clay cottage to a marble palace. The order of things that establishes a power and dominion guarded by sword and sceptre and regards reason and science as if they were as solid as the physical world itself must not, in his view, be so upset:

> The fierce Duke hung over the council; around him croud, weeping
>   in his burning robe,
> A bright cloud of infant souls; his words fall like purple autumn on
>   the sheaves.
>
> Shall this marble built heaven become a clay cottage, this earth an
>   oak stool, and these mowers
> From the Atlantic mountains, mow down all this great starry
>   harvest of six thousand years?
> And shall Necker, the hind of Geneva, stretch out his crook'd sickle
>   o'er fertile France,
> Till our purple and crimson is faded to russet, and the kingdoms of
>   earth bound in sheaves,
> And the ancient forests of chivalry hewn, and the joys of the
>   combat burnt for fuel;
> Till the power and dominion is rent from the pole, sword and
>   scepter from sun and moon,
> The law and gospel from fire and air, and eternal reason and science
> From the deep and the solid, and man lay his faded head down on
>   the rock
> Of eternity, where the eternal lion and eagle remain to devour?

Blake's satire here works in more than one way. Radical irony is directed against an authoritarianism which cannot bear to think that a marble-built palace might be the equal of a humble cottage or question the use of resources such as timber for the prosecution of warfare; there is equally a more imaginative irony, directed against the visionless philosophy that sets its standard according to the apparent permanence of the stars and an adherence to written texts rather than the life that should inform them.

Whereas Burgundy argues forcefully but from a mistaken view of things, the Archbishop of Paris, who rises 'In the rushing of scales and hissing of flames and rolling of sulphurous smoke', is evidently a more devilish figure, his serpentine energies perverted to a baser level as he hears an aged man, 'hovering in mist', expressing his own fears of what is to come:

> Nobles and Clergy shall fail from before me, and my cloud
>   and vision be no more;
> The mitre become black, the crown vanish, and the scepter and
>   ivory staff
> Of the ruler wither among bones of death; they shall consume
>   from the thistly field,
> And the sound of the bell, and voice of the sabbath, and singing
>   of the holy choir,
> Is turn'd into songs of the harlot in day, and cries of the virgin in
>   night.
> They shall drop at the plow and faint at the harrow, unredeem'd,
>   unconfess'd, unpardon'd;
> The priest rot in his surplice by the lawless lover, the holy beside
>   the accursed,
> The King, frowning in purple, beside the grey plowman, and their
>   worms embrace together

The Archbishop's horror is again to be viewed ironically by those who reflect that the priest and the lawless lover are alike human beings, and that if worms embrace in consuming both king and ploughman, this does no more than demonstrate the common humanity of the latter and the common life of all. In accordance with such an alternative view the horror of the nobles at what the Archbishop is showing them is eventually superseded by a visionary speech from 'Orleans generous as mountains'. When the Archbishop attempts to resume his discourse he discovers that, like Satan's at his lowest in *Paradise Lost*, his voice is transformed into a hiss. Orleans, by contrast, offers a more far-seeing vision, by which human beings fulfil the needs of their own energies and honour each other's individuality:

> Can the fires of Nobility ever be quench'd, or the stars by a stormy
>   night?
> Is the body diseas'd when the members are healthful? can the man
>   be bound in sorrow
> Whose ev'ry function is fill'd with its fiery desire? can the soul
>   whose brain and heart
> Cast their rivers in equal tides thro' the great Paradise, languish
>   because the feet
> Hands, head, bosom, and parts of love, follow their high
>   breathing joy?

And can Nobles be bound when the people are free, or God weep
   when his children are happy?
Have you never seen Fayette's forehead, or Mirabeau's eyes,
   or the shoulders of Target,
Or Bailly the strong foot of France, or Clermont the terrible voice,
   and your robes
Still retain their own crimson? mine never yet faded, for fire
   delights in its form.
But go, merciless man! enter into the infinite labyrinth of
   another's brain
Ere thou measure the circle that he shall run. Go, thou cold
   recluse, into the fires
Of another's high flaming rich bosom, and return unconsum'd,
   and write laws.[14]

Blake's vision of humanity at its best is here manifest. In subsequent
lines the army is commanded by the people to retire ten miles and the
book ends in a situation of stalemate as the King and nobles are left
wondering what to do next. But it is hard to see how the poem might
have proceeded, and indeed Blake may have decided it would be better
to leave it to one side and extend his vision to the whole of the contemporary scene, treating its past and future in terms which rendered
his prophetic intent more specific.

While the opening of 'The French Revolution' was a worthy attempt
to express some of his aims the first fruits of his enterprise in the
'prophetic' form were to be set out in the illuminated book *America*
of 1793, where he attempted to read the events of the recent War of
Independence in terms of a larger struggle, involving the figures that
had begun to dominate his mythology. Already he had produced the
figure of Los, who seems to have appeared first in the person of a
father seen in a design of 1792–3 binding his son to a rock, a figure of
active jealousy to match the more passive jealousy of Urizen. Now,
the group grew to include a companion for him, a female called
Enitharmon, along with another, a shadowy female who is here called
'the daughter of Urthona', while the son emerged as the rebellious
spirit 'red Orc'. These all appear prominently at the beginning of
America in a two-page 'Preludium', which sets the events to be
described into a larger mythological pattern, created by their disordered relationship. The rebellious Orc breaks the bonds imposed on
him by his jealous father and seizes the shadowy daughter, who
glimpses sexual fulfilment in his embrace at the very moment when

she feels herself being destroyed by pain:

> I know thee, I have found thee, & I will not let thee go;
> Thou art the image of God who dwells in darkness of Africa;
> And thou art fall'n to give me life in regions of dark death.
> On my American plains I feel the struggling afflictions
> Endur'd by roots that writhe their arms into the nether deep:
> I see a serpent in Canada, who courts me to his love;
> In Mexico an Eagle, and a Lion in Peru;
> I see a Whale in the South-sea, drinking my soul away.
> O what limb rending pains I feel. thy fire & my frost
> Mingle in howling pains, in furrows by thy lightnings rent;
> This is eternal death; and this the torment long foretold.

This death-dealing ravishment, in which the very energy expended gives a negative image of what true sexual fulfilment might be, is not an event preliminary to what is to happen in the book itself, but an interpretative enactment of the meaning inherent in all those events. The revolutionary violence involved in achieving independence is the distorting of an energy that might have made the union between Britain and America a fruitful marriage.

In considering this version of 'prophecy' one should take into account the general dangers accompanying political publication at this time. 'The French Revolution', although set up in proof by Joseph Johnson, had never seen the light of day as a finished publication, and this fact, if due to anything other than a failure to develop the narrative further, may reflect a fear on Johnson's part of possible prosecution. It may have been such fears, similarly, that led to the cancellation of a plate for *America*, describing the destruction of George III's house of 'council' – a thin disguise for Parliament. As the 'Prophecy' proper now follows, on the other hand, the protagonists are explicitly named as the tyrannical King of England and the American leaders, and it again becomes clear that for the book as a whole he was taking a wider sweep, linking his view of the break between America and England with his sexual critique. A fragment composed at this time makes the connection evident:

> As when a dream of Thiralatha flies the midnight hour:
> In vain the dreamer grasps the joyful images, they fly
> Seen in obscured traces in the Vale of Leutha, So
> The British Colonies beneath the woful Princes fade.
> But tho' obscur'd, this is the form of the Angelic land.

In this little cameo the experience of a fleeting sexual dream that leaves the male dreamer with nothing but a residue of expelled semen as evidence of what has happened is made the paradigm of the failed relationship between Britain and the American colonies. The same idea of a lapse of the angelic powers that might have led a different result is expressed in the opening illustration to the book, showing an angelic figure totally shut up in self-absorption while the woman he should be cherishing looks on in extreme anxiety, clutching a child who is showing the first signs of rebellion. Again, the implication is that if the English and the Americans had treated each other with the same shared insight that characterizes a good and fully consummated marriage they might have been spared the outbreak of war and the subsequent political severance.

In pursuance of a similar satirical end Blake sometimes counterpoints his text with an illustration that comments satirically on it. This is so of the lines that describe the failed and angry angel:

> Albion's Angel wrathful burnt
> Beside the Stone of Night; and, like the Eternal Lion's howl
> In famine and war, reply'd: 'Art thou not Orc, who serpent-form'd
> Stands at the gate of Enitharmon to devour her children?
> Blasphemous Demon, Antichrist, hater of Dignities ...

These are illustrated ironically by a design showing a paradisal scene, with a male and female figure lying on a sleeping ram, emblematic of sexual fulfilment. On the other hand, the lines devoted to Orc express his bid for freedom:

> The morning comes, the night decays, the watchmen leave their
>   stations;
> The grave is burst, the spices shed, the linen wrapped up;
> The bones of death, the cov'ring clay, the sinews shrunk & dry'd.
> Reviving shake, inspiring move, breathing! awakening!
> Spring like redeemed captives when their bonds & bars are burst;

These are counter-illustrated by a design of Urizen himself, spreading his arms and casting the forbidding presence of his clouds over the fulfilment of any such vision.

The last design in the volume is dominated by a great figure, so frozen into rigidity that sheep can graze on his sides and small liberated figures stroll above him, while his beard streams off from him like a great waterfall. At the foot of the plate, meanwhile, the forms of serpent and vegetation are artfully combined together so as to suggest vegetable and serpentine energies interweaving harmoniously and peacefully together, any threatening horrors having disappeared.

Immediately after *America* came the prophetic book *Europe* in 1794, which followed the same pattern: a two-page section led into the prophecy itself. In this case the 'Preludium' takes the mythological story beyond the rape of the shadowy female by Orc to record her cries of lamentation in the face of the unlimited energy that has been released – an unending succession of 'howling terrors, all devouring fiery kings'. Impregnated by Orc with his infinite energy, she can see no hope of a happy outcome:

> ... who shall bind the infinite with an eternal band?
> To compass it with swaddling bands? and who shall cherish it
> With milk and honey?
> I see it smile & I roll inward & my voice is past.

There is a supreme irony here, for even as she poses her question of the impossible, she glimpses a possible reply. Her mention of 'swaddling bands' and 'milk and honey' reminds an alert reader of the coming of the infinite divine being – whether it is the Messiah as prophesied by Isaiah or the infant Jupiter of classical mythology, both of whom were fed on milk (or butter) and honey. The infant Jesus was of course wrapped in swaddling bands. The infinite can redeem humanity, in other words, but only through the feat of realizing itself in human form – a fact which she glimpses – and is mystified – when she sees it *smile*.

What Blake sees in the history of Europe, however, is that when the divine is born (as illustrated on the plate in the form of a radiant child) all the powers of convention immediately set to work to bind it down to a religion of law by imposing restrictions. According to his own interpretation of European history this has been achieved by the imposition of a 'Female Will' and by a cult of virginity. The result has been a culture of 'Thou shalt not' and of 'Fear' in which even 'Albion's Angel' no longer has the power to end the misery by blowing the trumpet of the Last Judgment.

The drift of the argument in *Europe* is to show how a Christian message that has been veiled, and cults exalting virginity, have together fostered the so-called Enlightenment philosophy which left no place for the visionary. The frontispiece (Figure 4) is one of Blake's best-known designs, its depiction satirizing the Creator who, in *Paradise Lost*,

> ... took the Golden Compasses, prepared
> In God's eternal store, to circumscribe
> This Universe, and all created things.[15]

4 'The Ancient Days', frontispiece to *Europe*, Fitzwilliam Museum, Cambridge

This Urizenic figure is not depicted as a villain, since with his limited vision he is doing his best to prevent humanity from being swallowed up by the abyss. And this is evidently how, in terms of his developing mythology, Blake sees the course of events in Europe also: as the fear of the destructive energy represented by Orc has led his mother Enitharmon to establish the domination of Woman by proclaiming the sinfulness of sexual love, so cults of chastity have arisen in the Christian Church and a limited philosophy, restricted to what can be perceived by the five senses, has been promulgated by European thinkers. The tale that is developed through the plates of *Europe* is one of increasing gloom, therefore. In the course of it comes a passage of intense and intricately intellectual speculation, which encapsulates much that Blake had come to believe concerning the development of Enlightenment philosophy. In lines already quoted from he describes the fate of the senses once the angels of reason have chosen to abandon their debate and follow the king:

> In thoughts perturb'd, they rose from the bright ruins silent
>   following
> The fiery King, who sought his ancient temple serpent-form'd
> That stretches out its shady length along the Island white.
> Round him roll'd his clouds of war; silent the Angel went,
> Along the infinite shores of Thames to golden Verulam.
> There stand the venerable porches that high-towering rear
> Their oak-surrounded pillars, form'd of massy stones, uncut
> With tool; stones precious; such eternal in the heavens,
> Of colours twelve, few known on earth, give light in the opake,
> Plac'd in the order of the stars, when the five senses whelm'd
> In deluge o'er the earth-born man; then turn'd the fluxile eyes
> Into two stationary orbs, concentrating all things.
> The ever-varying spiral ascents to the heavens of heavens
> Were bended downward; and the nostrils golden gates shut
> Turn'd outward, barr'd and petrify'd against the infinite.

Once this has happened, the temple of a philosophy inspired by that of Bacon, Lord Verulam, has been established, and any sense of the infinite abolished in consequence, the energies residing in the infinite take their revenge, turning into flaming terror:

> Thought chang'd the infinite to a serpent; that which pitieth:
> To a devouring flame; and man fled from its face and hid
> In forests of night; then all the eternal forests were divided
> Into earths rolling in circles of space, that like an ocean rush'd

And overwhelmed all except this finite wall of flesh.
Then was the serpent temple form'd, image of infinite
Shut up in finite revolutions, and man became an Angel;
Heaven a mighty circle turning; God a tyrant crown'd.

The image of the 'Infinite shut up in finite revolutions' is displayed wittily by the figure of a serpent constrained into a series of descending circles which dominates the left-hand side of the page. Meanwhile the process by which human beings are confined to the use of their 'angelic' reason is expounded further: the heavens are explained purely in Newtonian terms, while the rule of God is the exact mirror-image of a crowned tyrant – the tyrants themselves assuming by the same token that they are thus authorized to rule by Divine right. The human head, in turn, is depicted as having lost its true aura:

Once open to the heavens and elevated on the human neck,
Now overgrown with hair and coverd with a stony roof,
Downward 'tis sunk beneath th' attractive north, that round the feet
A raging whirlpool draws the dizzy enquirer to his grave

This repeats the idea developed in an illustration to *America* (figure 5); the coiling serpent into which a human being was there seen peering, its vision lost in trying to follow its endless revolutions, has now been transposed into the vortex which is its analogue and which swallows it into death.

5 Detail from *America*, plate 7, Fitzwilliam Museum, Cambridge

The book now turns to comedy as a 'red-limbed angel' tries to resolve the situation by blowing the trumpet to signal the Last Judgment but finds that he cannot, so that it is left to a 'mighty Spirit' named Newton to achieve the task. The immediate result is to call all the children of Enitharmon to the sports of night 'beneath the solemn moon', while Enitharmon herself mourns her lost dominion, Orc finds his future to lie in the revolutionary fields of France, and Los, in turn, calls 'all his sons to the strife of blood'.

In both *America* and *Europe* the play of symbols between text and illustration was at its most intense – though as has been pointed out Blake would sometimes achieve an effect of counterpoint by putting on one plate a design which was more clearly relevant to another. The imagery of the serpent was made to work hard in these designs – indeed, Blake made several attempts to work into the title-page of *Europe* a gigantic snake. The result was to interpret the history of Europe in terms of misused energies and misunderstood reason. It is time, then, to look more generally at the place of symbolism in his literary thinking as a whole.

7
Thinking Allegorically, Imaging Symbolically

In reading Blake's work one is sometimes struck by the sense of an underlying wonderment, or even perplexity, on his part: it is as if it were difficult for him fully to understand the world in which he found himself. Endowed with marvellous visionary powers, he could not easily comprehend how his fellow human beings, while betraying signs of possessing similar powers in themselves, could so rarely live in accordance with them but stumbled through their lives harming one another and themselves, completely disregarding the rich imaginative powers at their disposal – which instead were neglected to their own hurt.

Although he made his living through visual art and practised it all his life Blake is remembered today first and foremost for his poems, where the response of his readers continues to substantiate his imaginative appeal. Even when he was producing his designs, moreover, he could always be regarded as being, in one sense at least, a very literary artist. Most of his images were produced to illustrate texts – often, as we have seen, through combining on the same page text and 'illumination'. The relationship between word and image offered a dual means of probing the bemusement referred to above by exploring further the possibilities of symbolism, which could involve ideas of his own that did not exist squarely in either field of discourse – though if they were presented in visual designs they might, for a full understanding of their significance, need the addition of an elucidating verbal text – particularly in cases where symbols were related to one another in terms of connections which he himself made. Such aids he did not always provide.

The development was reflected in his poetry. Having tried his hand at both conventional lyric and at the sharply satiric style of *An Island in the Moon*, he began to experiment with a style of creation closer to what he had been imbibing from the Swedenborgians, in which familiar elements re-formed themselves into statements with symbolic significance. In his first two poems in this mode, he reordered well-known mythical narratives, particularly that of the Garden of Eden, to fit his own developing view of the world as a place that was forever closing its eyes to its own capabilities.

'Tiriel', his first attempt, was only partly successful – which is probably why, though made the subject of several of his illustrations, it remained in manuscript. There, more than in any of his subsequent works, he drew on recognizable sources for his nomenclature. Tiriel, the chief and eponymous character, derived his name from the quality figuring in alchemical works as 'the intelligence of mercury' and this is no doubt a key to the part he plays in the poem's plot, which can be viewed as an allegorical narrative about the loss of human visionary powers. Every human being, in other words, is to be viewed as born with the potentiality of the winged Mercury, but in the course of human life and the circumstances that constrain it, this survives only as the dull substance that we know by the same name: notable for its power of endless self-division and instantaneous reassembly – to be associated with a 'mercurial' personality as much as with mercury itself – but in its ultimate nature no more than an insidious poison. (We might compare Coleridge's account of himself as 'delving in the unwholesome quick-silver mines of metaphysic depths'.[1]) In his fallen condition Tiriel wanders out of his once beautiful palace and curses his sons. Just as Lear addressed Goneril and Reagan as 'Tigers, not daughters'. so Tiriel curses his offspring as 'Serpents, not sons' – and this is not the only apparent reference in the poem to Shakespeare's play. Indeed, the sightless Tiriel has things in common with the blinded Gloucester (not to mention, of course, Sophocles' Oedipus).

The details of Tiriel's dealings, however, have closer links with the Old Testament. His former associates Har and Heva, whom he meets in his wanderings, are thinly disguised embodiments of the biblical Adam and Eve, appearing as the versions of their originals remaining when the wisdom and energy emblematized in Tiriel's original were cast out of Eden. The result is that they are more like Swift's Struldbrugs, faded beings grown old in etiolation: a foolish old pair who must still use their limited intelligence as best they can, while remaining touchingly beautiful and childlike. At the end of the poem their identities are more sharply defined when Tiriel asserts bitterly, 'Thy laws O Har and Tiriels wisdom end together in a curse' – dividing his realm equally into a world of Har's law-bound reasoning and his own sub-world of serpentine wisdom, the mercurial power in the subconscious that would allow abstract thought to be complemented into effective mental activity. The very division, however, negates a desirable multiplicity: if the mental processes delivered were to be truly rewarding the interplay of both would be needed.

An important problem with 'Tiriel' – and probably the main reason for its abandonment – was its dominant tone, which throughout remained negative. The chief positive achievement, in fact, was to be found in the implications behind a passage of despairing questions from Tiriel towards the end, including the lines:

> Dost thou not see that men cannot be formed all alike
> Some nostrild wide breathing out blood. Some close shut up
> In silent deceit. poisons inhaling from the morning rose ...

These lines, suggesting by contrast a humanity that is richer in nature than analysis of it according to narrow rules would suggest, follow the question 'Why is one law given to the lion & the patient Ox' and are evidently intended to indicate the hidden possibilities of the mercurial, which, if once cultivated, could transform all sense of the human condition.

Instead of printing or engraving any of the text – deleted or otherwise – Blake turned to a different project, *The Book of Thel*. A single line from the deleted passage in 'Tiriel' was now expanded into a quatrain entitled 'THEL'S Motto' and given a separate page:

> Does the Eagle know what is in the pit?
> Or wilt thou go ask the Mole:
> Can Wisdom be put in a silver rod?
> Or Love in a golden bowl?

This, though in Blake's best riddling style, is not an enigma without a possible solution. It marches with the questioning of cultivated uniformity that is also to be found in the earlier poem, coupled with a sense that use of reason, to be of any worth, must combine with a grasp of the material world if it is to acknowledge the truly human. Even one's mode of eating should recognize that dishes or bowls are best made – like the humanity derived from it – of clay, not of precious metals.

Thel herself is to be viewed as a figure of innocence facing experience, a being still retaining her visionary nature, but contemplating descent into the materiality of the world – including entry into a human form. The whole mode, this time, is of question and answer. First, Thel asks how she can achieve usefulness. So long as her questions are posed within the natural world the answers are all satisfactory: Lily, Cloud and Worm each protest their useful place in the scheme of things; finally the Clay herself offers an invitation to enter. When Thel accepts it, however, she finds that what she is entering is the human body – which, since it subsists only in its fallen state, she cannot accept.

Despite the assurance of the writing in this new form, there was evidently room for afterthought: the last page was subjected to revision and included a passage of questioning similar to the one deleted from 'Tiriel', as the assenting voices of natural things gave place to a different one of human cries and complaints, expressing the condition of the body in its confined state:

> Why cannot the Ear be closed to its own destruction?
> Or the glistning Eye to the poison of a smile!
> Why are Eyelids stord with arrows ready drawn,
> Where a thousand fighting men in ambush lie?
> Or an Eye of gifts & graces, show'ring fruits & coined gold!
> Why a Tongue impress'd with honey from every wind?
> Why an Ear, a whirlpool fierce to draw creations in?
> Why a Nostril wide inhaling terror trembling & affright.
> Why a tender curb upon the youthful burning boy!
> Why a little curtain of flesh on the bed of our desire?

The voice is that of a humanity labouring under the effects of imposed uniformity and the rule of law, so that the cry of protest at its suffering state and at the restraints placed on human desires comes naturally. Nor is it surprising if the virgin, unpractised in such matters, can do no more than utter a shriek and retreat hurriedly to regain the Vale of Har and the security she left there.

The Book of Thel was more successful than 'Tiriel', since Blake could employ his mythology more simply, taking over the vale of Har as an emblem of innocence and introducing a name such as 'Mne Seraphim' – an adaptation apparently from a name in the pages of *The Conjuror's Magazine*.[2*] He also decided that the text afforded an opportunity to present his writing in the 'illuminated' form that was to be his favoured mode from now on: it was thus a first fruit of the development that he had foreshadowed in *An Island in the Moon*, where he spoke of his plan to 'have all the writing Engraved instead of Printed & at every other leaf a high finishd print all in three Volumes folio'.[3] The new version of the last page was in fact accompanied by one of Blake's best designs, showing a serpent, happily bridled, carrying children who play on it without fear.

The production of *The Book of Thel* in such an elaborate form is a reminder that during these years he was not simply pursuing his career as an engraver and beginning to produce the works already discussed, in which literary effects would be extended by blending text with visual design, as in the *Songs of Innocence and of Experience*, but already exploring ways of using symbolism. As he did so, certain motifs were increasingly employed to register his interest in the interplay of vision and energy. Exactly how he came across the particular images he employed is not clear, since there are not many obvious sources, but some were available in existing iconography,[4] alongside others that might be suggested by the contemporary keen interest in electrical phenomena and chemical discoveries such as Priestley's work on oxygen.

In terms of the interplay between vision and energy, the motifs that refer to the first are those of light and vegetation, particularly trees and foliage. Energy, by contrast, is usually expressed in flames – animal energy being particularly focused in the serpent. The two can be wittily combined, as when serpentine foliage is depicted round a tree, or a flower is given flame-like petals. Such imagery is rarely used in a static, or simply allegorical, fashion, however: there is usually some further pattern. A good instance is Blake's use of the saying 'God out of Christ is a consuming fire'.[5] The sense that divinity actually needs to find human expression in order to reveal the fullness of its nature can be seen as embodying an idea that controls much of his dealing with the notion of human destructive wrath, also.

In the *Songs of Innocence*, the use of symbolic imagery is fairly simple. The motifs are of objects such as trees with tendrils, fruits, beasts and flowers (some flame-like), any of which might be seen in a child's picture-book. The nearest approach to complexity is in the motifs of a child bowling a hoop (figure 9) and children dancing in a ring which, with awareness of Blake's imagery elsewhere of circles and planets, might encourage the reader to find a resonance, or the presence of overshadowing trees ('The Little Boy Lost' and 'The Little Boy Found') which betray the darker elements inherent even in an apparently innocent world.

The visual world of *Songs of Experience* is a good deal more complex. The varying frontispieces for the combined *Songs* and this collection give one key to the iconography, the first showing patriarchal man and woman, Adam and Eve figures, being beaten down by flames, while in the second, similar figures – probably the same – lie dead, mourned by

7 Detail from Illustration to Thomas Gray's 'The Descent of Odin', Yale Center for British Art, Paul Mellon Collection

6 Detail from *Songs of Innocence and of Experience* 38

8 Detail from *Songs of Innocence and of Experience* 40

9 Detail from Illustration to Thomas Gray's 'Ode on a distant Prospect of Eton College', Yale Center for British Art, Paul Mellon Collection

a younger pair. In the subsequent collection almost every design sees an innocent interpretation being undercut by another conveying the more bitter accents of experience. If sheep and oxen appear by a stream, they are bowing their heads to the water, apparently in disregard of anything else. If there is a tree with light serpentine tendrils it is matched across the page by two heavy trunks, intertwining like great serpents but producing more darkness. The chimney sweeper plods through snow, suffering from the cold weather; the rose is dominated by its thorns; the nurse, instead of looking on at the playing children, is combing the hair of a lad into rectitude (Figure 6); elsewhere she is also guiding one child into uprightness while the other is playing with a flying shuttlecock (Figure 8). These last two contrasts between the spirit of play and the seriousness of experience are to be reinforced in the later illustrations to Gray's Poems by a similar juxtaposition between the boy that 'chases the rolling cycle's speed' and the one 'on serious business bent' in the 'Ode on a Distant Prospect of Eton College' (Figure 9) – the theme of disciplinary combing being picked up also by the 'wondrous boy' and his 'raven hair' in 'The Descent of Odin' (Figure 7).[6]

Despite its attractiveness, pure energy is not to be thought of as being in itself humane. It is this reflection that perhaps determines the unexpected modification of the best-known image of all. In one of Blake's most disappointing designs he ignores the various depictions of the tiger that were available from contemporary sources to produce a rather foolish apology for a tiger. It is as if he is answering the question 'Did he who made the lamb make thee?' satirically, suggesting that if he *had* done so, to produce a 'humanized' tiger, this is what the result might have looked like.

Such complexities of attitude, like the development of the serpentine imagery in the text and illustrations for *America* and *Europe*, suggest that even while he was producing all these works the action of his symbolizing mind was taking him beyond their confines. His concerns were moving away from those that had caused him to focus on a particular geographical area, even one as large as a continent, just as earlier he seemed to have reached the end of Experience. The object of his more sustained effort at this time, after all, stretched beyond both social and political issues: it was rather an inquiry into why its supreme being had achieved such dominance if, as Blake believed, the ultimate reality in the universe was one of light and energy, colour and music. In the long run, he was suspecting, Urizen was enabled to stay in power through some deep failure in human beings themselves, which caused them not only to suppose such a being in charge but to form themselves in his image.

Accordingly, he began to fashion a history for Urizen, one of tragedy rather than of evil: presenting him, indeed, as a noble figure, pioneering a means of survival for all human beings who shared his dark sense of the world, rather in the way that Milton's Satan set out on his heroic journey when the other fallen angels had refused to accept the challenge. This view of Urizen dominates the 1794 *First Book of Urizen*, (already touched on), one of the darkest of the prophetic books and evidently written as a conscious pastiche of the biblical book of Genesis. Creation is seen here as the result not of a sublime process, translating darkness and chaos into beautiful forms, but of a deliberate turning away from the true state of eternity. That withdrawal is the result of a monumental failure of perception in which all faith in movement, development, even change itself, has been lost. Instead, Urizen has the urge to create a universe of total permanence: he has sought, he says, for 'a joy without pain, | For a solid without fluctuation'. His 'Book', accordingly, contains all the Christian virtues, but reduced to laws: 'Laws of peace, of love, of unity: | of pity, compassion, forgiveness.' This satire is antinomian indeed, directed against a concept of the world where everything is reduced to standardization in order to impose an ineluctable stability.

In creating Urizen (like his cognate Nobodaddy), Blake evidently had in mind some of the more lurid portraits of God the Father that were current in his time. 'Thinking as I do that the Creator of this World is a very Cruel Being,' he once said, '& being a Worshipper of Christ I cannot help saying the Son, O how unlike the Father First God Almighty comes with a Thump on the Head Then Jesus Christ comes with a balm to heal it.'[7] Such a portrait was recognizable in the teachings of some Christian denominations, particularly the gloomier ones.

It was because he was dissatisfied with such simple versions of the world, and unwilling to proceed simply by inverting them, that the quest for a viable mythology came to play such an important part in his developing thought. Already, as we have seen, he had engaged with mythologies and allegories of all kinds, ranging from alchemy and Greek tragedy to Shakespeare, Milton and symbolic interpretations of the Bible, in the hope of discovering a reading of human nature more optimistic than the conventional one, the first results being found in the rather turgid 'Tiriel', where the sources were comparatively near the surface of the poem and where many of the names of the characters could be traced to literal sources. Now, however, he evolved his own mythology, in which the names, while still reflecting traditional themes, were purely his own, bearing the stamp of his distinctive thought.

At some point the reader has to decide whether to follow Blake into this idiosyncratic world – and if so, where to stop. One figure, nevertheless, so dominant in the writings and so absorbing in significance as to fascinate most readers has already been mentioned. This is Urizen, best known from the design in which he leans down with compasses into darkness out of the blank disk of a sun (Figure 4). When Blake looked at the behaviour of human beings in his world and asked himself what kind of God they really worshipped, this seemed to be the answer. Believing themselves to be in a world where their fate was to be overwhelmed by the darkness and death that surrounded all human existence, the only possible course they could pursue must be the building of an ordered world that might protect them from the prospect of so dire an end. Urizen, in Blake's designs, is not an ugly figure; he is graceful, even majestic. On the other hand, he is often also depicted with his eyes closed, suggesting his lack of true vision.

Blake, by contrast, believes the quest for an absolute permanence to be mistaken. In a world of life, fixity is impossible to achieve; the task of human beings is to learn how to inhabit a world where changes, shifts and transformations are part of the essential process. 'We are born to Cares and Woes,' Watts had written gloomily in one of his hymns. In contrast to this, Blake sees the human condition as one of necessary alternations:

> Man was made for joy & Woe
> And when this we rightly know
> Thro the world we safely go
> Joy & Woe are woven fine
> A Clothing for the Soul divine
> Under every grief & pine
> Runs a joy with silken twine[8]

He could not deny the existence of griefs and sorrows, of course, but he believed that a view of the world that made them central was at once mistaken and dangerous, fostering a defensive attitude in individuals and the very desire for permanence that was Urizen's great mistake, subjecting his eighteenth-century devotees to their current captivity.

Looking more closely at Urizen's activities, in fact, we see that, as elsewhere, Blake's purpose was not simply to attack his antagonist. In one sense he was on the side of Watts, whose vision possessed a grandeur – a visionary power even – that he could respect. The questions that were agitating him, on the other hand, deeper than any faced by

Watts, related to his own vision. How was it that the beauty and delight that he discovered everywhere in the world seemed not to be noticed at all by his fellows? Why did they persist in disregarding not just their own imaginative faculties but even the psychic experiences induced by terror, on the one hand, or by the free exercise of energy on the other?

At one level Blake found it easy to locate humanity's contemporary enemies. They formed the alliance of church and state attacked by eighteenth-century radicals such as Jean Messelier, who in his will, published by Voltaire, desired to see the last king strangled with the guts of the last priest. Looked at from a hostile point of view, the eighteenth-century church was lending supernatural backing to the authority of a law that amounted to nothing more than the will of an entrenched ruling class trying to secure its power more firmly. Some of Blake's most memorable writings were spurred on by his sense of the social iniquities resulting from such an imposition. But, as has already been pointed out, he seems to have suspected also that there was something in the human psyche that allowed it to accept complicity in such conspiracies. It was hard to believe that the whole human race would have allowed itself to be hoodwinked for so long if some power in the mind were not assenting to such law and such enforcement. Yet it remained difficult to see how the rule of solid law had come to be established within the setting of an eternity consisting of 'visionary forms dramatic'. In such terms it was possible to take a more sympathetic view of the ruling powers and to see them as representatives of a blinded humanity, seeking security in an incomprehensible world that constantly threatened it with dangers of all kinds. So he moved towards the development of a mythology of his own that might help resolve some of these puzzles.

Urizen, in this larger view, is not just a 'jealous god' whose purposes are inexplicably malignant, but a bewildered being who has lost his way in eternity and turned away from its light and energy to become wrapped in dark ruminations of his own. This view entails a total retelling of the Creation story as found in the Hebrew and Christian Scriptures. The creative 'brooding' of the Spirit on the face of the waters in Genesis is replaced by the self-enclosed 'brooding' of Urizen; the biblical Creation, commonly presented as the positive making of a firm basis in the midst of darkness and non-entity, by a work of desperation in the face of loss. Urizen begins to create the world we know, but in the hope of establishing ramparts against chaos in a universe where he feels increasingly lost. Because he has turned away from eternity, where vision and energy are harmonized, he must continue to suffer the despair of a darkened imagination and the fears of a thwarted energy that returns to threaten his stability.

It was his interest in these questions that led Blake away from the short lyrics in which he excelled to the longer enterprise that we now think of as the prophetic books. As already explained, his use of the word 'prophetic' did not involve claiming in any detailed sense to foretell the future.[9] Yet even while he was working through his shorter poems he was preoccupied by political matters. His efforts to work towards the cleansing of human perception until human beings should see the infinite in all things, went hand in hand with a belief that it was necessary to explore the political implications of what was actually happening in his world. He was looking, in other words, not to foresee future happenings but to discover the patterns of significance underlying all such events. By comparison with the Bible of his contemporaries, where the common assumption was that human ills were due to transgression of the divine law and that the God behind the universe was a great and gloomy lawmaker, Blake believed many of the ills of the world to result from a loss of imagination and an unwillingness to cultivate human energies in freedom. A mythology conceived in those terms would provide, he thought, a more convincing interpretation of human existence than those normally derived from the Bible; if universally accepted, moreover, it would offer greater possibilities of human amelioration.

Blake's course in concentrating on these ideas after producing *America* and *Europe* may also have been governed by a sober recognition. The two greatest contemporary events were after all the two 'Revolutions', American and French, and at one point it had been not unnatural to suppose (as indeed Thomas Paine assumed in *The Rights of Man*) that the sequence would continue as revolutions embracing not only the rest of Europe but Asia and Africa as well; now it became evident that revolutions were not after all going to spread to the rest of the world. Accordingly, his new works, 'Africa' and 'Asia', were presented not as separate books but as shorter sections in the next Prophetic Book, *The Song of Los*. Here the intense elaboration of mythological themes continues in an even more condensed form. In 'Africa' it takes in the development of philosophy and religion first in Greece (Trismegistus, Pythagoras, Plato) and then in the East and North, assuming the existence of a distorted sensualism in Islam and a cult of war in the Scandinavian and Germanic countries. The gospel of Jesus, meanwhile, does nothing to help the situation. Instead, the philosophy of the five senses established by Locke and Newton takes over, leading only to that of Rousseau and Voltaire; in the further mountains, meanwhile, the more sublime possibilities of the divine and angelic lie dead.

In 'Asia' the situation is still worse, as the kings extend their tyranny into oppressions of every kind. Their rule is not confined to the teaching of a philosophy of the five senses but to economic constraint in the form of imposed commercial rules and physical disasters, until the fire of revolution that has arisen in Europe spreads to the remaining continents, creating a caricature of sexuality where the grave itself reaches out for an orgasm engulfing all life itself – envisaged as a great male sexual organ plunging into her vacuity.

> The Grave shrieks with delight, & shakes
> Her hollow womb, & clasps the solid stem:
> Her bosom swells with wild desire:
> And milk & blood & glandous wine
> In rivers rush & shout & dance,
> On mountain, dale and plain.

To round off this vision of current negativity Blake makes use of the briefest sentence in the Bible; instead of 'Jesus', however,

> Urizen wept.

Urizen dominates the next prophetic book of this time – already produced, if we accept the dating on his own title-pages – as Blake begins to produce a Bible of his own – no doubt his promised 'Bible of Hell'. The title-page of *The First Book of Urizen* (figure 10) portrays its dominating figure with a pen in one hand and a graver in the other, sitting with his eyes closed and his back to a pair of gravestones, with the text he is writing from, available only to his feeling foot, enrooting itself into the ground as a basically illegible Book of Nature.

The text that follows is set, like a traditional Bible, in two columns throughout. The opening two pages contains the main hopeful images in the book as a whole: on the left-hand one a woman floats with a baby, while to the right (figure 3) a male figure runs through flames. After this, however, all the images are of pain and horror, division and deprivation, apart from one showing the child Orc falling through space, bright still in his illumination. The main thrust of the narrative is once again to present an alternative to the Genesis story of Creation, showing that account rather as depicting a process of withdrawal into

10 Detail from the title-page to *The Book of Urizen*. Courtesy of Library of Congress, Washington

solitude by its dominating figure, Urizen:

> Of the primeval Priests assum'd power,
> When Eternals spurn'd back his religion;
> And gave him a place in the north,
> Obscure, shadowy, void, solitary.

His next creative acts form a series of consequent divisions, to be hammered into shape by Los, who suffers equally, being essentially, as we have already said, a different aspect of the same figure. What is being created is recognisably a version of the human body, but it is a Urizenic version, constructed under law. Whereas the God of the Old Testament 'saw every thing that he had made, and, behold, it was very good', Urizen

> ... in darkness clos'd, view'd all his race,
> And his soul sicken'd! he curs'd
> Both sons & daughters; for he saw
> That no flesh nor spirit could keep
> His iron laws one moment.

Members of the resulting population are presented in terms of Blake's contemporaries, predicting the enslavement of their senses:

> For the ears of the inhabitants,
> Were wither'd, & deafen'd, & cold:
> And their eyes could not discern,
> Their brethren of other cities.

In the face of this dark and shrunken condition the only solution is revolt. It is led by a character, Fuzon, not encountered until now. He and the remaining children of Urizen abandon the 'pendulous earth': 'They called it Egypt and left it.'

The story of Fuzon's action returns to form the opening to the next book, *The Book of Ahania* – a parody of the Book of Exodus to follow the Urizenic Genesis. Fuzon is seen as a figure of unenlightened energy, rising up on a 'chariot iron-winged' and declaring his enmity to 'this abstract non-entity I This cloudy God seated on waters'. He even believes that his wrath has been enough in itself to slay Urizen, not realizing that in his cold jealousy the latter has been preparing silently and in agony a rock which he now launches against Fuzon to destroy his lightless corpse, nail him to the Tree of Mystery and leave him as a source of pestilence. The figure remaining is Ahania, Urizen's 'parted soul', a moon to his darkened body, now seized on his mountains of Jealousy, rejected as 'Sin' and abandoned. In her plight she sings a song of desolation, recalling the glory of Urizen in his former self and her happiness with him:

> Then thou with thy lap full of seed
> With thy band full of generous fire
> Walked forth from the clouds of morning
> On the virgins of springing joy,
> On the human soul to cast
>
> The seed of eternal science.
> The sweat poured down thy temples
> To Ahania return'd in evening
> The moisture awoke to birth
> My mothers-joys, sleeping in bliss.

Although her lament concludes with a protest against the 'Cruel jealousy! selfish fear!' who has cast her out, so that the final note renews the sense of desolation, the long passage of nostalgic recall here has lent a positive note to the book as a whole that *The Book of Urizen* lacked, which suggests that Blake was trying to find a way to move past that desolate negativity – a desire that may also account for his approach in the other prophetic book of this year, *The Book of Los*. This work seems an attempt to tell the story of the Urizenic creation concentrating not on Urizen, who as a figure of negativity could not really create except in his fantasies, but on Los – who had in any case already needed to be called in as the necessary agent to give embodiment to those fantasies. In the new work the note of nostalgia that had been struck by Ahania in her lament could be foregrounded by the speech of 'Eno aged Mother' which opens with an account of a time of 'Love and Joy' before the reign of Covet, Envy, Wrath and 'Curled Wantonness':

> Till Covet broke his locks & bars,
> And slept with open doors:
> Envy sung at the rich mans feast:
> Wrath was follow'd up and down
> By a little ewe lamb
> And Wantonness on his own true love
> Begot a giant race:

As soon as the focus is turned to Los, however, the keynote must be his frustration as he finds himself in a dark void, so that the whole of his energy is spent in frustration and anger at the 'Coldness, darkness, obstruction, a Solid | Without fluctuation' in which he is bound. When he succeeds in freeing himself, it is to find his state changed into a falling, not just like that of Mulciber in *Paradise Lost*, 'A summers day', but truly endless –

> Still he fell thro' the void, still a void
> Found for falling day & night without end …

After 'many ages of groans', the 'Human' begins to appear, organized into 'finite inflexible organs', and it is discovered that what is now being made is a body in the form of Urizen, to be bound down by the hammer of Los in his furnaces until it finally appears as 'a Human Illusion | In darkness and deep clouds involved'. Here we are presumably expected to recognize our own human ancestry. Once again, however, the dominant note is necessarily negative. We have gathered Blake's view of what he believes to be wrong with the human condition, not whether he can perceive a means of escape.

It is perhaps a sign of his uncertainty about such matters that from now on the use of symbols becomes more intense, some of Blake's images being stylized according to particular ideas of his. The use of combing to suggest adult regulation of the young has already been mentioned. Forms of hair are also significant: straight flowing hair suggests the predominance of visionary power, while tightly massed curls tip the scales in favour of energy. Baldness, meanwhile, indicates the absence of both qualities – and may even indicate idiocy. (Every time he happened to pass Bedlam, Blake would have seen the two bald figures that served as its guardian statues.[10])

In the writing of 'Tiriel' this was one of the most obvious emblematic images, developed also in the illustrations alongside that of his blindness. Tiriel himself tries to present his condition as one of pathos:

> Look at my eyes, blind as the orbless scull among the stones!
> Look at my bald head! Hark! listen, ye serpents, listen!

His sons see only an aged, grey-bearded tyrant, however: 'For every one of those wrinkles, each of those grey hairs | Are cruel as death & as obdurate as the devouring pit!' It is left to the childish elderly Har to see more clearly what he has now become:

> 'God bless thy poor bald pate! God bless thy hollow winking eyes. ...
> Heva, come kiss his bald head, for he will not hurt us, Heva.'

The exhibiting of baldness as a negative but pathetic condition, a sign of hypocrisy or loss of wits, was thus early established. It goes along with an equally permanent dialectic between vision and energy, for the absence of which both blindness and baldness can be a kind of visual shorthand.

An even more intricate figure is that of the grid, or net. The idea that evidently possessed Blake was that the criss-crossing lines that thinkers such as mathematicians and map-makers produce as part of their working can, if concentrated on too exclusively, turn instead into an imprisoning reticulation – a net in which the captive mind actually finds itself struggling. This conception gives rise to the design for 'The Human Abstract', in which the inhumane version of thinking described in the poem finds embodiment in an elderly figure below, struggling with a rope that has turned into a net.

During subsequent years, his symbolism took a modified form, corresponding to the shifting role of his attitude to energy. As supreme stress

was no longer laid on the outburst of flame but moved to the transforming power of vision, the use of serpent imagery, which in the 1790s
had expressed the threat posed by energy's existence, shifted, until it
came to be normally used to express the potentially throttling power
of the selfhood, given its insidious presence in the human physique.
This is the version in which it now often appears, in illustrations
ranging from the Book of Job to the Miltonic – relating the renewed
Milton, in the prophetic book of that name, to the imaginative Jesus:

> Saviour pour upon me thy Spirit of meekness & love:
> Annihilate the Selfhood in me, be thou all my life![11]

In spite of this shift towards a more Christianizing morality, the social
criticism inherent in *Songs of Experience* evidently remained very much
alive in his mind, and from one point of view it is to be regretted that his
former free-playing intelligence, ready to direct itself, in alternate breaths
as it were, towards satire or vision did not survive more vigorously. By
contrast, the urge to symbolize seemed to become even stronger. It
survived most vigorously, perhaps, in his sense of the contrast between
'classic' art and the 'Gothic', further defined in his statement

> Mathematic Form is Eternal in the Reasoning Memory. Living Form
> is Eternal Existence. Grecian is Mathematic Form Gothic is Living
> Form[12]

When he reworked a former print, already discussed, about 1808 he
embellished the inscription on it with the words:

> JOSEPH of Arimathea among The Rocks of Albion
>   This is One of the Gothic Artists who Built the Cathedrals in what
> we call the Dark Ages Wandering about in sheep skins & goat skins.
> of whom the World was not worthy such were the Christians in
> all Ages[13]

A similar devotion to Gothic art was evident in his design for the
Canterbury Tales, where the gateway of the inn from which the pilgrims
set out is clearly Gothic in style, while the landscape beyond also reveals
Gothic spires.[14] The argument which he was pursuing by this time
involved the assumption that the Gothic was the truly Christian, its
rising arches representing aspirations to a version of humanity that
included its sublimity. Against this was to be envisaged the art of the

Druids as shown in their temple architecture, which was for him as tellingly indicative of *their* state of mind. Against the soaring invitation of the Gothic, the unimaginative squaredness of the trilithon set one rock firmly across the other two, cutting off any possibility of sublimity, just as the limitations of mathematical calculation constantly acted as a bar to humanity from moving outside mathematically fixed forms and expanding into the visionary. As he put it when contemplating the fate of Albion at the opening of *Jerusalem*,

> His Sublime & Pathos become Two Rocks fixd in the Earth
> His Reason, his Spectrous Power, covers them above[15]

The grand image of the trilithon, already figured by the deceptive square entry to the grave as 'Death's Door' in *The Gates of Paradise*, would become another permanent part of his iconography, a Stonehenge image to be rendered memorably not only in *Milton* and *Jerusalem*,[16] but indicating also the decline of Job's state in his illustrations to that Book.[17] He also took the imagery further. As he mentioned in his *Descriptive Catalogue*,[18] he knew the work of antiquaries such as Jacob Bryant, and believed that such researches might confirm his belief that Britain had been 'the primitive Seat of the Patriarchal Religion',[19] with Abraham, Noah and others the original Druids. His own interest in the Druids, in the course of which he noted that the engaged attention of the erudite of the previous century had looked back as far as Caesar's Gallic Wars, was of long standing. He seems to have ignored contemporary claims (as sometimes invoked in Wordsworth's poetry, for example[20]) that the Druids had been a primitive, peace-loving cult, whose pursuits constituted a strange contrast to the cruelties of later religions, and to have taken up instead the implications of their recorded practices of human sacrifice. For him, therefore, Druidism was essentially a cruel cult, redeemed only by the presence of the more enlightened figures among them known as the Bards. Above all, as we have seen, he found in the stone remains they left a kind of sublimity that was also forbidding, anticipating the devotion to law that he distrusted in his own contemporary civilization. This grim portent, when depicted in *Milton*[21] and *Jerusalem*, dominated the whole design of a page (Figure 11). It would reappear in his illustrations whenever he wanted to emphasize what he saw as the anti-visionary bias of his contemporary civilization.

A further elaboration in his criticism responded to a development in contemporary Druid cultivation. William Stukeley, a noted antiquary

11 Jerusalem, plate 70, Yale Center for British Art, Paul Mellon Collection

of the time, had observed the Druids' fondness for arranging their rock-temples in circles, as at Stonehenge and Avebury. Sharing the current interest in comparative religions, he had formed the theory that these temples were originally designed to imitate the Egyptian hierogram that brought together sun, serpent and wings. Moreover, when he studied the local landscapes, he even believed that he could detect wavy avenues leading away from the stone circle, which might be thought to have originally corresponded to the serpents of the Egyptian pattern. This design he could reconcile with Christian orthodoxy by supposing that in Egyptian religion it had itself represented a dim shadowing of the Christian Trinity.[22] (In much the same fashion Stukeley had argued that the Druid cult of human sacrifice might have resulted from a misunderstanding of the need for redemption and the story of Abraham's sacrifice of his son Isaac.[23]) At the end of *Jerusalem* Blake would follow this line of ideas to the extent of depicting wavy serpentine avenues, made up of many more trilitha, leading away from a Stonehenge (Figure 12). Had he been told that there were in fact no such avenues at the sites in question he would no doubt have retorted that this simply reinforced his critique of a Druidism that devoted itself to visionless, square-shaped trilitha and to temples shut up into imprisoning circles, leaving no place for the energy of the serpent or the soaring of wings and substituting a scene of imprisonment, a lack of vision that was in danger of assuming total control and against which only the artist's vision, as expressed by Los, could hope to flourish.

The single-mindedness and determination with which Blake pursued his unusual view of the world was in certain respects idiosyncratic, yet the reader who engages with it will discover that it carries rewards of its own, particularly for those who are attracted by its combination of imagination and energy. When one is puzzled by a piece of text or by an unusual design, it is often helpful to ask whether a point of imaginative illumination or a moment of energy is prominent. These can take many forms. To repeat they may be simply stylized, as when a figure with long, flowing locks of hair is connected with imagination, while one with closely coiled curls is seen to express energy. Vision and energy may sometimes work in alternation, as with some of the lyrics in *Songs of Innocence* that find their counterparts in *Songs of Experience*. It is in the interplay of the two qualities, however, that Blake's complexities are often at their most active.

At all times, however, it is his most vivid statements, whether in his poetry or in his designs, that must attract attention. Obscure passages

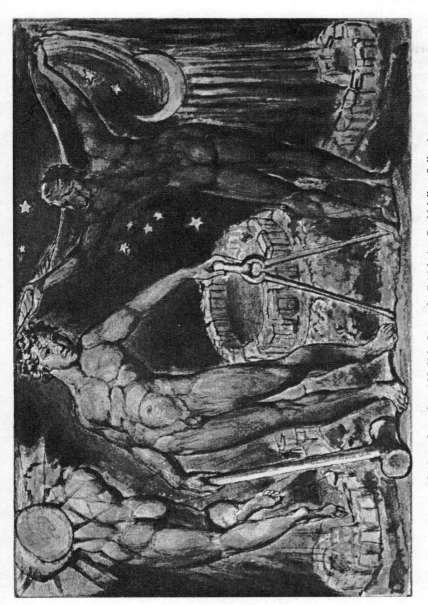

12 *Jerusalem*, plate 100, Yale Center for British Art, Paul Mellon Collection

sometimes reveal their significance when considered in the light of powerful positive images, whether of enthralment (as in the illustrations to *The Book of Urizen*) or of human energy and joy – a figure running through fire, angels singing for joy, faces bearing the lineaments of gratified desire. These are the images and statements by which he lived, and for which – whether or not they were heeded by his audience – he remained content to work in isolation and obscurity.

8
'Vala' and the Fate of Narrative Epic

Even a cursory examination of the illuminated books dated in 1795 conveys the impression that Blake's sense of engagement was fading. The striking illuminations that characterized *The Book of Los* give place to designs limited in extent by comparison with the amount of text, which is now crowded into a few pages. Such a decline of boldness suggests that towards the end of the century Blake passed through some process of disturbance: how far this may have been precipitated by possible private events such as those hinted at in the chapter on his marriage, how far by other, more public factors, is impossible to determine. We are left to draw our own conclusions by inference from the scanty evidence that survives and from indications of developments that were taking place in his own state of mind, including further reflections on his own beliefs.

One significant factor in inducing a change of mood was certainly the course of contemporary events. During the decade initial excitement in parts of the country created by the events of the French Revolution and subsequent revulsion (which he shared) at the events of the Terror had given place to a growing patriotism, stimulated by the war against the French. The Treason Trials of 1794, though ending in the acquittal of those charged, initiated a mood of caution among similar figures, who feared setting themselves at risk. This was intensified by events such as the trial of Richard Brothers in the following year and his committal to a madhouse. Prophecy was a dangerous pursuit, particularly if it seemed in any way to condone the Revolution.[1] By 1798 the *Anti-Jacobin* (to be followed by the *Anti-Jacobin Review*) had taken up the patriotic and anti-Gallican sentiments and was in full cry. Though it was not until 1808 that the *Review* would earn Blake's bitter contempt by its scathing dismissal of his designs for Blair's *Grave*, the general conservative policy of the journal had long been answering to a perceptible change of temper in the country at large.

One effect of the new, hostile mood was for writers increasingly to look inward. Instead of risking the possible effects of attempting prophetic statements in a political setting where events might in any case prove one wrong, it might be safer to turn one's mind to study of the human faculties and what lay in their capabilities. In March 1798 Coleridge wrote:

> I have for some time past withdrawn myself almost totally from the consideration of *immediate* causes, which are infinitely complex & uncertain, to muse on fundamental & general causes ... to the seeking with patience & a slow, very slow mind ... what our faculties are & what they are capable of becoming.[2]

In much the same manner, turning away from efforts to create poetical works of political prophecy, Blake had increasingly turned to the shorter books just described in which he worked in terms of a controlling mythology designed among other things to account for the nature of human behaviour. He now embarked on a more ambitious project: to try to consolidate his thoughts on the topic into a long poem, which would be presided over by the illusory vision of nature to which he gave the name Vala. The new poem was at first given her name as title – evidently with the expectation that other, already achieved segments of his mythology would be subsumed into the new narrative.

A sense of the way in which Blake's mind was moving during the intervening years can be gathered from his annotations to *An Apology for the Bible*, produced by Richard Watson, the Bishop of Llandaff,[3*] the first of which reads: 'To defend the Bible in this year 1798 would cost a man his life. The Beast & the Whore rule without control.' The next sentences begin to exhibit his own reply to the bishop, which is then developed by way of further annotations:

> It is an easy matter for a Bishop to triumph over Paines attack but it is not so easy, for one who loves the Bible
>
> The Perversions of Christs words & acts are attackd by Paine & also the perversions of the Bible; Who dare defend either the Acts of Christ or the Bible Unperverted?
>
> But to him who sees this mortal pilgrimage in the light that I see it. Duty to his country is the first consideration & safety the last
>
> Read patiently take not up this Book in an idle hour the consideration of these things is the whole duty of man & the affairs of

life & death trifles sports of time But these considerations business of
Eternity
   I have been commanded from Hell not to print this as it is what
our Enemies wish[4]

An important feature of Blake's many comments on Watson's book is
that they show him absorbing the impact of current scepticism concerning the accuracy of the biblical record – until then little considered
critically in England but now in Germany the subject of increasingly
widespread concern. The last of the opening comments just recorded
suggests, however, a nervousness at thought of the effect liable to be
produced by the reproduction of any such critical comments in his own
publications.

   As E. P. Thompson pointed out, his attitude to Watson did not mean
that he altogether sided with Paine, whose criticisms he regarded as
directed not against the Gospel but against 'Antichrist'.[5] And whatever
his attitude to Paine's critical comments, he continued to insist on
his own adherence to Christianity. He also felt, evidently, that Paine's
criticisms did not justify the Bishop's censure that he was undermining
the bases of morality; on the contrary, he argued, much behaviour
recorded in the Old Testament – including the massacres undertaken in
the belief that they were commanded by the Lord – was notably
immoral. 'To me who believe the Bible and profess myself a Christian,'
he wrote, 'a defence of the Wickedness of the Israelites in murdering
so many thousands under pretence of a command from God is altogether Abominable & Blasphemous.' And again, 'To Extirpate a nation
by means of another nation is as wicked as to destroy an individual
by means of another individual which God considers (in the Bible) as
Murder & commands that it shall not be done.'[6]

   Another clear shift in Blake's attitudes at this time is to be traced in his
attitude to Milton. The radical reinterpretation of him in *The Marriage of
Heaven and Hell* had now modulated to a dual respect, closer to the
attitude found in Wordsworth's sonnet addressed to him, which allowed
for celebration of his aspiration to sublimity while offering equal respect
for his humility, his willingness to take on himself the lowliest human
duties.

   His attitude to energy, likewise, was becoming more complex, focus-
ing no longer on the power of out-bursting flame but moving to a
stress on vision. The use of serpent imagery, which in the early 1790s
had expressed the threat posed by energy, shifted accordingly: the
dominance of the selfhood, given its insidious presence in the human

physique and its potentially throttling force, was now emphasized. Above all, he was increasingly possessed by his belief in Vision as the supreme value. Its cultivation, nevertheless, could not be undertaken in a passive frame of mind; it relied for success on the cultivation of active powers:

> That which can be made Explicit to the Idiot is not worth my care. The wisest of the Ancients considerd what is not too Explicit as the fittest for Instruction because it rouzes the faculties to act. I name Moses Solomon Esop Homer Plato ...

Once invoked, the visionary power could be totally transforming. To Dr Trusler, who complained that his 'Fancy' seemed to be in 'the World of Spirits', he wrote defending the 'Spiritual World':

> I know that This World Is a World of Imagination & Vision I see Every thing I paint In This World, but Every body does not see alike. To the Eyes of a Miser a Guinea is more beautiful than the Sun & a bag worn with the use of Money has more beautiful proportions than a Vine filled with Grapes. The tree which moves some to tears of joy is in the Eyes of others only a Green thing that stands in the way. Some See Nature all Ridicule & Deformity & by these I shall not regulate my proportions, & Some Scarce see Nature at all But to the Eyes of the Man of Imagination Nature is Imagination itself. As a man is So he Sees. As the Eye is formed such are its Powers You certainly Mistake when you say that the Visions of Fancy are not be found in This World. To Me This World is all One continued Vision of Fancy or Imagination & I feel Flatterd when I am told So. What is it sets Homer Virgil & Milton in so high a rank of Art. Why is the Bible more Entertaining & Instructive than any other book. Is it not because they are addressed to the Imagination which is Spiritual Sensation & but mediately to the Understanding or Reason Such is True Painting and such <was> alone valued by the Greeks & the best modern Artists. Consider what Lord Bacon says 'Sense sends over to Imagination before Reason have judged & Reason sends over to Imagination before the Decree can be acted.' See Advancem^t of Learning Part 2 P 47 of first Edition
>
> But I am happy to find a Great Majority of Fellow Mortals who can Elucidate My Visions & Particularly they have been Elucidated by Children who have taken a greater delight in contemplating my Pictures than I even hoped. Neither Youth nor Childhood is Folly or Incapacity Some Children are Fools & so are some Old Men. But There is a vast Majority on the side of Imagination or Spiritual Sensation[7]

Given such beliefs, how could he make a great epic for the new age that was dawning? He had already made attempts towards the kind of mythology that needed to be formed. In two poems, he had created mythical narratives with a strong resemblance to the Garden of Eden story, presenting in 'Tiriel' a doomed landscape where an aged and tyrannical figure whose experience had lost touch with his innocence gave up trying to impose his law and in *The Book of Thel* a further, and in some ways alternative, attempt in this mode, with a figure of pure Innocence endeavouring to find her way through the tortuous paths of Experience. By now, however, he was evidently feeling the need to make larger trial of the myth-making mode. Following the writing of *America* and *Europe*, in which he had concentrated on offering his own interpretations of recent history against a mythical background, and the other Lambeth books noticed above, his attempts came to a climax with his drafting of a long manuscript poem in which he would try to produce a mythical pattern that could be applied to the whole of human history as well as to every individual human life. Central to this was his concept of 'the Eternal Man', the human being existing in every human being, whose disorders reflect on a grand scale failings from which all in their several ways suffer.

The fragmentary poem thus created is one of the most interesting and extraordinary in English literature. Before his time, it could be said, such imaginative structures were normally geared to the structure of existing mythologies, and especially to the Bible; afterwards it would be more common for writers to produce fantastic worlds or universes of their own creation, though such writers would still find it necessary to draw in some way on existing traditions, whether it was C. S. Lewis falling back on Christian theology or Philip Pullman drawing on lore of the North. Blake, however, was striking out more boldly. As we have seen, he had brought together echoes of Sophocles, Shakespeare, Norse mythology and alchemy for his first prophetic books, but he discarded even these props for his later compositions, so that apart from the hint of an illusion of unity in the name 'Enion' or the possible reversal of 'SOL' in 'LOS',[8*] the names in his later mythology are innocent of locatable verbal roots. What is particularly unusual in Blake's scheme, indeed, is its extraordinary autonomy – even if he pays dearly for it so far as communication with his readers is concerned. Lacking the handholds offered by reference to known and familiar traditions, they are likely to find themselves frequently struggling as they try to elucidate the offered scenario. This is particularly true of the Eternal Man, since the question immediately arises, what is *his* status? Can he have associates that are equally eternal? And if the Zoas are only functions or parts of him, is it possible for them to have distinctive personalities?

For this reason, and despite the obvious and immediate appeal of 'Vala' when approached from many angles, readers who confront it more directly, in one of the complete editions, may find it confusing; and if they then turn to the original manuscript, or a facsimile, they will come upon even more causes for puzzlement. What was originally written on the page has in many cases been erased and overwritten; even the original planned order is not clear. According to one reading, the initial opening would have been at what is now headed as Night Two, so that the poem would have begun with the lines:

> Man calld Urizen & said. Behold these sickning Spheres
> Take thou possession! Take this Sceptre! Go forth in my might
> For I am weary. & must sleep in the dark sleep of Death ...

There followed various emendations, including the insertion of a line above the first,

> Turning his Eyes outward to Self. losing the Divine Vision

and then, later and above that, in its turn, another possible opening:

> Rising upon his Couch of death, Albion beheld his Sons

where 'Albion' replaces the original word 'Man'.

Piecing together the implications of Blake's alterations, it seems that the original idea for his long poem had been to present the 'dream of Vala' as a sequence involving the decline of 'Man', or the 'Eternal Man', from his full humanity. The process was to be imagined as a dream in which our own mortal lives are forever implicated, showing how they came to suffer from the domination of Reason. While there were various ways in which the rise to dominance of Urizen, protagonist of Reason, could be rendered, however, the organization of the poem as a whole presented increasing difficulties. The first great development was to change the ordering so that it did not begin with the moment of failure in Man, but instead presented the resulting state of the four Zoas, corresponding to the major faculties of the human body – thought of as the head, the heart, the genitals and the hands and feet – and portrayed their activities as they wander around, their lost unified relation with each other replaced in this disordered state by strife and misunderstanding.

This was one reason, no doubt, why the title 'Vala' came to be supplemented or replaced by that of *The Four Zoas*.

At the time of the poem's inception Blake was also working on several hundred illustrations to Edward Young's *Night Thoughts*, a series which he created by allowing his designs to surround the text of the poem, so adding to its epic status. For his own poem he decided to take over Young's form and organize it into 'Nights', rather than Spenser's 'Cantos' or Milton's 'Books'. In most respects, however, Blake's poem differs from Young's, which has a recognizable human figure, that of the narrator, at the centre of its reflections and an even firmer figure to which it is addressed, 'Lorenzo'. It resembles *Night Thoughts* further only at the deepest level: its serious concern with questions of life, death, and immortality. Since Blake rejects the normal Christian postponement of immortality as a condition to be grasped only after death, in favour of an eternity that lies about us all the time if we could only open our eyes to it, he adopts a different approach, which takes some colouring from *Paradise Lost*. In Milton's poem we are made to feel not only that Satan has fallen from heaven, but also that he is gradually forgetting even what it was like, to be reminded only when he glimpses its light in the distance or meets again one of its inhabitants. The participants in Blake's poem are not 'characters' in the normal sense, since each of them embodies only one of the four main living principles in the human being, yet they are in a state not dissimilar to Satan's, resenting the disorders of the world in which they are moving about, yet haunted by the sense that things were once otherwise. From time to time one of the characters will have a dream or vision in which some part of the story of their disruption is recaptured, so that the reader can gradually build up, through these flashbacks, a full picture of that state and what it was like.

These Zoas cannot be fully formed human beings, since the subject of Blake's poem is, precisely, the lost presence of an integrating power that should work in the human psyche and harmonize it. Instead, each Zoa embodies one of its conflicting functions, Urizen being associated with the head, Luvah with the heart, Tharmas with the genitals and Urthona with the shaping powers generally. At times it may seem that Urizen is primarily to blame for the disruption, with his substitution of eighteenth-century mathematical rationality for a more creative and imaginative kind of thinking. At other times it will be the lost genital innocence of Tharmas that seems responsible. At times, again, it is the unbridled energy of the figure Orc, a burning boy who threatens destruction from another central region, that will appear most frightening.

In the course of the work, though, it becomes clear that all three are diminished by an overriding further catastrophe: Urizen's rationality, Tharmas's lost innocence and Orc's uprising are the result of a deeper failure, to be localized, if anywhere, in the heart, Orc's fiery revolt being the result of Luvah's decline there into impotence.

Gradually, moreover, the flashbacks make it clear that the failure does not rest even there, but with the Eternal Man of whom they are parts, who allowed himself to be deluded by an illusion of impossible purity and holiness, and so failed 'in the noonday sun', sinking into a sleep within which all the events troubling the Zoas are nightmares. The implication throughout is that if the Eternal Man could once reawaken, the heart would be the place where recall of his powers would be experienced first and foremost, while simultaneously vision would be renewed in the reasoning powers and sexual innocence recovered as 'organized experience'.

One power has not been discussed so far. Urthona, associated with the earth forces, has been rendered even more impotent than the others by the failure of the Eternal Man. His powers can be expressed only by his representative Los, who lives primarily in his hands and feet, and can use them either to express his rage and frustration in a mad dance or to create into form anything that comes within reach. His is a visionless creativity, valuable for its positive energy but powerless in itself to redeem the situation. Nevertheless his status has changed for this epic presentation: he is less a figure of jealousy, and rather the great Smith, whose energy is essential for the whole.

Eventually, in the last Night, an apocalypse takes place. In a rending of the universe, the Zoas find themselves pitched into a turmoil through which they recover a sense of their lost significance. Subsequent scenes of reconciliation are followed by a conclusion in which they are all seen and heard working in their ancient harmony and serving a restored humanity.

In some ways this is a fitting conclusion to what has all the makings of a successful romantic epic. It substitutes for the idea of a fall of man into states of sin and guilt, the sense of a lost integration of the personality that many psychoanalysts, particularly those of a Jungian persuasion, would regard as a valid account of the human condition. In other respects, however, the achievement is necessarily fragmentary. The manuscript that survives has a number of unusual features, for which Blake left no explanation. It began with pages in fine, copperplate handwriting which were, however, much emended in the course of time, while the later pages were written in a swift cursive script, giving a more makeshift impression. There are other signs of confusion, such as the existence of Night the Seventh in two successive versions – the result perhaps of an oversight, or possibly of a late decision to revise. After a certain point also Blake began to use proof-sheets of the pages already engraved on which the printed design could survive while his own writing was then written into the spaces originally left to contain the printed text of Young's poem. Were the designs selected for their relevance to the inserted text, or taken simply at random in the absence of a stock of clean paper? We can only surmise. In addition, while some of the designs on the manuscript take the form of direct illustrations to the text, others have an obvious sexual content, often depicting human genitals, and some have subsequently been erased. It is not clear whether these have a bearing on the text or were simply later and unrelated additions on Blake's part. Nor is it clear whether they were intended as illustrations making satiric comments on human sexual behaviour or as a straightforward attempt to include it among the topics included in the sweep of his vision. As a result, editors have been left to decide for themselves what to make of them, some deciding firmly that everything now on the pages has been left as part of a coherent purpose which remains only to be elucidated and expounded, while others suspect that they are witnessing the relicts of a series of shifting plans, ranging from the desire to create a noble long poem rivalling *Paradise Lost* or the *Night Thoughts* to a gallimaufry taking in human aspirations to the sublime at one extreme and the vagaries of sexual deviance at the other.

However interpreted, the poem is unique in its time for the range of its representations of human behaviour. Sexual fulfilment is seen as an important factor when considering psychic health, yet as needing to be kept in proportion – at least if one takes seriously the words of Luvah in the last Night: 'Attempting to be more than Man We become less', following the injunction to him and Vala to 'return, & Love in peace, I Into your place, the place of seed, not in the brain or heart'.[9]

Blake's decision not to publish the poem suggests that he was not fully satisfied with it, a feeling that may be associated with the form he had chosen; what he had come to see, on this interpretation, was that any attempt at a mythical interpretation for the whole of experience *was in itself a work of Urizen*. Some scholars have argued that Blake's work embodied a continuous struggle between the visitations of his imagination and the struggle towards order that he caricatured in Urizen; in such a case, it might be argued, the very aim to produce a large and ordered epic was inevitably doomed.

In any case, however, the shape he chose for his conception was bound to run into difficulties. To have main 'characters' who were not full human beings was to give rise to shadowy forms of action; even more difficult was the task of writing in terms of a mythology that readers needed to discover (or even invent for themselves) as they went along. By comparison with Milton, who could take for granted readers who would know the basic story of the Creation and the Fall of man from the Bible and other accounts, Blake was telling a story founded largely in his own ideas about the meaning of human existence. The central conception – that of finding an interpretation of human civilization that would also interpret the history of every individual human being – was brilliant, but the structural difficulties that resulted were proportionately immense. As the poem proceeded, Blake seems to have found himself steadily more imprisoned by the terms he had set himself.

But if there is in one sense a failure here, it is the kind of failure that reaches well beyond most poetic successes. One cannot read *The Four Zoas* without a sense of the strong intelligence and imagination that are being brought into play. In the early Nights the depiction of Urizen trying to construct a permanent world in the midst of a desolate space and time that he does not comprehend is particularly brilliant. The character Tharmas comes off well, similarly, through having qualities vivid enough to facilitate visualization. While his language has a rough honesty, his association with the sea has touches of Neptune, visually reinforced when he announces his domination with the claim that the Eternal Man has become a 'Dreamer of furious oceans, cold sleeper of weeds and shells',[10] having previously expressed his wrath in the cry:

> ... Fury in my limbs! destruction in my bones & marrow!
> My skull riven into filaments, my eye into sea jellies
> Floating upon the tide wander bubbling & bubbling
> Uttering my lamentations & begetting little monsters ...[11]

The most successful extended achievement in this mode is created in terms not only of geometric images but of their even more controlled movement:

> Thus were the stars of heaven created like a golden chain
> To bind the Body of Man to heaven from failing into the Abyss
> Each took his station, & his course began with sorrow & care
> In sevens & tens & fifties, hundreds, thousands, numberd all
> According to their various powers. Subordinate to Urizen
> And to his sons in their degrees & to his beauteous daughters

Travelling in silent majesty along their orderd ways
In right lined paths outmeasurd by proportions of number weight
And measure. mathematic motion wondrous. along the deep
In fiery pyramid. or Cube. or unornamented pillar
Of fire far shining. travelling along even to its destind end
Then falling down. a terrible space recovring in winter dire
Its wasted strength. it back returns upon a nether course
Till fired with ardour fresh recruited in its humble season
It rises up on high all summer till its wearied course
Turns into autumn. such the period of many worlds
Others triangular right angled course maintain. others obtuse
Acute Scalene, in simple paths. but others move
In intricate ways biquadrate. Trapeziums Rhombs Rhomboids
Paralellograms. triple & quadruple. polygonic
In their amazing hard subdued course in the vast deep[12]

For the general reader, however, the most memorable passages of all are likely to be the laments of the main victims as they describe their deprivation. Blake knew well that to those who are comfortably situated, the world looks very different from the way it looks to victims of injustice and need. In the early Nights of the poem the victim's view is expressed in several passages of unforgettable poignancy:

What is the price of Experience do men buy it for a song
Or wisdom for a dance in the street? No it is bought with the price
Of all that a man hath his house his wife his children
Wisdom is sold in the desolate market where none come to buy,
And in the witherd field where the farmer plows for bread in vain.

It is an easy thing to triumph in the summers sun
And in the vintage & to sing on the waggon loaded with corn.
It is an easy thing to talk of patience to the afflicted
To speak the laws of prudence to the houseless wanderer
To listen to the hungry ravens cry in wintry season
When the red blood is filld with wine & with the marrow of lambs.

It is an easy thing to laugh at wrathful elements
To hear the dog howl at the wintry door, the ox in the slaughter
    house moan
To see a god on every wind & a blessing on every blast;
To hear sounds of love in the thunder storm that destroys our
    enemies house;

To rejoice in the blight that covers his field, & the sickness that
cuts off his children
While our olive & vine sing & laugh round our door, & our
children bring fruits & flowers
Then the groan & the dolor are quite forgotten & the slave
grinding at the mill
And the captive in chains & the poor in the prison, & the soldier
in the field
When the shatterd bone hath laid him groaning among the
happier dead
It is an easy thing to rejoice in the tents of prosperity
Thus could I sing & thus rejoice, but it is not so with me![13]

Blake adopted various expedients in his attempts to find a viable
ordering for his conception; he even tried renaming the Eternal Man
'Albion' and imaging his Emanation as 'Jerusalem'. Eventually – though
not till some years later[14]* – he seems to have stopped work on his
attempt at an epic, and left it permanently in manuscript.

There was, however, one happy consequence of this. In retreating
from his attempt to produce a total epic formation for his vision, Blake
was forced to fall back on a more fragmentary mode for his utterances –
and this in fact turned out not only to suit them well but also to predict
the nature of future work by others.

In the meantime, however, his personal affairs were passing through a
period of crisis. The call for engraving had fallen off, and where it arose
it was tending to be met by engravers more orthodox in their methods.
In these circumstances his position was saved by his new friendship
with Thomas Butts, a minor civil servant who was impressed by his
abilities and who agreed to commission paintings from him. How far
Blake refused more commercially based offers of work as a result is not
clear, but the payments for this long series of designs, usually on biblical
subjects, certainly provided a basic means of livelihood to sustain him
during long years of neglect.

At the same time he suffered from some nervous affliction, the 'deep
pit of Melancholy' he described to George Cumberland in July 1800,[15]
probably to be identified with the 'Nervous Fear' of which he wrote in a
letter to Flaxman of September.[16] On this occasion it was Flaxman who
came to his rescue through the good offices of his friend William
Hayley, who lived at Felpham in Sussex; after visiting him that summer
Blake agreed to move there for a period and take a cottage nearby.
Hayley, whose liberalism in politics would have appealed to Blake, had

offered him the opportunity of working side by side; only gradually would Blake see that Hayley was picturing himself in the dominant position, proposing works for him to carry out and betraying impatience towards his own claims. As often, however, Blake's enthusiasm carried all before it for the time being and on 18 September the Blakes, together with William's sister Catherine, made the difficult journey to Felpham. Since they had sixteen heavy boxes and portfolios full of prints, and needed seven different chaises on the way, they did not arrive until nearly midnight, but they found the cottage even better than they had hoped. Soon they were to settle happily into what they hoped would be a new life.

9

'A Slumber on the banks of the Ocean'

For a time Felpham was all that Blake might have hoped for when he arrived. The London he had left now seemed a dark dungeon, a 'Web' and 'Veil' that resisted 'every beam of light', or, as his wife put it, a 'terrible desart'.[1] Although the countryside was not too far from the city's centre and its scenes could still be glimpsed from within its developing wilderness of brick and stone, it was an exhilarating experience to have fields all about him now; still more to have light from the sea close at hand. They had passed through a country which they found 'most beautiful' to reach a cottage which exceeded their expectations. To Flaxman he wrote uninhibitedly to express his belief that Felpham was 'a sweet place for Study, because it is more spiritual than London':

> Heaven opens here on all sides her golden Gates her windows are not obstructed by vapours ... voices of Celestial inhabitants are more distinctly heard & their forms more distinctly seen ...[2]

Flaxman he felt he could speak to as his 'Companion from Eternity', 'before this Earth appear'd in its vegetated mortality to my mortal vegetated eyes'. He could use terms, in other words, that partly reflected the two men's familiarity with the spiritual language of Swedenborgianism. Writing to the more traditional and Anglican Butts, on the other hand, he would be more restrained, describing the same events in a fashion attuned to their immediate worldly effect:

> Our Cottage is more beautiful than I thought it & also more convenient, for tho small it is well proportiond & if I should ever build a Palace it would be only My Cottage Enlarged. Please to tell Mrs Butts that we have dedicated a Chamber for her Service & that it has a very

fine view of the sea. Mr Hayley recievd me with his usual brotherly affection. My Wife & Sister are both very well & courting Neptune for an Embrace, whose terrors this morning made them afraid but whose mildness is often Equal to his terrors.[3]

He still retained a strong sense of his own spiritual destiny, nevertheless.

Work will go on here with God speed –. A roller & two harrows lie before my window. I met a plow on my first going out at my gate the first morning after my arrival & the Plowboy said to the Plowman, 'Father, the Gate is Open' – I have begun to Work & find that I can work with greater pleasure than ever. Hope soon to give you a proof that Felpham is propitious to the Arts.[4]

A week or so later he wrote again to Butts, thanking him for reprehending his 'follies' and declaring that in future he would be 'the determined advocate of Religion and Humility'; he went on to transcribe verses recording how in his new surroundings he had had his 'first Vision of Light':

> The Sun was Emitting
> His Glorious beams
> From Heavens high Streams
> Over Sea over Land
> My Eyes did Expand
> Into regions of fire
> Remote from Desire
> The Light of the Morning
> Heavens Mountains adorning
> In particles bright
> The jewels of Light
> Distinct shone & clear –
> Amazd & in fear
> I each particle gazed,
> Astonishd Amazed
> For each was a Man
> Human formd. Swift I ran ...

So the poem runs on, full of his sense of seeing the forms of light in nature humanized. It is replete with the sense of illumination afforded by their new location –

> My Eyes more & more
> Like a Sea without shore
> Continue Expanding
> The Heavens commanding ...[5]

His delight in the place continued to grow, including his pleasure in the inhabitants: 'The Villagers of Felpham are not meer Rustics they are polite & modest'[6] (a view which was supported, as it happens, by a description of Felpham a few years later in the local guidebook: 'All orders and descriptions of people in this favored spot are remarkable for the amenity and cheerfulness of their manners and for civility and hospitality.'[7])

The move, it seems, was proving such a good therapy for the crises that had been besetting him during the previous years that he felt that he could now move forward. For a time, moreover, the friendship with Hayley seemed fully beneficial. In September 1801 he wrote to Butts,

Time flies faster, (as seems to me), here than in London I labour incessantly & accomplish not one half of what I intend because my Abstract folly hurries me often away while I am at work, carrying me over Mountains & Valleys which are not Real in a Land of Abstraction where Spectres of the Dead wander. This I endeavour to prevent & with my whole might chain my feet to the world of Duty & Reality. but in vain! the faster I bind the better is the Ballast for I so far from being bound down take the world with me in my flights & often it seems lighter than a ball of wool rolled by the wind Bacon & Newton would prescribe ways of making the world heavier to me & Pitt would prescribe distress for a medicinal potion. but as none on Earth can give me Mental Distress, & I know that all Distress inflicted by Heaven is a Mercy. a Fig for all Corporeal Such Distress is My mock & scorn.

Later in the same letter he went on:

I continue painting Miniatures & Improve more & more as all my friends tell me. but my Principal labour at this time is Engraving Plates for Cowpers Life a Work of Magnitude which Mr Hayley is now Labouring with all his matchless industry & which will be a most valuable acquisition to Literature not only on account of Mr Hayleys composition but also as it will contain Letters of Cowper to his friends Perhaps or rather Certainly the very best letters that ever were published.[8]

In addition to such works Blake was also devoting himself that autumn to languages he was studying for the first time: Latin, Greek and Hebrew. He would write to his brother a year later that he wished he had learned them earlier, since he found them so easy.[9]

The mood of sunny enlightenment did not persist, however, and by 1802 he was writing in a different vein. The burst of creativity that had marked his early years in Sussex was now supplemented by moods of despondency about his prospects and the attitude of his friends, so that he was conscious of an alternative voice of admonition:

> '... Poverty Envy old age & fear
> Shall bring thy Wife upon a bier
> And Butts shall give what Fuseli gave
> A dark black Rock & a gloomy Cave.'[10]

In the midst of these and other gloomy apprehensions he remained defiant, however, arguing against the fears of Los in his spectral form,

> 'My hands are labourd day & night'
> 'And Ease comes never in my sight'
> 'My Wife has no indulgence given'
> 'Except what comes to her from heaven'
> 'We eat little we drink less'
> 'This Earth breeds not our happiness'
> 'Another Sun feeds our lifes streams'
> 'We are not warmed with thy beams'
> 'Thou measurest not the Time to me'
> 'Nor yet the Space that I do see'
> 'My Mind is not with thy light arrayd'
> 'Thy terrors shall not make me afraid'[11]

At intervals in this bravado there intervene passages which reveal the intricacy of his thinking about his art, including a statement of the four levels of vision by which he believes himself to work: 'single', 'twofold', 'threefold' and 'fourfold'. Exactly when this conception was elaborated in his mind is not clear, though it may have owed a good deal to a four-fold scheme which is depicted among the engravings to Jacob Boehme's works – engravings which he once claimed to be equal to the work of Michelangelo.[12] Single vision was the dead vision of contemporary mathematical rationalism, whereas the vision by which he customarily worked was the twofold, which customarily sought to find inner significance within the normal everyday, but which, as he is explaining, carried its own dangers of fear of the future along with the delights of creativity. Above the fear and vision granted to artists like himself he envisaged two further realms: the 'threefold' vision of innocent pleasure given to those enjoying the pleasures of marriage and domesticity (termed 'Beulah' from his reading of Isaiah and *The Pilgrim's Progress*[13]) and the supreme 'fourfold' of supreme vision – at once absolute in its certainty and essentially unseizable for purposes of immediate visual representation. The effects of these levels of vision, each of which subsumes those below it, are summarized in the closing lines of the letter:

> Now I a fourfold vision see
> And a fourfold vision is given to me
> 'Tis Fourfold in my supreme delight
> And threefold in soft Beulah's night
> And twofold Always. May God us keep
> From Single vision & Newtons sleep[14]

He emerges from his doubt and defiance, that is, confident in the rightness of his spiritual vision. Already on the same day he had proclaimed his confidence to Butts:

> Nothing can withstand the fury of my Course among the Stars of God & in the Abysses of the Accuser My Enthusiasm is still what it was only Enlarged and confirmed.[15]

The slightly truculent note of this went along with some disquiet about his future. The kindness which Hayley had shown him in welcoming him to Sussex had begun to be diminished by a sense that he was being increasingly patronized by his benefactor. In this respect it is important to begin taking some account of the surroundings in which both men found themselves. As a part of Sussex, Felpham belonged to the traditional life of England: it was dominated by Tory landowners who looked to their tenants for compliance with the old order. William Cowper, whose life, as Blake mentioned, Hayley was engaged in writing, had been a part of this order and members of his family, who were at once proud of his stature as a poet and embarrassed by his later descent into madness, lived in the neighbourhood. His relative Lady Hesketh, who was particularly anxious on these scores and in constant communication with William Hayley, was concerned to retain a surveillance over the picture that was being presented in his 'Life'.

She regarded his new friendship with Blake with particular unease. Perhaps some tidings had reached her concerning his association with the radicals of the metropolis; or she may simply have picked up signs of danger from his directness of manner. She could perhaps sniff something of the republicanism that we know still lurked in his veins.[16] More important from an immediate point of view was the fact that he showed no signs of compliance with her desire that her cousin's later condition should not be acknowledged or recognized. When she saw a miniature which Blake had executed from a portrait of Cowper by Romney, her immediate reaction was horror: 'I cannot restrain my Pen from declaring that I think it dreadful! shocking!' No doubt she felt that the signs of madness had not been sufficiently veiled.

Lady Hesketh also communicated some disquiets concerning Blake's gifts, arguing from what she no doubt took to be a compassionate point of view (though her comments were based largely on the remarks of an artistic old gentleman of eighty-two who had expressed his criticisms to her):

> if Mr. Blake is but new in the world, may it not be in reality kinder, to point out his failings, than to suffer him to think his performances faultless – surely it may, as it may stimulate his endeavours after Perfection!

In reply, Hayley sought to defend his protégé firmly and persuasively:

> Pray suffer no mortal, my dear Lady, however you may give them credit for refined taste in Art, to prejudice you against the works of that too feeling artist, whose Designs met with so little mercy from your Octogenaire admirable! ... [There is] great spirit and sentiment in the engravings of my friend. ... Whatever the Merits, or the Failings, of my diligent and grateful artist may be, I know I shall interest your Heart and soul in his Favour, when I tell you, that he resembles our beloved Bard in the Tenderness of his Heart, and in the perilous powers of an Imagination utterly unfit to take due care of Himself. With admirable Faculties, his sensibility is so dangerously acute, that the common rough treatment which true genius often receives from ordinary minds in the commerce of the world, might

not only wound Him more than it should do, but really reduce Him to the Incapacity of an Ideot, without the consolatory support of a considerate Friend – From these excesses of Feeling, and of irregular Health, (forever connected with such excesses) His productions must ever perhaps be unequal, but in all He does, however wild or hasty, a penetrating eye will discover true Genius, and if it were possible to keep his too apprehensive spirit for a Length of Time unruffled He would produce works of the pencil, almost as excellent and original, as those works of the pen, which flow'd from the dear poet, of whom He often reminds me – when his mind is darkened with any unpleasant apprehension – He reminds me of him also by being a most fervent Admirer of the Bible, and intimately acquainted with all its Beauties –

Hayley continued with the account of the Blakes' married happiness quoted from earlier,[17] expressing his wish that Cowper, their 'beloved Bard', had been as happy in a wife, and stating his intention of being as kind as possible to them, since he considered it

a point of devotion to the two dear departed angels [Cowper and Tom Hayley] to be so, for I am confident I could gratify their spirits in nothing so much, as in befriending two wonderful Beings, whom they both, were they still on earth, and possess'd of Health, would peculiarly delight to befriend ...[18]

His attempt to align Blake with Cowper was probably not well judged in view of Lady Hesketh's sensitivity on the point of her cousin's madness, and she showed little sign of relenting. Indeed, her antipathy to Blake may in time have ricocheted on Hayley himself, who in any case thought himself fully qualified to pronounce judgment on his works and to dismiss those that he found wanting – which may account for some of the comments that Blake found particularly irritating.

Blake's desire to produce writing on an epic scale had meanwhile not only returned but (as will shortly be described) was gradually being transposed into a new kind of writing, the product of which was a verse that might bewilder a contemporary reader such as Hayley. He seems to have relied increasingly on a mode of writing that verged on the trancelike: as he would come to describe it, he would write 'from immediate Dictation twelve or sometimes twenty or thirty lines at a time without Premeditation & even against my will'.[19]

The situation between the two men was not improved by differences of temperament. In contrast to Blake's directness Hayley was polite to a fault – as Leigh Hunt observed in *The Feast of the Poets*:

> The worst part of Mr. Hayley is that smooth-tongued and over-wrought complimentary style, in addressing and speaking of others, which, whether in conversation or writing, has always the ill-fortune, to say the least of it, of being suspected as to sincerity.[20]

Hayley had befriended him and gone out of his way to seek commissions for him, but this had initially been a result of recommendations from Flaxman, who admired his gifts as a visual artist. Hayley might accept these but was less likely to appreciate his achievements as a writer: a fact not surprising once one considers that he was not only himself a poet, but also the biographer of Cowper, whose work he strongly admired – regarding it, like many of his contemporaries, as having achieved the high-water mark of what was possible in poetry. Cowper's ability to write a sensitive poetry without at any point pandering to the excesses of the fashion for 'sensibility' was welcome to members of upper-middle-class society who deplored the cult of writers such as Rousseau and Goethe. The title of Jane Austen's *Sense and Sensibility* indicates accurately where contemporary literary taste had arrived. To readers looking for a continuation of the discrimination between these two qualities – by which they could feel that Cowper had disciplined contemporary poetry – Blake's evident tendency to extravagance would have seemed both irrelevant and tiresome.

The poetic world was changing, however. It was not Blake but Hayley himself who would shortly find himself dismissed impatiently by members of the younger generation such as Byron:

> His style in youth or age is still the same;
> For ever feeble and for ever tame.
> Triumphant first see 'Temper's Triumphs' shine!
> At least I'm sure they triumph'd over mine.
> Of 'Music's Triumphs', all who read may swear
> That luckless Music never triumph'd there.[21]

From shafts such as these, Hayley's reputation never really recovered, and in time was to sink only lower when some of Blake's epigrams on him eventually reached print. He was indeed to acquire a reputation as something of a ludicrous buffoon. He had a fatal propensity for simple and copious verse-making, which could be brought into service all too quickly when an epitaph was called for but which proved fatal to his claims to a serious poetic reputation. Yet his poetic shortcomings should not be allowed to obliterate recognition of his human qualities as a benevolent friend to the oppressed – not only to major figures such as Cowper and Romney but to poor people such as the Widow Spicer. Oliver Stonor, who considered the question carefully, came to believe that in judging him on the basis of some of Blake's epigrams and branding him immoderately posterity had been unfair, the most just verdict being that of Southey, who warned Coleridge against embarking on criticizing his verses on the grounds that it would prove an invidious exercise, in view of his manifold virtues: 'Everything about that man is good except his poetry.'[22]

Blake's own view was certainly more charitable than those of some of his successors. Reading through the letters of 1801 one is struck by the warmth of his references to his patron: Hayley, he says, has acted 'like a Prince'. It is not until January 1803 that signs of discontent appear:

> ... you have so generously & openly desired that I will divide my griefs with you that I cannot hide what it is now become my duty to explain – My unhappiness has arisen from a source which if explord too narrowly might hurt my pecuniary circumstances. As my dependence is on Engraving at present & particularly on the Engravings I have in hand for Mr H.& I find on all hands great objections to my doing any thing but the meer drudgery of business & intimations that if I do not confine myself to this I shall not live. this has always pursud me. You will understand by this the source of all my uneasiness This from Johnson & Fuseli brought me down here & this from Mr H will bring me back again for that I cannot live without doing my duty to lay up treasures in heaven is Certain & Determined & to this I have long made up my mind & why this should be made an objection to Me while Drunkenness Lewdness Gluttony & even Idleness itself does not hurt other men let Satan himself Explain – The Thing I have most at Heart! more than life or all that seems to make life comfortable without. Is the Interest of True Religion & Science & whenever any thing appears to affect that Interest. (Especially if I myself omit any duty to my Station as a Soldier of Christ) It gives me the greatest of torments, I am not ashamed afraid or averse to tell You what Ought to be Told. That I am under the direction of Messengers from Heaven Daily & Nightly but the nature of such things is not as some suppose. without trouble or care. Temptations are on the right

hand & left behind the sea of time & space roars & follows swiftly he who keeps not right onward is lost & if our footsteps slide in clay how can we do otherwise than fear & tremble ...

He also mentioned that they were 'determind not to remain another winter here but to return to London':

> I hear a voice you cannot hear that says I must not stay
> I see a hand you cannot see that beckons me away

Naked we came here naked of Natural things & naked we shall return. but while clothd with the Divine Mercy we are richly clothd in Spiritual & suffer all the rest gladly[23]

He and Catherine were still basically happy ('We are very Happy sitting at tea by a wood fire in our Cottage the wind singing above our roof & the sea roaring at a distance'), but he explained his current concerns frankly and at some length in a letter to his brother a few weeks later:

My Wife has had Agues & Rheumatisms almost ever since she has been here, but our time is almost out that we took the Cottage for. I did not mention our Sickness to you & should not to Mr Butts but for a determination which we have lately made namely To leave This Place – because I am now certain of what I have long doubted Viz [that H] is jealous as Stothard was & will be no further My friend than he is compelld by circumstances. The truth is As a Poet he is frightend at me & as a Painter his views & mine are opposite he thinks to turn me into a Portrait Painter as he did Poor Romney, but this he nor all the devils in hell will never do. I must own that seeing H. like S Envious (& that he is I am now certain) made me very uneasy, but it is over & I now defy the worst & fear not while I am true to myself which I will be.

By this time he had become convinced that he could make an excellent living on his own:

The Profits arising from Publications are immense & I now have it in my power to commence publication with many very formidable works, which I have finishd & ready A Book price half a guinea may be got out at the Expense of Ten pounds & its almost certain profits are 500 G. I am only sorry that I did not know the methods of publishing years ago & this is one of the numerous benefits I have obtaind by coming here for I should never have known the nature of Publication unless I had known H & his connexions & his method of managing. It now <would> be folly not to venture publishing. I am now Engraving Six little plates for a little work of M^r H's for which I am to have 10 Guineas each & the certain profits of that work are a fortune such as would make me independent supposing that I could substantiate such a one of my own & I mean to try many ...

In addition to his own work, Catherine had been offering to print the plates for Cowper's work and doing it to perfection, so that he felt increasingly optimistic concerning their future: 'My only Difficulty is to produce fast enough.' Hayley had also encouraged him to learn more languages, which to his surprise and pleasure he had found he could do much more easily than he expected:

I go on Merrily with my Greek & Latin: am very sorry that I did not begin to learn languages early in life as I find it very Easy. am now learning my Hebrew ... I read Greek as fluently as an Oxford scholar & the Testament is my chief master. astonishing indeed is the English Translation it is almost word for word & if the Hebrew Bible is as well translated which I do not doubt it is we need not doubt of its having been translated as well as written by the Holy Ghost.[24]

The decision to return to London, more fully explained and expounded in this same letter of January, remained constant, and by the spring was prompting preparations which had Hayley's blessing. In July, Blake felt able to enlarge privately on the growing tension between them:

As to M^r H I feel myself at liberty to say as follows upon this ticklish subject. I regard Fashion in Poetry as little as I do in Painting. so if both Poets & Painters should alternately dislike (but I know the majority of them will not) I am not to regard it at all but M^r H approves of My Designs as little as he does of my Poems and I have been forced to insist on his leaving me in both to my Own Self Will. for I am determind to be no longer Pesterd with his Genteel Ignorance & Polite Disapprobation. I know myself both Poet & Painter & it is not his affected Contempt that can move me to any thing but a more assiduous pursuit of both Arts. Indeed by my late Firmness I have brought down his affected Loftiness & he begins to think I have some Genius. as if Genius & Assurance were the same thing. but his imbecile attempts to depress Me only deserve laughter – I say thus much to you knowing that you will not make a bad use of it But it is a Fact too true That if I had only depended on Mortal Things both myself & my Wife must have been Lost – I shall leave every one in This Country astonishd at my Patience & Forbearance of Injuries upon Injuries & I do assure you that if I could have returnd to London a Month after my arrival here I should have done so, but I was commanded by my Spiritual friends to bear all to be silent & to go thro all without murmuring & in firm hope till my three years should be almost accomplishd at which time I was set at liberty to remonstrate against former conduct & to demand Justice & Truth which I have done in so effectual a manner that my antagonist is silencd completely. & I have compelld. what should have been of freedom My Just Right as an Artist & as a Man. & if any attempt should be made to refuse me this I am inflexible & will relinquish Any engagement of Designing at all unless altogether left to my own Judgment. As you My dear Friend have always left me for which I shall never cease to honour & respect you[25]

The news that they had arranged for their return, said Blake, was welcomed by those who heard of it: 'I ought not to be away from the opportunities London affords of seeing fine Pictures and the various improvements in Works of Art going on in London.'[26]

If in one sense Felpham had been a haven of sleepy quiet for Blake and his wife, however, events were about to remind them that its situation, on the scale of the country as a whole, was very different. These were years of widespread fears of invasion from France, for which the obvious point of entry would have been the coastline of Kent and Sussex. The year before, Wordsworth had written his sonnet beginning 'Vanguard of liberty! Ye men of Kent ...'

It was against this background that even while he was planning to leave Sussex Blake's life was interrupted by an incident that would upset his composure for some time to come. On 12 August 1803 he found a soldier named John Scholfield in his garden (not knowing, he later said, that he had been invited there by a gardener) and in response to what he regarded as insulting behaviour told him to leave. He gave his own account a few days later to Butts:

I am at Present in a Bustle to defend myself against a very unwarrantable warrant from a justice of Peace in Chichester which was taken out against me by a Private in Capt[n] Leathes's troop of 1st or

Royal Dragoons for an assault & Seditious words. The wretched Man has terribly Perjurd himself as has his CoM^rade for as to Sedition not one Word relating to the King or Government was spoken by either him or me. His Enmity arises from my having turned him out of my Garden into which he was invited as an assistant by a Gardener at work therein, without my knowledge that he was so invited. I desired him as politely as was possible to go out of the Garden, he made me an impertinent answer I insisted on his leaving the Garden he refused I still persisted in desiring his departure he then threatend to knock out my Eyes with many abominable imprecations & with some contempt for my Person it affronted my foolish Pride I therefore took him by the Elbows & pushed him before me till I had got him out. there I intended to have left him but he turning about put himself into a Posture of Defiance threatening & swearing at me. I perhaps foolishly & perhaps not, stepped out at the Gate & putting aside his blows took him again by the Elbows & keeping his back to me pushed him forwards down the road about fifty yards he all the while endeavouring to turn round & strike me & raging & cursing which drew out several neighbours. at length when I had got him to where he was Quarterd. which was very quickly done. we were met at the Gate by the Master of the house. The Fox Inn, (who is [my] the proprietor of my Cottage) & his wife & Daughter. & the Mans CoM^rade. & several other people My Landlord compelld the Soldiers to go in doors after many abusive threats [*from the*] against me & my wife from the two Soldiers but not one word of threat on account of Sedition was utterd at that time. This method of Revenge was Plann'd between them after they had got together into the Stable.

It was now necessary for him to arrange his defence:

I have for witnesses. The Gardener who is Hostler at the Fox & who Evidences that to his knowledge no word of the remotest tendency to Government or Sedition was utterd, – Our next door Neighbour a Millers wife who saw me turn him before me down the road & saw & heard all that happend at the Gate of the Inn who Evidences that no Expression of threatening on account of Sedition was utterd in the heat of their fury by either of the Dragoons. this was the womans own remark & does high honour to her good sense as she observes that whenever a quarrel happens the offence is always repeated. The Landlord of the Inn & His Wife & daughter will Evidence the Same & will evidently prove the Comrade perjurd who swore that he heard me while at the Gate utter Seditious words & D--- the K--- without which perjury I could not have been committed & I had no witness with me before the Justices who could combat his assertion as the Gardener remain in my Garden all the while & he was the only person I thought necessary to take with me. I have been before a Bench of Justices at Chichester this morning. but they as the Lawyer who wrote down the Accusation told me in private are compelld by the Military to suffer a prosecution to be enterd into altho they must know & it is manifest that the whole is a Fabricated Perjury. I have been forced to find Bail. Mr Hayley was kind enough to come forwards & Mr Seagrave Printer at Chichester. Mr H. in 100£. & Mr S. in 50£. & myself am bound in 100£. for my appearance at the Quarter Sessions which is after Michaelmass. So I shall have the Satisfaction to see my friends in Town before this Contemptible business comes on I say Contemptible for it must be manifest to every one that the whole accusation is a wilful Perjury.

... Well I am content I murmur not & doubt not that I shall recieve Justice & am only sorry for the trouble & expense. I have heard that my Accuser is a disgraced Sergeant his name is John Scholfield. perhaps it will be in your power to learn somewhat about the Man I am very ignorant of what I am requesting of you. I only suggest what I know you will be kind enough to Excuse if you can learn nothing about him & what I as well know if it is possible you will be kind enough to do in this matter.[27]

Since Blake is not known ever to have forsaken his republican beliefs, it is by no means impossible that he allowed some anti-royalist expressions to escape him as he expelled Schofield from his garden; he may equally have made some derogatory remarks concerning the status of the soldiery in contemporary England. One can easily project an exchange in which Schofield protested that he must not be attacked physically, since he was a member of the King's army, to which Blake might well have answered 'Damn the King! – You soldiers think that you can walk into anyone's garden without permission, just because you have chosen to be the government's hirelings.' He might also have added some comments to the effect that they would be better employed in preparing themselves to resist Napoleon, whose forces were known to be very much better trained. This, together with an intervention from Catherine Blake on her husband's side, would have provided enough material on which Schofield could have fabricated his extended charge of sedition – which Blake, who had recently proposed designs for national monuments devoted to Pitt and Nelson, is unlikely to have been advocating at this time. Nevertheless, in the current national situation, such a charge was to be taken seriously; a coach-maker in nearby Dartford was indicted for saying 'Damn the King and those who wear his livery'.[28]

The military men to be found thronging the counties were not necessarily as popular with the villagers, however, as with the landowners who looked to them for their defence. In any case, the Blakes seem to have been well liked locally and the villagers of Felpham, who no doubt felt a strong loyalty to their neighbour William Hayley and were less likely to have been drawn along by the contemporary hysteria, were alarmed by the event for a quite opposite reason:

> … it has struck a consternation thro all the Villages round. Every Man is now afraid of speaking to or looking at a Soldier. for the peaceable Villagers have always been forward in expressing their kindness for us & they express their sorrow at our departure as soon as they hear of it Every one here is my Evidence for Peace & Good Neighbourhood & yet such is the present state of things this foolish accusation must be tried in Public.[29]

In October the case against Blake was brought to trial at the quarter sessions in the neighbouring town of Petworth, where several gentlemen of the neighbourhood served as Justices of the Peace. Blake, who had no doubt hoped that the case against him would immediately collapse, was incensed by a result in which the jury was brought to the point of declaring not only that he was 'a Wicked Seditious and Evil disposed person', but even that he had beaten, wounded and ill treated Schofield 'so that his Life was greatly despaired of': as a result he introduced the names of some involved at Petworth into plates of his *Jerusalem*. He found himself committed to the assizes at Chichester in the following January which, since he and Catherine had already left for London, meant that he would need to return.

While friends such as Flaxman rallied around and expressed their confidence that he would be acquitted, there were those who found themselves siding with the prosecution. Lady Hesketh, for example, wrote to Hayley expressing her concerns: 'Mr Blake appeard to me much to blame, even upon his own representation of the matter, but if I may give credit to some reports that reached me at the time, M^r B: was more Seriously to blame than you were at all aware of …'[30] She continued for some time to express her fears for Hayley's own safety, fearing that Blake might actually attack him.[31]

While he awaited his further arraignment, Blake, who after all had gone to Sussex as a refuge from his susceptibility to 'Nervous Fear', must have suffered sleepless nights at the thought of his likely fate if the charges against him were accepted. Even if he was not convicted of treason, he could still have faced imprisonment, or a fine, or both.

In the event the charges against him came to nothing. Whatever the villagers' motives, they refused to testify against Blake; and if any words that might bear a seditious interpretation had escaped his lips they had not in any case been uttered in the hearing of anyone apart from Schofield. Reflecting on his acquittal he could even find some pleasure in the thought that the experience might have been a source of benefit to him:

> Perhaps the simplicity of myself is the origin of all offences committed against me. If I have found this I shall have learned a most valuable thing well worth three years perseverance. I have found it! It is certain! that a too passive manner. inconsistent with my active physiognomy had done me much mischief I must now express to you my conviction that all is come from the spiritual World for Good & not for Evil.[32]

In spite of this, however, he felt that he seemed destined to suffer such blows:

> O why was I born with a different face
> Why was I not born like the rest of my race
> When I look each one starts! when I speak I offend
> Then I'm silent & passive & lose every Friend
>
> Then my verse I dishonour. My pictures despise
> My person degrade & my temper chastise
> And the pen is my terror. the pencil my shame
> All my Talents I bury, and dead is my Fame
>
> I am either too low or too highly prizd
> When Elate I am Envy'd, When Meek I'm despisd[33]

What has been suggested above about the lack of popularity in which the army seems to have been held in the neighbourhood may help to throw light on the local behaviour at the end of the trial. Blake's neighbours in Felpham could hardly have afforded the expense of going to Chichester, so that the populace which gathered to hear the result there may well have been moved by local popular sentiment rather than by immediate feeling for the accused. At all events, according to the local newspaper, the favourable verdict 'so gratified the auditory, that the court was, in defiance of all decency, thrown into an uproar by their noisy exultations'. There can be little doubt whose side they favoured.

Although he could share the jubilation of his friends at his acquittal, the affair as a whole meant that much of the charm of Sussex for Blake had been diminished. The memory of Chichester itself, despite his experiences there, would remain for him a haven, its cathedral an exemplar of the beauty of the Gothic to which he increasingly turned his attention.[34*] But the events of the previous weeks simply helped to confirm his view that his future must lie in London. Any latent animosity towards Hayley for his apparently envious attitude had, however, been swallowed up in gratitude for the support and assistance which had been given him so unstintingly during the trial. So far from offering criticisms of Hayley's poetry, moreover, he conveyed to him the praises of others in terms that would convict him of hypocrisy if his private views at the time had been decisively otherwise. During the two years or so after leaving Felpham he wrote frequently to his friend, without ever hinting at the criticisms he had been nursing concerning his attitude.

During the course of their relationship his affairs had, in any case, taken a new turn. It may well be that some of his animosity had been due to a sense that he was being held back from his true work – to refashion 'The Four Zoas' as a full epic – by the more mechanical demands of journeyman work. If so, by the time he left Felpham he seems to have accepted that that ultimate plan was too difficult to be carried out. The poem, in other words, was never going to be more than a collection of glorious fragments; instead, he would turn to the making of works moulded not in terms of a detailed narrative but of repeated insistences on the need for humanity to rise above its current confined vision.

10
Fragmentary Modes of Epic

The fact that the advent of the new millennium had not been marked by any apocalyptic turn in human events can hardly have escaped Blake's attention. He may well have reflected also that his scheme of accounting for human nature in terms of 'Four Mighty Ones' that 'are in every Man' might be over-simplistic – even, we have suggested, Urizenic – once one considered the full complexity of human nature.

Another element that had entered his thinking during these years was more directly physical: it concerned the rise of interest in phenomena such as mesmerism and animal magnetism, which had played a prominent part in the intellectual ferment of recent years.[1] Given that virtually no language had as yet developed for thinking about such matters it was still not easy to reach any kind of factual grasp, but as Robert Rix has pointed out, related interests had already led to the expulsion from the New Jerusalem Church of a branch of Swedenborgians that wished to explore them. Blake seems to have kept in touch with them: it was an area where some of Swedenborg's own followers, at least, could not be said to have 'written all the old false-hoods'.[2]

As Rix points out, Blake 'cast his support in favour of individual visionary experience, which later came to be considered a heresy in the New Jerusalem Church'.[3] He also thinks that during his stay in Felpham this interest drew the sympathy of William Hayley, who had been taking a keen interest in animal magnetism,[4*] and notes that while there Blake's attributing of the origin of his poetry to spirit communication, already mentioned, suggests that he may have cultivated something like a trance-like somnambulism: he is found, for example, confirming that he speaks daily and hourly with his dead brother Robert, who dictates to him,[5] and that he can 'converse with my friends in Eternity. See Visions,

139

Dream Dreams, & Prophecy'.[6] He also claims to be nothing but a 'Secretary', as the 'Authors' of his poetry are 'in Eternity'.[7]

From a letter of 1804 we know in addition that Blake believed his wife's rheumatism to have been cured with the use of electricity, praising a 'Mr. Birch' for his 'Electrical Magic'.[8]* He criticized three contemporary magnetizers, however, Richard Cosway, George Baldwin and an unknown Frazer, in a satiric Notebook poem of unknown date. They were attacked, claims Rix, because, as he put it, they 'Fear to associate with Blake' and were criticized by him for capitalizing on the popular market for magnetism at the expense of higher spiritual purposes: 'This Life is a Warfare against Evils | They heal the sick he [Blake] casts out Devils'.[9]*

From *The Four Zoas* onwards, dream visions take a more central place in Blake's poetry. In *Milton*, he returns several times to the poet's sleep and dreams in reference to somnambulistic visions, where his 'Sleeping Body' makes companion with the divine 'Spirits of the Seven Angels,' 'walking' with them 'as one walks | In sleep'.[10] Rix finds the reference to magnetic therapy in Blake's poetic vocabulary there 'unmistakable', in fact. In the beginning, Blake invokes his 'Muses' to 'Come into my hand | By your mild power; descending down the Nerves of my right arm'.[11] Albion's cure is figured in terms of electrical therapy: 'Now Albions sleeping Humanity began to turn upon his Couch; | Feeling the electrical flame of Miltons awful precipitate descent'.[12] In *Jerusalem*, similarly, the introductory address, 'To the Public', contains Blake's strongest commitment to the importance of spirit visitations: 'We who dwell on Earth can do nothing of ourselves, everything is conducted by Spirits, no less than Digestion or Sleep'.[13]

It certainly seems as if during these years Blake was developing an original form of self-hypnosis, which enabled him to mediate between his subconscious and his writing powers. It is in fact hard to think of anything in previous English poetry comparable to what he was now writing. Uncontrolled verse written from a disordered mind is by no means unknown; what is remarkable here is the extraordinary balance between impulsive versification and the imposition of continuous control. After the failed attempts to create an overall narrative in 'Vala', it seems, Blake settled for less rigorous, more thematically inspired sequences in *Milton*, to be succeeded by a mode in *Jerusalem* which dispensed with the sense of an ordered and detailed narrative, leaving only the opening sleep and the final reawakening to provide the semblance, at least, of an overall framing.

In the autumn of 1804 Blake wrote to Hayley of a new turn in his artistic fortunes:

> ... now! O Glory! and O Delight! I have entirely reduced that spectrous Fiend to his station, whose annoyance has been the ruin of my labours for the last passed twenty years of my life. He is the enemy of conjugal love and is the Jupiter of the Greeks, an iron-hearted tyrant, the ruiner of ancient Greece. I speak with perfect confidence and certainty of the fact which has passed upon me. Nebuchadnezzar had seven times passed over him; I have had twenty; thank God I was not altogether a beast as he was; but I was a slave bound in a mill among beasts and devils; these beasts and these devils are now, together with myself, become children of light and liberty, and my feet and my wife's feet are free from fetters. O lovely Felpham, parent of Immortal Friendship, to thee I am eternally indebted for my three years' rest from perturbation and the strength I now enjoy. Suddenly, on the day after visiting the Truchsessian Gallery of pictures, I was again enlightened with the light I enjoyed in my youth, and which has for exactly twenty years been closed from me as by a door and by window-shutters. Consequently I can, with confidence, promise you ocular demonstration of my altered state on the plates I am now engraving after Romney, whose spiritual aid has not a little conduced to my restoration to the light of Art. O the distress I have undergone, and my poor wife with me. Incessantly labouring and incessantly spoiling what I had done well. Every one of my friends was astonished at my faults, and could not assign a reason; they knew my industry and abstinence from every pleasure for the sake of study, and yet – and yet – and yet there wanted the proofs of industry in my works. I thank God with entire confidence that it shall be so no longer – he is become my servant who domineered over me, he is even as a brother who was my enemy. Dear Sir, excuse my enthusiasm or rather madness, for I am really drunk with intellectual vision whenever I take a pencil or graver into my hand, even as I used to be in my youth, and as I have not been for twenty dark, but very profitable years. I thank God that I courageously pursued my course through darkness.[14]

It is not clear what one should make of this new revelation, since it had no obvious or adequate sequel. Blake seems from this point, on the other hand, to display a new confidence in his engraving; yet he had not ceased from wanting to create poetry on an epic scale in the intervening years, and it might be thought that much of *Milton* had already been produced by the time that he left Felpham, since in 1803 he wrote:

> none can know the Spiritual Acts of my three years Slumber on the banks of the Ocean unless he has seen them in the Spirit or unless he should read My long Poem descriptive of those Acts for I have in these three years composed an immense number of verses on One Grand Theme Similar to Homers Iliad or Miltons Paradise Lost the Person & Machinery intirely new to the Inhabitants of Earth (some of the Persons Excepted) I have written this Poem from immediate Dictation twelve or sometimes twenty or thirty lines at a time without Premeditation & even against my Will. the Time it has taken in writing was thus renderd Non Existent. & an immense Poem Exists which seems to be the Labour of a long Life all producd without Labour or Study. I mention this to shew you what I think the Grand Reason of my being brought down here[15]

In his next letter he wrote to Butts of

> a Sublime Allegory which is now perfectly completed into a Grand Poem[.] I may praise it since I dare not pretend to be any other than the Secretary the Authors are in Eternity I consider it as the Grandest Poem that This World Contains. Allegory addressd to the Intellectual powers while it is altogether hidden from the Corporeal Understanding is My Definition of the Most Sublime Poetry. it is also somewhat in the same manner defind by Plato. This Poem shall by Divine Assistance be progressively Printed & Ornamented with Prints & given to the Public – But of this work I take care to say little to Mr H. since he is as much averse to my poetry as he is to a Chapter in the Bible He knows that I have writ it for I have shewn it to him & he had read Part by his own desire & has lookd with sufficient contempt to enhance my opinion of it. But I do not wish to irritate by seeming too obstinate in Poetic pursuits But if all the World should set their faces against This. I have Orders to set my face like a flint. Ezekiel iii C 9 v. against their faces & my forehead against their foreheads ...

All that can be said with certainty is that he had worked, and would now continue to work, on the poetry that would eventually see publication as the two poems *Milton* and *Jerusalem*. We know little about their composition (apart from the descriptions of his own, as mentioned above) or even the exact dates involved. In the case of *Milton*, the title-page originally announced a poem of twelve books and twenty-eight chapters; the final one, announcing two books, bore the date 1804 and introduced fifty pages of text. The title-page for *Jerusalem*, likewise, also bearing the date 1804, was set at the front of a work that would eventually run to four books of twenty-five pages each. The indications, however, are that both books took shape over a long period, during which even the order of plates sometimes changed. So far as one can judge, their working corresponded to the change of tactic on Blake's part suggested earlier, by which he no longer looked to create a long narrative poem with a plot readily discernible at every stage. Instead, he was now opting rather for a loose plot-like framework into which he could insert relevant plates as they came into being.

In the case of *Milton*, he was also participating in a movement common to various Romantic writers of the time, carrying them towards autobiography. Just as Wordsworth's 'Poem to Coleridge' turned into the epic self-examination we now know as *The Prelude*, and the work of Coleridge towards a philosophical masterpiece was diverted to his *Biographia Literaria*, so Blake's efforts in a similar vein led him to become increasingly self-focusing. It seemed, in other words, as if the truest achievement in a post-Miltonic age was not to attempt a poem that might surpass *Paradise Lost* but *to be a reincarnation of its author*. Milton, on this reading, was not so much a person as a spirit, who might descend on anyone at any time – simply assuming a form appropriate to the age in which he found himself. The Milton who is now Blake's model is a Milton for the new century, therefore, transforming his Puritan morals, which needed to be reappraised, and subduing the spectrous and rational devotion to law that rendered poems such as *Paradise Lost* inadequate for the future. In this way he might hope to release himself into the full vigour and self-giving illumination that could be regarded as Milton's underlying qualities. On this view, whereas the eighteenth-century world had been dominated by thinkers who wished to reduce it finally to quantitative measurement and the rule of law, the new dispensation would, by contrast, free the poetic genius to explore the moment of illumination that can never be organized into any time scheme, and to enter into the timelessness of certain sensuous experiences (the lark pouring out its song as it ascends the sky, the flower with its power to overwhelm the senses with its scent), finding in them the true significance of the world. This is the point of a mysterious saying such as

> There is a Moment in each Day that Satan cannot find
> Nor can his Watch Fiends find it; but the industrious find
> This Moment & it multiply. & when it once is found
> It renovates every Moment of the Day if rightly placed[16]

We may compare Wordsworth's 'There are in our existence spots of time, I Which with distinct preeminence retain I A renovating virtue ...'[17] Or, to quote more lines from *Milton*,

> Every Time less than a pulsation of the artery
> Is equal in its period & value to Six Thousand Years.
> For in this Period the Poet's Work is Done: and all the Great
> Events of Time start forth & are conceivd in such a Period,
> Within a Moment: a Pulsation of the Artery.[18]

In such a view of the world, time and space relax their relentless hold on the mind, yielding their domination to insights which are essentially timeless and placeless.

For Blake's other epic enterprise of the time, he took over from 'Vala' the idea of calling the Eternal Man Albion, and gave the poem the name of his Emanation, *Jerusalem*. *Milton* is primarily about inspiration, a manifesto for the role of the poetic genius in his time. Although as a whole poem it does not make for easy reading, it quivers with brilliant ideas and images, reordering the world in the image of a nature replete with momentary inspirations. *Jerusalem* is, by comparison, a more patient work, devoted to Blake's belief that the long-term work of the artist is to continue making, giving forms to things, since in the world as he has come to know it this is the only true work of redemption possible. Los becomes therefore no longer a threatening figure or simply one of four Zoas; his urge to create makes him the chief protagonist, the hero of the poem.

In the course of the book various passages are devoted to themes that had come to seem crucial to him. The issue of industrialism, for example, which often seems an issue of only minor concern, is suddenly foregrounded in the midst of a dire prophetic passage concerning Albion's fate, involving not only the rise of arms trafficking at the expense of peaceful uses of human work, but also the effects of division of labour – a topic which is commonly regarded as being first raised later in the century:

> Then left the Sons of Urizen the plow & harrow, the loom
> The hammer & the chisel, & the rule & compasses, from London
>   fleeing
> They forg'd the sword on Cheviot, the chariot of war & the
>   battle-ax,
> The trumpet fitted to mortal battle, & the flute of summer in
>   Annandale

And all the Arts of Life. they changed into the Arts of Death in
    Albion.
The hour-glass contemnd because its simple workmanship.
Was like the workmanship of the plowman, & the water wheel,
That raises water into cisterns: broken & burnd with fire:
Because its workmanship was like the workmanship of the
    shepherd.
And in their stead, intricate wheels invented, wheel without wheel:
To perplex youth in their outgoings, & to bind to labours in Albion
Of day & night the myriads of eternity that they may grind
And polish brass & iron hour after hour laborious task!
Kept ignorant of its use, that they might spend the days of wisdom
In sorrowful drudgery, to obtain a scanty pittance of bread:
In ignorance to view a small portion & think that All,
And call it Demonstration: blind to all the simple rules of life.

In the same passage the terrible fact of war itself is evoked in all its
cruelty, including the effects of such contemporary evils as the use of
the press-gang to enrol ordinary civilians into the forces needed for the
planned warfare:

Now: now the battle rages round thy tender limbs O Vala,
Now smile among thy bitter tears: now put on all thy beauty
Is not the wound of the sword sweet! & the broken bone delightful?
Wilt thou now smile among the scythes when the wounded groan
    in the field
We were carried away in thousands from London; & in tens
Of thousands from Westminster & Marybone in ships closd up:
Chaind hand & foot, compelld to fight under the iron whips
Of our captains; fearing our officers more than the enemy.[19]

In spite of this stark realism, Blake's purposes were by now moving from
an attempt to produce a great interpretative and epic narrative to a
poetic form that could aim at raising the consciousness of his readers by
inviting them to perceive the sublimity inherent in all things. He could,
for example, offer a picture of Britain that would focus less on the hum-
drum reality of industrial centres and more on its centres of beauty, such
as the cathedral cities. The linking of Albion to Jerusalem enabled him
to create a series of visions in which the counties of Britain and Israel
could be constantly juxtaposed to enforce the effect of geographical
sublimity. Meanwhile, he could return in a looser manner to the theme

of the Eternal Man's sleep, but no longer give it the status of a dramatic event. Instead, his poem could begin with a more general announcement of theme:

> Of the Sleep of Ulro! and of the passage through
> Eternal Death! and of the awaking to Eternal Life.

He was also enabled to present developed ideas concerning his conception of Christianity. In these later prophetic books there are many references to it – so many that at first sight Blake might appear simply to have been converted back to the established religion of his fellow Englishmen. Many of his paintings, similarly, were devoted to biblical subjects, corresponding to the shift in his attitude at the turn of the century discussed earlier. His new attitude was more complicated, however. He seems to have decided that, whatever its shortcomings, Christianity was the religion by which the forces of imagination were most successfully nurtured and for the rest of his life he would support it. The terms of his acceptance would still be very much his own, however. The Bible was to be read not, as was common in his time, for its promulgation of the moral law, but for its dreams and visions and for its accounts of visionaries and prophets. He numbered himself amongst their modern successors, his affirmations meeting with incomprehension even from those who might have been expected to welcome them.

> Trembling I sit day and night, my friends are astonish'd at me.
> Yet they forgive my wanderings, I rest not from my great task!
> To open the Eternal Worlds, to open the immortal Eyes
> Of Man inwards into the Worlds of Thought: into Eternity
> Ever expanding in the Bosom of God. the Human Imagination
> Saviour pour upon me thy Spirit of meekness & love:
> Annihilate the Selfhood in me, be thou all my life!
> Guide thou my hand which trembles exceedingly upon the
>   rock of ages ...[20]

Blake's use of the expression 'My friends are astonish'd at me' suggests that he was recalling a particularly apposite prophetic passage, describing the suffering 'servant' in Isaiah: the words there, 'many were astonied at him', would carry on with them the natural run of the sentences, culminating in the words 'He shall see of the travail of his soul and shall be satisfied'.[21]

Blake's idea of warfare combined a rejection of physical war – always imagined in horror – with a glad acceptance of human relations that did not shrink from contention. The climax of poetic warfare must have been for him the heavenly war described in *Paradise Lost*, including the climactic moment when the Son of God finally intervened in his chariot. (It can hardly have escaped his notice that this moment follows on the attempts by the devils to win the conflict by introducing mechanical means, looking forward to industrialism, in the shape of an explosive engine.)

Meanwhile rejection of such physical destruction might be complemented by acceptance of Jerusalem, pictured as a beautiful woman: an image deriving from both Isaiah at the prophetic climax of the Old Testament ('put on thy beautiful garments O Jerusalem') and the Book of Revelation in the penultimate chapter of the New ('And I John saw the holy city, new Jerusalem ... prepared as a bride adorned for her husband'). The contrasting images of destruction – physical warfare and an anatomising reductionism, as against creativity; Jerusalem's visionary beauty and Los's hammering into form – could thus be set over against the details of the fragmentary poem, offering a larger interpretative pattern. The looseness of the new organization is confirmed by the fact that many of the etched plates carry a catch-word at the end that does not correspond to the anticipated first word of the next plate as set into the final sequence: it would seem that as inspiration took him, Blake would write and etch one or two plates which could then be set aside until, when he had accumulated a sufficient number, he felt ready to attempt a final ordering according to his looser general conception. A tighter form could finally be imposed but only by the ordering of the text into four symmetrical books of twenty-five plates, each given a title-page of its own and addressed to the one of the four audiences that Blake thought most relevant to it.

The unusual nature of this arrangement calls for an equally unusual mode of response from the reader. In his previous work, it has been pointed out, the mythological burden of the meaning is intense, justifying an equally intricate effort to unravel its significance. This intensity, particularly rewarding in the case of prophetic books such as *America* and *Europe*, had continued to be a feature of some parts of 'Vala' – where indeed parts of the earlier books are repeated – yet increasingly one is there conscious of lapses into incoherence, the more so as Blake introduces further attempts at new organizing concepts, such as that of 'the Council of God'. In these two last poems, by contrast, it is as if incoherence has actually been built in to a larger envisaged coherence. One can accept Los's heroic status, especially in *Milton* – in any case a more heroic poem – but his dealings with other figures become harder to follow. The role of Reuben in *Jerusalem* is a good case in point. In some sense he can claim to be a version of 'vegetated man', as shown by his biblical origins in the mysterious incident when he brought mandrakes from the field to his mother, Leah.[22] Yet no one has so far read this riddle in a manner which fully explains his presence in Blake's poem, and it is likely that he stands with much else that belongs to the visionary writing of his final years. What is called for, therefore, is something more on the lines of Keats's 'negative capability', where the reader desists from irritable reaching after fact and reason and responds to the sweep of the poetry, as set against the larger epic aspiration – expressed particularly in the designs. The more one learns to read the poems in this unusual way, the richer they become. As has already been suggested, Blake seems to be calling for a raising of one's own register in sympathy, involving not a search for detailed security of interpretation but the evocation of a harmonising response. To some readers this will no doubt be foolishness; to others it may seem like the beginning of poetic wisdom.

That something of this was in his mind is shown by the prose address with which he began the work:

> When this Verse was first dictated to me I consider'd a Monotonous Cadence like that used by Milton & Shakspeare & all writers of English Blank Verse, derived from the modern bondage of Rhyming; to be a necessary and indispensable part of Verse. But I soon found that in the mouth of a true Orator such monotony was not only awkward, but as much a bondage as rhyme itself. I therefore have produced a variety in every line, both of cadences & number of syllables. Every word and every letter is studied and put into its fit place: the terrific numbers are reserved for the terrific parts – the mild & gentle, for the mild & gentle parts, and the prosaic, for inferior parts: all are necessary to each other. Poetry Fetter'd, Fetters the Human Race! Nations are Destroy'd, or Flourish, in proportion as Their Poetry Painting and Music, are Destroy'd or Flourish! The Primeval State of Man, was Wisdom, Art, and Science.[23]

In dealing with a long work where so many passages may, in the beginning at least, and sometimes long after, strike the reader as a barren waste, the best procedure, as Gilchrist showed, is to concentrate on the passages that are most undeniably rewarding. He draws attention, for instance, to a few lines in *Jerusalem*:

> The Vegetative Universe, opens like a flower from the Earths center
> In which is Eternity. It expands in Stars to the Mundane Shell
> And there it meets Eternity again, both within and without ...[24]

The impact of such lines is actually diminished if read with what comes before and after: they need to resonate within the bounds of their own suggestiveness. It can sometimes be the same with even a single line:

> I behold London; a Human awful wonder of God![25]

A sentence like this – discovered, it may be, by serendipity – will remind one of Fuseli's saying that Blake was *'damned good to steal from'*.[26]

London was in any case strongly present to his mind in writing *Jerusalem*, as the city most readily corresponding to the Hebrew capital. Glimpses of it appear from time to time in this poem, as in its Plates 46 [32], where the mathematically organized dome of St Paul's is set against buildings of Gothic beauty, and 84, where a similar juxtaposition illustrates the lines:

> I see London blind and age-bent begging through the streets
> Of Babylon led by a child ...

Plate 45 [31] of the poem carries an even more intricate account of London, a survey there running from 'Highgate thro Hackney & Holloway' to various districts of the East End and on to 'where the Tower of London frownd dreadful over Jerusalem'. He continues:

> thence to Bethlehem where was builded
> Dens of despair in the house of bread: enquiring in vain
> Of stones and rocks he took his way, for human form was
> none ...

The surprising appearance of Bethlehem in the midst of a London geography which later moves on to 'Westminster & Marybone' gives plausibility to the suggestion that Blake was thinking not just of the New Testament town (literally, the 'house of bread'), but of the Bethlehem Royal Hospital (or Bedlam) in Moorfields, which had only recently ceased to be a place for the public exhibition of lunatics – who might

13 'Caius Gabriel Cibber, 'Raving Madness': sculpture from the Bethlem Hospital, Bethlem Royal Hospital Archives and Museum

14 Detail from 'Europe: a Prophecy', Fitzwilliam Museum, Cambridge

15 Detail from *Jerusalem*, plate 51, Yale Center for British Art, Paul Mellon Collection

16 William Hogarth, 'The Reward of Cruelty', Yale Center for British Art, Paul Mellon Collection

17 Detail from *Jerusalem*, plate 69, Yale Center for British Art, Paul Mellon Collection

18 Detail from *Jerusalem*, plate 25, Yale Center for British Art, Paul Mellon Collection

justly claim to be seeking bread and being offered a stone; this lay in the City, and so between the Tower and Westminster. The case for this identification is strengthened by the fact that if Blake passed the hospital in his early years, he would have seen outside Cibber's striking statues of 'Melancholy Madness' and 'Raving Madness' (Figure 13) on their mats[27*] – both of them, but particularly the second, resembling the bald figure of 'Skofield', as depicted by him on his design six pages later in *Jerusalem*, and resembling other figures in the prophetic books (see e.g. Figures 14 and 15).[28*]

A common theme in the poem is the need to attack habits of analysis that deprive the mind of possible food through the admission of vision and harmony. The effects of this might be seen in some of the harsher elements in eighteenth-century London life. Just as rational men could countenance the building of dark Satanic mills in industrial cities because they could already be said to have minds in the form of mills, so minds that were always anatomizing could easily tolerate cruel versions of dissecting for the purposes of science. Blake must have known Hogarth's design, 'The Reward of Cruelty' (Figure 16), which shows the body of a condemned criminal being handed over for dissection in a scene presided over by a figure of unfeeling justice. This can be matched by designs in *Jerusalem* (Figures 17 and 18) which show similar acts of dissection – the second no doubt having its own relevance to lines such as 'You accumulate Particulars, & murder by analyzing' or 'The Infant Joy is beautiful, but its anatomy | Horrible ghast & deadly!'[29]

Haunted by such effects of a world dominated by destructive analysis, Blake felt increasingly the need to portray the delights of one informed by Genius, as he showed in his account of the female in Beulah:

> The Female searches sea & land for gratification to the
> Male Genius: who in return clothes her in gems & gold
> And feeds her with the food of Eden. hence all her beauty beams
> She Creates at her will a little moony night & silence
> With Spaces of sweet gardens & a tent of elegant beauty:
> Closed in by a sandy desart & a night of stars shining.
> And a little tender moon & hovering angels on the wing.
> And the Male gives a Time & Revolution to her Space
> Till the time of love is passed in ever varying delights
> For All Things Exist in the Human Imagination[30]

A passage in *Milton* gives similar status to Los:

> Los is by mortals nam'd Time Enitharmon is nam'd Space
> But they depict him bald & aged who is in eternal youth
> All powerful and his locks flourish like the brows of morning
> He is the Spirit of Prophecy the ever apparent Elias
> Time is the mercy of Eternity; without Times swiftness
> Which is the swiftest of all things: all were eternal torment ...[31]

There are also in *Milton* occasions of pure poetic bonus such as the following passage of straightforward sensuous beauty:

> Thou hearest the Nightingale begin the Song of Spring;
> The Lark sitting upon his earthy bed: just as the morn
> Appears; listens silent; then springing from the waving Corn-field!
>   loud
> He leads the Choir of Day! trill, trill, trill, trill,
> Mounting upon the wings of light into the Great Expanse:
> Reecchoing against the lovely blue & shining heavenly Shell:
> His little throat labours with inspiration; every feather
> On throat & breast & wings vibrates with the effluence Divine
> All Nature listens silent to him & the awful Sun
> Stands still upon the Mountain looking on this little Bird
> With eyes of soft humility, & wonder love & awe.
> Then loud from their green covert all the Birds begin their Song
> The Thrush, the Linnet & the Goldfinch, Robin & the Wren
> Awake the Sun from his sweet reverie upon the Mountain:
> The Nightingale again assays his song, & thro the day
> And thro the night warbles luxuriant; every Bird of Song
> Attending his loud harmony with admiration & love,
> This is a Vision of the lamentations of Beulah over Ololon!
>
> Thou percievest the Flowers put forth their precious Odours!
> And none can tell how from so small a center comes such sweets
> Forgetting that within that Center Eternity expands
> Its ever during doors, that Og & Anak fiercely guard
> First eer the morning breaks joy opens in the flowery bosoms
> Joy even to tears, which the Sun rising dries; first the Wild Thyme
> And Meadow-sweet downy & soft waving among the reeds.
> Light springing on the air lead the sweet Dance: they wake
> The Honeysuckle sleeping on the Oak: the flaunting beauty

Revels along upon the wind; the White-thorn lovely May
Opens her many lovely eyes: listening the Rose still sleeps
None dare to wake her, soon she bursts her crimson curtain bed
And comes forth in the majesty of beauty; every Flower:
The Pink, the Jessamine, the Wall-flower, the Carnation
The Jonquil, the mild Lilly opes her heavens! every Tree,
And Flower & Herb soon fill the air with an innumerable Dance
Yet all in order sweet & lovely, Men are sick with Love!
Such is a Vision of the lamentation of Beulah over Ololon.[32]

Some lines shortly before provide a visionary account of the relation
between human beings and the sky above them

The Sky is an immortal Tent built by the Sons of Los
And every Space that a Man views around his dwelling-place:
Standing on his own roof, or in his garden on a mount
Of twenty-five cubits in height, such space is his Universe;
And on its verge the Sun rises & sets. the Clouds bow
To meet the flat Earth & the Sea in such an orderd Space:
The Starry heavens reach no further but here bend and set
On all sides & the two Poles turn on their valves of gold:
And if he move his dwelling-place, his heavens also move.
Wher'eer he goes & all his neighbourhood bewail his loss.
Such are the Spaces called Earth & such its dimension:
As to that false appearance which appears to the reasoner,
As of a Globe rolling thro Voidness, it is a delusion of Ulro
The Microscope knows not of this nor the Telescope. they alter
The ratio of the Spectators Organs but leave Objects untouchd
For every Space larger than a red Globule of Mans blood.
Is visionary: and is created by the Hammer of Los
And every Space smaller than a Globule of Mans blood. opens
Into Eternity of which this vegetable Earth is but a shadow:
The red Globule is the unwearied Sun by Los created
To measure Time and Space to mortal Men. every morning.
Bowlahoola & Allamanda are placed on each side
Of that Pulsation & that Globule, terrible their power.[33]

The lines describing 'every space that a Man views around his dwelling-
place', which continue

And if he move his dwelling-place, his heavens also move
Where'er he goes, & all his neighbourhood bewail his loss.[34]

are surprisingly close to a passage in Wordsworth's *Excursion*:

> ... when we stand upon our native soil,
> Unelbowed by such objects as oppress
> Our active powers, those powers themselves become
> Subversive of our noxious qualities,
> And by the substitution of delight,
> And by new influxes of strength suppress
> All evil, then the Being spreads abroad
> His branches to the wind, and all who see
> Bless him rejoicing in his neighbourhood.[35]

The same striking metaphor is used by Wordsworth in his original man-uscript, though in the final version he seems to have become uneasy with the image, substituting the lines 'whence the Being moves | In beauty through the world ...' The convergence of imagery, and even the common word 'neighbourhood', are no doubt to be regarded as coinci-dence, since Blake could hardly have seen Wordsworth's manuscript, but they show a remarkable meeting of minds that have come from dif-ferent starting-points: Wordsworth's 'neighbourhood' rejoices in the sta-bility of the man's rooted Being, whereas Blake's enjoys the work of his energetic Genius as a 'son of Los', to be mourned if lost.

Attempting to read Blake's later poetry on such a high visionary plane sometimes means, however, that one must give less attention to the more obvious ways of reading a text. When, for example, he introduces a list of the cathedral cities of Britain into his verse it is tempting either to retire baffled, or to look for a range of symbolic meanings correspon-ding to each (as did Damon in his *Blake Dictionary*). Yet on the kind of interpretation presented in this chapter they might all be viewed simply as sites where the visionary potentiality locked up in Gothic architecture could, for a willing reader, be released. When, similarly, he names vari-ous of the mountains of Wales and other British areas, he may well have wished to do no more than alert the reader to the possibility of viewing them in the same light of sublimity as the Hebrew mountains which the Psalmist had found it quite natural to venerate.

Blake employed increasingly in his later poetry two terms that he had first devised for 'Vala': those of the 'Spectre' and 'Emanation'. In their original setting, they were particularly well adapted to the theme that the initial human tragedy had resulted from an act of separation. Once that first division had taken place, all human beings must suffer from the resulting dislocation. Most notably, the human being could be thought of as riven between a male energy of doubt and destruction on the one hand and a female power of pity and lost vision on the other. In 'Vala' this condition is first proclaimed dramatically in the cry, 'Lost! Lost! Lost! are my Emanations'.[36]

For Blake, the Spectre and Emanation were not simply characters in his epic drama, but evidently to be regarded as presences in a more personal and immediate sense. The most striking evidence for this comes in a notebook poem:

> My Spectre around me night & day
> Like a Wild beast guards my way
> My Emanation far within
> Weeps incessantly for my Sin[37]

Spectre and Emanation in his poetry are ambivalent. In his extroverted mode the Spectre acts as a defensive power; in the introverted, he becomes a source of fearful doubt. In the first mode, similarly, the Emanation can float before him as a lovely image of beauty, but in the second it becomes a source of pity, reflecting his guilt for acts of sin. In both cases they act out or suffer his divided nature: a twofold deficiency that is a necessary result of his failing humanity has set up a separation within him that is only to be resolved, if ever, in rare experiences of fourfold vision. The twin Blake of the Frontispiece above again shows himself.

Whereas Blake's version of the Druids is a dispensable part of his ideas, bound largely into his interpretation of the past and useful mainly as a source of certain designs, the lore of Spectre and Emanation is worked more intricately into his poetic thinking. The idea of the Emanation, as has more than once been pointed out, is remarkably close to Jung's concept of the 'anima', showing Blake drawn to an idea of the human being as originally androgynous, so that in some way every human born reflects anew a fall into sexual division.

His account of the human condition, in other words, was becoming more complex the more he studied it.

11
Years of Resentment, Hints of Paradox

It was not likely that two such men as Blake and Fuseli would remain close friends permanently. Although he was an immediate source of fascination for Blake, who wrote in 1800, 'When Flaxman was taken to Italy, Fuseli was given to me for a season',[1] the exact phrasing of that tribute probably covers an indication that the 'season' had now passed, at least in its fullness. He may even have picked up some hint of Fuseli's opinion, voiced to Farington in 1796, that he had 'something of madness about him'.[2] His grateful acceptance of the fact that Flaxman's bounty was now to include a share in the friendship of William Hayley was accompanied by acknowledgement of a recent slighting, imagined or otherwise, on the part of Fuseli, among other associates: the year before he had written to Cumberland bitterly that since his illustrations to Young's *Night Thoughts* had been published, 'even Johnson & Fuseli have discarded my Graver'.[3] What kind of falling out this may or may not cover is impossible to know, but the believed lack of employment, however boldly greeted by an 'I laugh at Fortune', meant that he was relieved when offered the chance of going to Sussex for a time to live under Hayley's patronage. Two years later he was still mindful of his gratitude – even if it was now tempered by the growing belief that he was being hindered from pursuing his prime artistic aims by demands that he devote himself to other tasks already quoted:

> As my dependence is on Engraving at present ... & I find on all hands great objections to my doing any thing but the meer drudgery of business, & intimations that if I do not confine myself to this I shall not live, this has always pursud me. You will understand by this the source of all my uneasiness This from Johnson & Fuseli brought me down here & this from M^r H will bring me back again, for that

I cannot live without doing my duty to lay up treasures in heaven is Certain …[4]

A couple of months later he elaborated on his fears by voicing them to Butts in the form of spectral doubts (also quoted above) that

> … Butts shall give what Fuseli gave
> A dark black Rock & a gloomy Cave.[5]

Again, there seems to be a despairing suspicion that Fuseli had somehow failed to provide support at a crucial juncture. Fortunately for his material prospects, however, Butts did not fulfil his fears on this occasion or any other, continuing to provide a secure income in return for regular biblical illustrations. And if he had thought that his gifts as an engraver were being disprized by those who had previously supported him, this too proved mistaken: by 1803 he could write to Hayley that he had now 'got to work after Fuseli for a little Shakespeare' and that Johnson had told him that there was no want of work.[6]

Although he might be disappointed by his failure of support, Blake never abandoned his judgement that Fuseli was among the foremost artists of his age, to be mentioned in the same breath as his own hero Michelangelo. In one of his notebook epigrams, addressed to 'H' (presumably Robert Hunt), he wrote:

> You think Fuseli is not a Great Painter Im Glad
> This is one of the best compliments he ever had[7]

In the same way, he held that the neglect of Fuseli's *Milton* had been a disgrace to the country and a 'Sufficient Apology' for his own vigorous indignation.[8] In 1806 he wrote a spirited defence of Fuseli's portrait of Count Ugolino in the Royal Academy Exhibition, dismissing a reviewer's criticisms and quoting the opinion of a visitor that Fuseli was 'a hundred years beyond the present generation'.[9]

Little is known of the later relations between the two men, apart from Fuseli's already quoted comment on Blake that he was '*damned good to steal from*',[10] Blake's report (apparently without rancour) that Fuseli had been made 'Master of the Royal Academy'[11] and Tatham's story that when in 1815 Blake went to the Academy to copy the Laocoön group, Fuseli came in and cried, 'What! you here, Meesther Blake? We ought to come and learn of you, not you of us!'[12] – suggesting that their relationship, if sometimes barbed, remained respectful on both sides.

His respect for Fuseli, citizen of Switzerland, had always kept alive his latent republicanism. When he read and annotated Bacon's *Essays*, for instance, this side of him was roused to anger and contempt. Bacon's statement that 'A king is a mortal god on earth, unto whom the living god hath lent his own name as a great honour' was greeted by him with the comment, 'O Contemptible & Abject Slave'.[13] On the previous page he drew a line of excrement, leading from 'The Devil's Arse' to the inscription 'A King'. The gesture was fully in line with political satires of the time, one of which showed Pitt being excreted from the Devil's hind parts,[14] though if Blake's particular refinement had been known openly at the time, he might have faced another charge of sedition.

At the same time there was a simple patriotism about him which could go along with such scurrilous expressions of scorn. One need think only of the lines in which he inveighed against the German poet Klopstock:

> When Klopstock England defied
> Uprose terrible Blake in his pride
> For old Nobodaddy aloft
> Farted & Belchd & coughd
> Then swore a great oath that made heavn quake
> And calld aloud to English Blake
> Blake was giving his body ease
> At Lambeth beneath the poplar trees ...

After an account of the terrible effect on Klopstock's bowels created by Blake's turning round 'three times three', the lines conclude:

> If Blake could do this when he rose up from shite
> What might he not do if he sat down to write[15]

Whatever scorn Blake might feel for the rule of kings and priests – or for that matter a Lord Chancellor such as Bacon – he was ready to come to the defence of his country when it was threatened by foreign enemies. He could therefore produce some years later two designs representing 'The Spiritual Form of Nelson guiding Leviathan' and 'The spiritual form of Pitt, guiding Behemoth', which he claimed to be 'compositions of a mythological cast, similar to those Apotheoses of Persian, Hindoo, and Egyptian Antiquity, which are still preserved on rude monuments' and which he offered to produce 'on a scale that is suitable to the grandeur of the nation, who is the parent of his [the Artist's] heroes'.[16]

Some scholars have been so bemused by finding an erstwhile opponent of war, and in particular of Pitt, so pandering, apparently, to the current taste that they have urged their readers to look for a deep irony. Yet the language of Blake's descriptions is so open, so devoid of the little pointers that one would expect to find for such an interpretation, that it is hard to accept that he was behaving with such flat-footed guile as to support a public gesture the true satire of which would be discernible only to a select few – many of them not living till a century later. Even David Erdman, doughty champion of Blake's radicalism, is forced to concede that 'in many respects the irony, the political satire, is as inscrutable as that in Blake's early drama'.[17] One is forced to ask whether in both cases we may be dealing not with a convoluted irony, but with simple lack of long-term consistency. Forgetting his political animus of the 1790s, on this reading, Blake was by now impressed by the simple and lasting enthusiasm of his countrymen for their recently deceased heroes and wished to express the essence of that in his designs. It was, after all, the 'Spirit' of Pitt and the 'Spirit' of Nelson that he had chosen for his subjects. The other remarkable feature of these and other designs, and his accounts of them, is his evident desire at this time to create on a grand scale congruent to the extent of his aspirations in poetry.

Perhaps, in any case, he had never had much interest in the details of politics. One thinks of lines in his 'Public Address' of 1809–10:

> I am really sorry to see my Countrymen trouble themselves about Politics. If Men were Wise the most arbitrary Princes could not hurt them If they are not wise the Freest Government is compelld to be a Tyranny Princes appear to me to be Fools Houses of Commons & Houses of Lords appear to me to be fools they seem to me to be something Else besides Human Life.[18]

During these years Blake was unfortunate enough to fall foul of the contemporary journals from more than one direction. Southey, writing anonymously a review of Hayley's *Ballads*, which he found 'incomparably absurd', could not resist the temptation to satirize both men simultaneously:

> The poet has had the singular good fortune to meet with a painter capable of doing full justice to his conceptions; and, in fact ... we know not whether most to admire the genius of Mr William Blake or of Mr William Hayley.[19]

The *Anti-Jacobin Review* had of course been setting itself for some years against any publications that could be associated with the Revolution, and some memories of the set in which Blake had moved in the early 1790s may actually have increased their hostility to any who showed that their attitude had shifted. A review there of the illustrations to Blair's *Grave* in November 1808 concluded:

> The dedication ... to the Queen, written by Mr. Blake, is one of the most abortive attempts to form a wreath of poetical flowers that we have ever seen. Should he again essay to climb the Parnassian heights, his friends would do well to restrain his wanderings by the strait waistcoat. Whatever licence we may allow him as a painter, to tolerate him as a poet would be insufferable.

Meanwhile, the *Examiner* embarked on a campaign of hostility against all that it associated with 'methodism'. The event that caused Blake particular anger – even, perhaps, to the point of temporary mental breakdown – was the publication there of a review of his *Descriptive Catalogue* which questioned his sanity:

> If beside the stupid and mad-brained political project of their rulers, the same part of the people of England resquired [*sic*] fresh proof of the alarming increase of the effects of insanity, they will be too well convinced from its having lately spread into the hitherto sober region of Art. ... When the ebullitions of a distempered brain are mistaken for the sallies of genius by those whose works have exhibited the soundest thinking in art, the malady has indeed attained a pernicious height, and it becomes a duty to endeavour to arrest its progress. Such is the case with the productions and admirers of WILLIAM BLAKE, an unfortunate lunatic, whose personal inoffensiveness secures him from confinement, and, consequently, of whom no public notice would have been taken, if he was not forced on the notice and animadversion of the EXAMINER, in having been held up to public admiration by many esteemed amateurs and professors as a genius in some respect original and legitimate.

Blake responded angrily in his Notebook 'Public Address':

> The manner in which my Character has been blasted these thirty years both as an artist & a Man may be seen particularly in a Sunday Paper cald the Examiner Publishd in Beaufort Buildings. (We all know

that Editors of Newspapers trouble their heads very little about art & science & that they are always paid for what they put in upon these ungracious Subjects[)] & the manner in which I have routed out the nest of villains will be seen in a Poem concerning my Three years Herculean Labours at Felpham which I will soon Publish. Secret Calumny & open Professions of Friendship are common enough all the world over but have never been so good an occasion of Poetic Imagery. When a Base Man means to be your Enemy he always begins with being your Friend Flaxman cannot deny that one of the very first Monuments he did I gratuitously designd for him at the same time he was blasting my character as an Artist to Macklin my Employer as Macklin told me at the time   how much of his Homer & Dante he will allow to be mine I do not know as he went far enough off to Publish them even to Italy. but the Public will know & Posterity will know ...

Events at Felpham were still clearly simmering in his sub-consciousness; and when he worked on *Jerusalem* both polarities of his personality expressed themselves in a general appeal to a nobler vision and a sardonic undertow, such as Milton had sometimes employed. So the persons who had figured in his trial could return, lightly disguised, as players in *Jerusalem*. Gilchrist caught something of this when he noticed the resemblance between the names of Skofeld in Blake's poem and the Private John Schofield whose accusations had led to the trial, and found himself wondering whether other real names might not be lurking behind those in the narrative such as 'Hand & Hyle & Coban', or 'Kwantok, Peachey, Brereton, Slayd & Hutton', or 'Kox, Kotope & Bowen'.[20] His suspicions proved well founded when later research revealed that the participants in the trial had included among their number Schofield's companion John Cook and the Justices of the Peace John Peachey, William Brereton, Major Hulton and John Quantock.[21] 'Hand', similarly, sounds rather like John Hunt, who with his brothers had mounted the smear campaign against him in the *Examiner*. These are understandable strokes of revenge, though it is a relief that they were not carried on too far, particularly on occasions when they put Blake in danger not only of boring his readers, but of sounding like a man suffering from a persecution obsession.

Not everyone was concerned to disprize him. Benjamin Heath Malkin, whom he met in 1805, having recently lost a son who had already revealed himself to be a child prodigy, engaged him to engrave his portrait for his own *Memoir*, into which he introduced a reprinting of poems from *Poetical Sketches* and from the *Songs of Innocence*. These latter (the first publishing of them for the public at large) were reproduced in several journals, one incidental beneficial result being that by these means they for the first time reached William and Dorothy Wordsworth.[22]

Despite such commissions from men such as Malkin and Butts, not to mention the commercial engravings he continued to undertake, Blake caused many to believe in his lack of ambition for worldly goods – an impression which was largely justified. He spoke to Robinson of his horror of money, and of his turning pale when it was offered to him;[23] he also claimed seldom to carry money in his pockets:[24] 'Were I to love money, I should lose all power of original thought; desire of gain deadens the genius of man. I might roll in wealth and ride in a golden chariot, were I to listen to the voice of parsimony. My business is not to gather gold, but to make glorious shapes, expressing god-like sentiments.'[25] His disciple Samuel Palmer spoke of him as having believed that he would always be supplied with it when it was needed:

> he worked on with serenity when there was only a shilling in the house. Once (he told me) he spent part of one of these last shillings on a camel's hair brush.
>
> ... while engrossed in designing, he had often an aversion to resuming his graver, or to being troubled with money matters. It put him out very much when Mrs Blake referred to the financial topic, or found herself constrained to announce, 'The money is going, Mr. Blake.' 'Oh, d----- the money!' he would shout; 'it's always the money!' Her method of hinting at the odious subject became, in consequence, a very quiet and expressive one. She would set before him at dinner just what there was in the house, without any comment until, finally, the empty platter had to make its appearance: which hard fact effectually reminded him it was time to go to his engraving for a while. At that, when fully embarked again, he was not unhappy; work being his natural element.[26*]

His attitude to money was not quite as simple-minded as such reports might suggest, however. The plan of his character Quid, quoted earlier, was to 'have all the writing Engraved instead of Printed & at every other leaf a high finished print all in three Volumes folio, & sell them a hundred pounds a piece. they would Print off two Thousand ...' As we have seen, Quid seems to represent one side of Blake himself. Since the whole of the *Island* involves some self-satire, it is not necessary to take such a speech too seriously; yet it involves an amount of worldly knowledge that is not readily associated with Blake, and there are other indications of complexity in his monetary dealings. He could be straightforward in his refusal of worldly goods, as he claimed in a letter already quoted:

> 'My hands are labourd day & night'
> 'And Ease comes never in my sight'
> 'My Wife has no indulgence given'
> 'Except what comes to her from heaven'
> 'We eat little we drink less'
> 'This Earth breeds not our happiness'[27]

If, on the other hand, he felt he was being cheated of his proper financial reward, the independent side of his nature would readily come to the surface. Morton Paley, who has considered some of the uncompromising statements that later accompanied the Laocoon design, such as 'Christianity is Art | & not Money | Money is its Curse', along with Blake's endorsement of the communitarianism encouraged in the Gospels and early Church, sets these against the evidence, from price lists sent to Dawson Turner in 1818 and to George Cumberland in 1827, that Blake was not averse from asking a high price for his own work if he thought that appropriate.[28]

His sense of the importance of receiving a fair price ('unprofitable enough to me, tho Expensive to the Buyer', as he put it to Turner[29]) was never clearer than in his dealings with Robert Cromek, the young Yorkshire engraver and entrepreneur who commissioned him to produce illustrations for Blair's *Grave*. The understanding was that Blake would be responsible not only for the designs, but for the engravings to be made from them – which would have given him several hundred pounds, as opposed to the guinea apiece paid for the designs. In the event, however, the work of engraving Blake's designs was given to Schiavonetti, and when Blake requested some recompense for the verses to the Queen which he had written to accompany them he received a contemptuous reply from Cromek, who asserted that he had performed him a considerable service by employing him at all.

Looking at the events from this distance of time, it seems likely that Cromek made a verbal proposal to Blake that he should both design and engrave his designs – though without making any formal contract. That was certainly Blake's impression, since he reported to Hayley that Cromek had been so well pleased by the designs that he had made the commission for the engravings. Cromek may then have had cold feet about Blake's engraving capabilities, since he told Stothard that he had looked at the etching of one of the subjects and found it executed so carelessly that he decided to employ Schiavonetti instead. As an engraver himself Cromek could not be accused of ignorance on such matters, but it may be that his training (like that of certain wood engravers who later reworked some of Blake's Virgil illustrations) caused him to be blind to Blake's technical prowess. At all events, there was clearly an element of sharp practice in his actions, and the impression was to be reinforced some years later when Cromek employed Stothard to execute a design for Chaucer's *Canterbury Pilgrims* which was suspiciously close to what Blake had been planning. Although it is again difficult now to sort the rights and wrongs of the affair, it has to be reported that others apart from Blake found Cromek less than trustworthy. Allan Cunningham's son commented that he 'had rather lax ideas about meum and tuum' and recorded his father's anecdote of an occasion when Sir Walter Scott said of a Ben Jonson letter he had once possessed, 'the last person I showed the letter to was Cromek, and I have never seen it since'.[30*]

Cromek's sharp practice reinforced Blake's impression that he had been badly served by Hayley. When he felt himself driven too far by the patronizing attitudes of such men he could set down his feelings in pithy epigrams – again in private; the satirical power of the early writings would then re-emerge in a more virulent form:

> A petty sneaking Knave I knew
> O Mr Cr----- how do ye do[31]

> Thus Hayley on his Toilette seeing the sope
> Cries, Homer is very much improvd by Pope

> Of Hs birth this was the happy lot
> His Mother on his Father him begot[32]

Yet in spite of such pungent remarks, there can be little doubt, as we have seen, of the general goodwill that was shown to him by Hayley throughout the relationship, or indeed of his recognition of the fact during and after the trial.

Hayley, or someone who shared his nature, was the victim of another shaft:

> He has observd the Golden Rule
> Till hes become the Golden Fool[33]

He was aimed at explicitly in another:

> Thy Friendship oft has made my heart to ake
> Do be my enemy for Friendships sake[34]

Another way of expressing his complaints was to raise his treatment of
them to epic status: in *Milton* one recognizes the sentiment just quoted
as part of Palamabron's prayer in the Great Assembly:

> God, protect me from my friends, that they have not power
>   over me
> Thou hast giv'n me power to protect myself from my bitterest
>   enemies.[35]

In the same way, a vestigial echo of his resentment against Hayley may
be traced in the cry of the Gnomes against Satan in *Milton*:

> To do unkind things in kindness! with power armd, to say
> The most irritating things in the midst of tears and love[36]

His own directness and honesty were not universally approved – nor
indeed were they invariably in evidence. Samuel Palmer was to call Blake
'a man without a mask', but the characterization cannot be accepted
quite without question, since the private notebooks and letters make it
clear that at the very least the 'face' itself did not always remain consistent. Hayley cannot have known some of the things that Blake thought
of him or he would hardly have continued to refer to him (albeit with
continuing patronization) as 'our good Blake'. What is being referred to
is, rather, his unswerving sincerity, resulting from a determination to say
what he feels, when he chooses to say it, without curtainings of Augustan
decorum or concessions to the demands of current propriety.

When Blake did make more public statements of his bitterness, they
were often in aid of the depressed arts of his time, as in his Public
Address and Descriptive Catalogue, where he campaigned for his own
kind of visionary art. In private marginal comments on Sir Joshua
Reynolds's first Discourse, he attacked the rich men of England, who, he
said, 'form themselves into a Society to Sell and Not to Buy Pictures':

> When Nations grow Old. The Arts grow Cold
> And Commerce settles on every Tree
> And the Poor & the Old can live upon Gold
> For all are Born Poor. Aged Sixty three.[37]

Meanwhile he pressed firmly on, producing designs based on his visionary understanding of human existence and asserting in private the lasting quality of his work:

> Still admird by Noble minds,
> Followd by Envy on the winds,
> Re-engravd Time after Time,
> Ever in their youthful prime,
> My Designs unchangd remain.
> Time may rage but rage in vain.
> For above Times troubled Fountains
> On the Great Atlantic Mountains,
> In my Golden House on high
> There they Shine Eternally[38]

His insistence on the need for cultivation of Vision and for rational thinking to be transformed by the workings of the imagination remained steady: in his view even the dust of the ground could either be an irritating substance or be transformed by the eye into a visionary sight:

> Mock on Mock on Voltaire Rousseau
> Mock on Mock on! tis all in vain!
> You throw the sand against the wind
> And the wind blows it back again
>
> And every sand becomes a Gem
> Reflected in the beams divine
> Blown back they blind the mocking Eye
> But still in Israels paths they shine
>
> The Atoms of Democritus
> And Newtons Particles of light
> Are sands upon the Red sea shore
> Where Israels tents do shine so bright[39]

This is in fact one of Blake's most successful lyrics, riddling (as they often are), yet not hard to decipher, given our knowledge of his obsessive philosophy. It is another refusal of the reductive claims of a purely rational and scientific outlook in favour of restoring a sense of glory, well in line with the poem beginning, 'To see a world in a grain of sand', which again seeks to redeem perception from the bonds of an exclusive devotion to the bounds of time and space by opening it out to the condition where a wild flower can show heaven, the palm of one's hand enclose infinity and an hour reveal the nature of eternity.

Another lyric which springs largely from Blake's own ideology yet is readily comprehensible is 'The Crystal Cabinet'. In this piece he draws heavily on the idea set forth in a letter quoted above, that in the hierarchy of levels of perception, the 'threefold', identified there as corresponding to 'soft Beulah's night', was the realm of affectionate love.

> The Maiden caught me in the Wild
> Where I was dancing merrily
> She put me into her Cabinet
> And Lockd me up with a golden Key
>
> This Cabinet is formd of Gold
> And Pearl & Crystal shining bright
> And within it opens into a World
> And a little lovely Moony Night
>
> Another England there I saw
> Another London with its Tower
> Another Thames & other Hills
> And another pleasant Surrey Bower
>
> Another Maiden like herself
> Translucent lovely shining clear
> Threefold each in the other closd
> O what a pleasant trembling fear
>
> O what a smile a threefold Smile
> Filld me that like a flame I burnd
> I bent to Kiss the lovely Maid
> And found a Threefold Kiss returnd
>
> I strove to sieze the inmost Form
> With ardor fierce & hands of flame
> But burst the Crystal Cabinet
> And like a Weeping Babe became
>
> A weeping Babe upon the wild
> And Weeping Woman pale reclind
> And in the outward air again
> I filld with woes the passing Wind[40]

To a reader of Blake's other work the point will be evident: it follows in the wake of the lines:

> He that binds to himself a joy
> Does the winged life destroy

and those concerning the impossibility of permanently enjoying 'fourfold vision'. The attempt to do so, indeed, corresponds to what the lover in the poem has done: he has tried to make permanent the experience of threefold vision created by affectionate love which proves just as essentially elusive as fourfold vision, flying as soon as an attempt is made to grasp it (like the Cupid brought to the light by Psyche in the ancient myth).

Threefold vision has rather the essential fragility of thin glass or a bubble: it cannot be seized by a grasping hand without being immediately destroyed. The lover who attempts this will find himself immediately delivered into the bleak world of single vision, while for himself and the woman the magic world they have briefly been inhabiting falls apart again, leaving them as 'weeping babe' and 'weeping woman'.

'The Mental Traveller',[41] another poem of the kind, is more riddling. It too can be read as the depiction of a spirit moving between the possibilities of single, twofold and threefold vision, while lacking the overall illumination that would be afforded by the illumination of fourfold vision. The dominant note, however, is of paradox, as shown in the first two stanzas:

> I traveld thro' a Land of Men
> A Land of Men & Women too
> And heard & saw such dreadful things
> As cold Earth wanderers never knew
>
> For there the Babe is born in joy
> That was begotten in dire woe
> Just as we Reap in joy the fruit
> Which we in bitter tears did sow[42]

The core of the poem's paradoxical structure as it develops reveals itself in the shifting relationship between male and female personae, moving on from that between the lovers in 'The Crystal Cabinet' to reveal a persistent lack of fit between the genders: the single incident of that poem gives place to a long cycle of events in which the male is first a Babe, given to an old woman who, in a sequence recalling the Christian Passion, makes him experience the cruelty of the law, binding iron thorns round his head, piercing his hands and feet and cutting out his heart. By the process of analysing every nerve and feeding on his cries of suffering she herself grows steadily younger while he grows to the stage reached by Orc in the Preludium to *America*, when he re-enacts the incident described there, rending his bonds and ravishing her. But from now on the events are increasingly unexpected, as if at every point Blake deliberately turns away from natural consequence, to move off at a tangent. The 'bleeding youth', for instance, does not follow a path of revenge or of further suffering, but plants the female to become a garden where he himself can grow old living on the fruits of his own charitable industry.

The next events are equally unexpected: the objects of his charity live lives that accord with their own desires; a Female Babe springs from their fire who takes a man for herself, then turns on the ageing benefactor – who in turn is forced to find a maiden of his own:

> And to Allay his freezing Age
> The Poor Man takes her in his arms
> The Cottage fades before his Sight
> The Garden & its lovely Charms

At this point the verse is handled with particular brilliance, as the descent into a world of single vision is described, with the natural perception of a flat earth transformed by the eye of reason into a Newtonian organization – rather as if both eye and what is seen by the eye were behaving like a giant wary hedgehog. Male and female, abandoned to live in this dark and desert state, are left to play sexual games with one another that reduce them to infancy while exposing them to the dangers resulting from unrestrained natural wildness.

> The Guests are scatterd thro' the land
> For the Eye altering alters all
> The Senses roll themselves in fear
> And the flat Earth becomes a Ball
>
> The Stars Sun Moon all shrink away
> A desart vast without a bound
> And nothing left to eat or drink
> And a dark desert all around

The honey of her Infant lips
The bread & wine of her sweet smile
The wild game of her roving Eye
Does him to Infancy beguile

For as he eats & drinks he grows
Younger & younger every day
And on the desart wild they both
Wander in terror & dismay

Like the wild Stag she flees away
Her fear plants many a thicket wild
While he pursues her night & day
By various arts of Love beguild

By various arts of Love & Hate
Till the wide desart planted oer
With Labyrinths of wayward Love
Where roams the Lion Wolf & Boar

This wilderness state gives place in turn to a more civilized one, in which there is room for the development of cities and peaceful agriculture, until the presence of the male – by now transformed back into a 'wayward Babe' – is recognized by the other characters: striking terror around like Orc, he is experienced as a figure of pure energy, purely destructive and mortally unapproachable:

For who dare touch the frowning form
His arm is witherd to its root
Lions Boars Wolves all howling flee
And every Tree does shed its fruit

And none can touch that frowning form
Except it be a Woman Old
She nails him down upon the Rock
And all is done as I have told

Perhaps the best word to use in connection with this extraordinary set of verses is one that occurs twice in the poem itself: 'wayward'. It is as if Blake is engaged in a game of hide-and-seek with his readers, in which he wantonly refuses to allow the possibility of a firm breakthrough into organized meaning. Yet this does not seem to have been a part of his deliberate purpose; certainly the approach to total meaning seems often to be on the point of achievement. Without the relief of such moments, the spirit would be bound into an inexorable cycle of promise plagued by tormenting denial, passing successively through the levels of vision, in an unending cycle and leaving the reader apprehensive lest 'the desart vast without a bound' should after all prove to be the only reality. As a result of the oblique method used, on the other hand, the poem achieves resonance from this constant presence of near-meaning. In the end, indeed, it derives power from this very refusal to insist on fully coherent significance, which benefits from the process described earlier, where as a shifting grasp on possible meaning is combined with a relaxed creativity the reader's mind is stimulated into activity of its own.

It also relies to an unprecedented extent on an effect that has been previously noted in more limited terms. I have previously drawn attention to the manner in which a poem will at some point change direction quite unexpectedly. Here the effect operates more widely, as almost every stanza seems to take the poem yet another way. It is as if the move away from narrative in 'Vala' has turned itself into something more like an artistic method on its own account.

Other poems in the Notebook operate more straightforwardly: the haunting line 'O why was I born with a different face?', a quatrain on his own predicament which has already been quoted,[43] became here the pivot of a poem entitled 'Mary', which tells the story of a girl whose looks are so beautiful that although she captivates all at the first village ball she attends she arouses so much envy as actually to forfeit her good looks through obsession with the faces that have raised themselves about her:

> With Faces of Scorn & with Eyes of disdain
> Like foul Fiends inhabiting Marys mild Brain
> She remembers no Face like the Human Divine
> All Faces have Envy sweet Mary but thine[44]*

The most curious feature of all this is that the combination of control of development with waywardness of line was not exhibited in the same manner when Blake was producing his visual art. Sometimes a similar effect could be achieved when he retained a firm hold on a design while parts of the picture were allowed to riot into wildness, but these could not really compare with what happens in, say, 'The Mental Traveller'.

All such effects could be said to bear witness not only to the perpetual struggle between the restraining Urizen and the flame of energy that was forever re-enacting itself in his psyche, but to the persistent influx of bitterness, verging on cynicism, that would return to possess him as he contemplated human experience. His most successful works, as a result, were those in which he wrought those contradictions into some direct-ness of statement. These could sometimes produce arrangements of frag-mentary lines that would leave future editors bemused at the task of reducing them to a single poem. One well-known example is 'Auguries of Innocence', which begins with the lines, inviting the reader to see the world in a grain of sand and a heaven in a wild flower, that were cited earlier as epitomizing permanent elements in Blake's philosophy.[45] Further lines from this poem would become famous for their direct indignation:

> A Robin Red breast in a Cage
> Puts all Heaven in a Rage

Or

> A dog starvd at his Masters Gate
> Predicts the ruin of the State

As in other cases cited earlier, the poem as a whole is full of unexpected turns, so that one couplet will only rarely fall into logical sequence with another – though many can profitably be read or quoted in isolation. The most coherent sequence is in fact the series of lines addressing doubt:

> The Emmets Inch & Eagles Mile
> Make Lame Philosophy to smile
> He who Doubts from what he sees
> Will neer Believe do what you Please
> If the Sun & Moon should Doubt
> Theyd immediately Go out

Once again these lines end in a bold assertion that takes readers far from the point where they set out and for which if there is a justification it is to be sought in the anti-rational assertion of two preceding lines:

> A Riddle or the Crickets Cry
> Is to Doubt a fit Reply

The sentiments of such lines reflect the position that he had reached as a result of the confusions of recent years. Just as Coleridge, in the same period, wrote notebook poems that followed the wavering line of his thoughts – poems that eventually found their way, truncated, into his collected works with titles such as 'Limbo' and 'Ne Plus Ultra' – so poems of the kind just examined are notable for the manner in which they refuse to be bound into a directional pattern but are left free to turn in any direction where the mind of the poet draws them. This did not mean that his poetic mind could be contentedly resigned to total anarchy, however. Blake's ultimate aim was rather to leave it free to be guided by the prophetic spirit – which might indeed prove absolute in its demands. By now, however, he had worked his way through the years of resentment sufficiently to be able to accept, with a touch of resignation, that

> Do what you will this lifes a fiction
> And is made up of Contradiction

12
A Persisting Visionary

From 1818, Blake enjoyed a time of increasing serenity. The end of the war no doubt assisted this: in previous years the struggle against Napoleon had not only offered support for the anti-Jacobin movement, but led to a strongly conservative mood in politics and art that thrust work such as Blake's into the background and covertly fuelled his resentment. Although there seems to have been no open breach, moreover, he had no longer been seeing Flaxman and Fuseli with the frequency that had marked their former acquaintance. Now, however, as art became fashionable again, there was more sympathy for innovative ideas.

His own isolation was relieved, moreover, by the advent of new friends such as John Linnell, who introduced him to a wider circle. As a result, he was increasingly influential on young painters of the time, including Samuel Palmer, Frederick Tatham, Edward Calvert and George Richmond, the group calling themselves the Ancients. Another young disciple, Francis Finch, declared that Blake struck him as '*a new kind of man*, wholly original, and in all things'.[1] He was widely respected; but except for one or two grants from benevolent funds, little assisted in his poverty.

The number of his notable new acquaintances included John Constable, who, in a memorable anecdote, showed Blake one of his sketchbooks:

> Blake ... said of a beautiful drawing of an avenue of fir trees on Hampstead Heath, 'Why, this is not drawing, but *inspiration*;' and Constable replied, 'I never knew it before; I meant it for drawing.'[2]

An interesting glimpse of Blake from the outside at this time appears in the diary of Lady Charlotte Bury, who at a dinner party given by

Lady Caroline Lamb found herself sitting between him and Sir Thomas Lawrence. She recorded her impressions of this unknown artist:

> There was another eccentric little artist, by name Blake; not a regular professional painter, but one of those persons who follow the art for its own sweet sake, and derive their happiness from its pursuit. He appeared to me full of beautiful imaginations and genius; but how far the execution of his designs is equal to the conceptions of his mental visions, I know not, never having seen them. *Main d'oeuvre* is frequently wanting where the mind is most powerful.

She was struck both by his unworldliness and by the evident distinction of his mind:

> He looks care-worn and subdued; but his countenance radiated as he spoke of his favourite pursuit, and he appeared gratified by talking to a person who comprehended his feelings. I can easily imagine that he seldom meets with any one who enters into his views; for they are peculiar, and exalted above the common level of received opinions.

She found herself struck by his lack of 'that worldly wisdom and that grace of manner which make a man gain an eminence in his profession, and succeed in society' – which her other neighbour so evidently possessed, and which she thought made the latter privately despise her for 'conversing with so insignificant a person'. Whether or not she was correct in her assumption, Sir Thomas Lawrence admired Blake's art and was shrewd enough to buy several of his works. 'The Wise and Foolish Virgins' (to be considered shortly) became his favourite.[3*]

Another particularly significant relationship was with John Varley, Linnell's teacher. Varley was a large man, large also in his pecuniary debts, which he shrugged off claiming in a manner that might have appealed to Blake, that it was necessary for him to have his troubles, since if it were not for them he would burst with joy.[4] His prolific enterprises included landscape painting and astrology – to the last of which he was particularly devoted. He was fascinated by the strength of Blake's visionary powers, which asserted themselves when he drew a series of visionary heads from various figures – historical, such as William Wallace or Wat Tyler, or more fanciful, such as 'The Man who built the Pyramids' or 'The Ghost of a Flea' – claiming in each case that they were sitting for him.

Several interesting accounts from Blake's contemporaries of this practice survive:[5] no one provided a convincing rational explanation, though some were predictably ready to set them down to simple madness. Perhaps the most interesting account was Crabb Robinson's, which came in the course of a discourse concerning the proper mode of understanding the Bible, Blake claiming that efforts to read it in a natural sense had been destroyed by Voltaire and that he had been commissioned by God to expose it:

> I have had much intercourse with Voltaire and he said to me I blasphemed the Son of Man and it shall be forgiven me But *they* (the enemies of V:) blasphemed the Holy Ghost in me and it shall not be forgiven them – I asked in what lang[e] Voltaire spoke he gave an ingenious answer – To my Sensations it was English – It was like the touch of a musical key – he touched it probably French, but to my ear it became English –[6]

Linnell commented:

> Even when John Varley to whom I had introduced Blake & who readily devoured all the marvellous in Blakes most extravagant utterances even to Varley Blake would occasionally explain unasked how he beleived that both Varley & I could see the same visions as he saw making it evident to me that Blake claimed the possession of some powers only in a greater degree that all men possessed and which they undervalued in themselves & lost through love of sordid pursuits – pride, vanity, & the unrighteous mammon[7]

Another acquaintance was rather more surprising, since the intuition that sometimes warned him against dangerous new friends evidently failed to come into play. Had it done so it would probably have lacked general credibility, since in his time Thomas Wainewright was one of the most successful men about town, notable for a light-hearted approach to life. As a contributor to the *London Magazine*, he made a memorable offer to the editor in 1826:

> Dear, respected, and respectable Editor!
> ... my exertions to procure crack-contributors have been nearly as zealously unremitting as your own. ... my learned friend Dr. Tobias Ruddicombe, M.D. is, at my earnest entreaty, casting a tremendous piece of ordnance, – *an eighty-eight pounder!* which he proposes to

fire off in your next. It is an account of an ancient, newly discovered, illuminated manuscript, which has to name 'Jerusalem the Emanation of the Giant Albion!!!' It contains a good deal anent one '*Los*', who, it appears, is now, and hath been from the creation, the *sole* and fourfold dominator of the celebrated city of *Golgonooza*! The doctor assures me that the redemption of mankind hangs on the universal diffusion of the doctrines broached in this M.S.

The promised essay never, however, appeared; Wainewright himself, on whose physiognomy Blake's gaze proved to have been much less effectively piercing than in the case of William Ryland,[8] turned out a forger and poisoner, finishing his days in Tasmania. For Blake this was all the more unfortunate since before his fall Wainewright had firmly defended his achievements, declaring the neglect of his art to be a disgrace to the country, since its pious content was a 'national example'.[9]

In 1821 Blake and his wife had moved to what was to be his final dwelling, a small apartment in Fountain Court, just off the Strand, where the Ancients took delight in visiting him. George Richmond left a vivid and detailed account of the setting:

> The fire-place was in the far right-hand corner opposite the window; their bed in the left hand, facing the river; a long engraver's table stood under the window (where I watched Blake engrave the *Book of Job*. He worked facing the light), a pile of portfolios and drawings on Blake's right near the only cupboard; and on the poet-artist's left – a pile of books placed flatly one on another; no bookcase.[10*]

Samuel Palmer, meanwhile, drew attention to the difference between Blake as seen in public, and indoors, where

> he was careful, for economy's sake, but not slovenly: his clothes were threadbare, and his grey trousers had worn black and shiny in front, like a mechanic's. Out of doors he was more particular, so that his dress did not, in the streets of London, challenge attention either way. He wore black knee breeches and buckles, black worsted stockings, shoes which tied, and a broad-brimmed hat. It was something like an old-fashioned tradesman's dress. But the general impression he made on you was that of a gentleman, in a way of his own.
>
> In person, there was much in Blake which answered to the remarkable man he was. Though low in stature, not quite five feet and a half,

and broad-shouldered, he was well made, and did not strike people as short. ... The head and face were strongly stamped with the power and character of the man. There was great volume of brain in that square, massive head, that piled up brow, very full and rounded at the temples ... His eyes were fine – 'wonderful eyes', some one calls them; prominently set, but bright, spiritual, visionary; not restless or wild, but with 'a look of clear heavenly exaltation'. The eyes of some of the old men in his *Job*, recall his own to surviving friends. His nose was insignificant as to size, but had that peculiarity which gives to a face an expression of fiery energy, as of a high-mettled steed, – a little *clenched*; nostril that opened as far as it could, but was tied down at one end.' His mouth was wide, the lips not full, but tremulous, and expressive of the great sensibility which characterized him. He was short-sighted, as the prominence of his eyes indicated. ... he wore glasses only occasionally.[11]

More than one visitor had commented on the impression of squalor that greeted them on entering earlier habitations of his: George Cumberland, for instance, wrote on 3 June 1814, 'Called Blake – still poor still Dirty' – commenting, however, that Stothard was 'still more dirty than Blake yet full of Genius'.[12] On 21 April 1815 he reported to his father,

> We call upon Blake yesterday evening found him & his wife drinking Tea durtyer than ever however he received us well ...[13]

A perhaps apocryphal anecdote by George Richmond struck a different, if slightly quizzical note: 'once Mrs Blake, in excuse for the general lack of soap and water, remarked to me: "*You see, Mr. Blake's skin don't dirt!*" '[14] When Samuel Palmer, on the other hand, met with the word 'squalor' in connection with Blake he replied indignantly that it gave a notion 'altogether false':

> whatever there was in Blake's house, there was no squalor. Himself, his wife, and his rooms were clean and orderly; everything was in its place. His delightful working corner had its implements ready – tempting to the hand.

Gilchrist, who quotes this, adds that 'nobody, to look at or listen to him in society, would have taken him for the knock-me-down assertor he was in his writings. ... In more intimate relations, again, his own goodness and sweetness of nature spoke still more eloquently.'[15]

This strong impression of 'goodness' was matched by a new wealth of references to Christianity on his part – so many, in fact, that at first sight Blake might appear to have been fully converted back to the established religion of his fellow Englishmen – all the more since many of his paintings were now devoted to biblical subjects. As mentioned earlier, he seems to have decided that for all its shortcomings Christianity, being the religion by which the forces of imagination had been most successfully nurtured, deserved his continuous support. His acceptance would be very much on his own terms, however. In his view the Bible was to be read centrally not, as was commonly the case, for its promulgation of the moral law, but for its dream-poetry and for its accounts of visionaries and prophets, some of whom had suffered for their beliefs. In its historical form Christianity was to be seen as dominated, like many religions, by priests intent on maintaining the existing order; yet it had also been founded in the life of a supreme visionary, Jesus of Nazareth, who had had little respect for either priests or conventions. Whenever the substance of his message was attended to it could, in Blake's interpretation, be said to be serving the human condition by its nourishing of the free imagination.

His feeling for the teaching of Jesus is well illustrated in a reminiscence of Samuel Palmer's, recalling how, when expounding the parable of the Prodigal Son and reaching the words 'When he was yet a great way off, his father saw him', he was completely overcome by emotion. His respect for certain religious practices is equally well shown in George Richmond's memory of finding his own invention flagging and going to Blake for advice:

> To his astonishment, Blake turned to his wife suddenly and said, 'It is so with us, is it not, for weeks together, when the visions forsake us? What do we do then, Kate? 'We kneel down and pray, Mr Blake.'[16]

The setting out of his later attitude to Christianity in 'The Everlasting Gospel' was that of a Notebook poem fragmentary in presentation, some passages being written more than once, in different formations. It is a work better to be thought of, indeed, in terms of a musical composition, themes being repeatedly newly thought and recast into different patterns. Such a mode corresponds well with the mode of *Jerusalem* and its re-weavings of particular themes to fit the varying patterns of successive plates. One particular plate in that work which stands out from the others in the mode of its lettering, suggesting composition on a separate occasion from most, presents Blake's interpretation of

Christianity particularly vividly as he pictures the female emanation Jerusalem looking into the relationship between Mary and Joseph:

> She looked & saw Joseph the Carpenter in Nazareth & Mary
> His espoused Wife. And Mary said, If thou put me away from thee
> Dost thou not murder me? Joseph spoke in anger & fury. Should I
> Marry a Harlot & an Adulteress? Mary answerd, Art thou more
>   pure
> Than thy Maker who forgiveth Sins & calls again Her that is Lost
> Tho She hates. he calls her again in love. I love my dear Joseph
> But he driveth me away from his presence. yet I hear the voice of
>   God
> In the voice of my Husband. tho he is angry for a moment, he
>   will not
> Utterly cast me away. if I were pure, never could I taste the sweets
> Of the Forgiveness of Sins! if I were holy! I never could behold the
>   tears
> Of love! of him who loves me in the midst of his anger in furnace
>   of fire.

In reply Joseph perceives, to Mary's delight, that he should instead grasp the necessity for forgiveness:

> Then Mary burst forth into a Song! she flowed like a River of
> Many Streams in the arms of Joseph & gave forth her tears of joy
> Like many waters ...

The plate concludes with a line that recalls Blake's sexual aphorism (expressed also below in the second version of 'The Gates of Paradise'): 'Every Harlot was once a Virgin: every Criminal an Infant Love'.

As one considers such passages, the infernal proclamations of *The Marriage of Heaven and Hell* can be seen as having been forerunners to a developed reading of the New Testament where, in contradistinction to the doctrines often taught in the churches, an enlightened humanity is set at the centre of things – a humanity rooted in love and forgiveness:

> Thou art a Man God is no more
> Thine own Humanity learn to adore ...[17]

In this later redaction Energy retains importance but must now be mod- ified in the light of Blake's predominating insight that what truly counts is Imagination (the quality to be identified above with Jesus) – in the light of which all moral concerns are subordinate. The overall need, he now sees, is for the practice of forgiveness.

When he is thinking of vision in *Jerusalem* and elsewhere, nevertheless, he is also dwelling on the nature of sublimity. His use of names and places from the Bible will not be undertaken to refer the reader inertly back to Christianity in its common acceptance, but to encourage a refreshed interpretation. (He may also have hoped to make his poem more readily comprehensible by using familiar names and terms, though when, as here, such names are not used with their normal connotations, they can at first sight be more, rather than less, bewildering.)

As has already been stressed, a single, coherent narrative is not to be looked for in this new mode. The indications are that various of the single plates and sequences of plates were engraved over many years and then assembled into the four symmetrically arranged chapters of the final version. There is a general overall theme, the sleep and ulti-mate awakening of the Eternal Man; there is also a special motif for each chapter, announced in the prefaces. But much else is also at work, so that readers will do best not to worry in the first instance about unusual names and terms, but to read the poem steadily with a sense of Blake's general themes and his loftiness of approach. If there is a list of English counties, with their equivalents among the tribes of Israel, this is likely to be not an attempt to make a series of detailed parallels or symbolic references, but a hint to the reader that if the poets and prophets of Israel could find splendour and sublimity in the provinces and landscapes of their own land, there is no reason why English readers should not find similar qualities in the landscapes and cities of the British Isles. The more radical ideas at work in the poem are subtly deployed, sometimes surfacing in a particular name or unusual word. Readers who choose to ignore them and read at a more general level will find much to admire, while investigation of them will sometimes increase still further their respect for Blake's intelligence and imagina-tive power.

Looking at the high visionary intent of the later poetry, we may well ask what had happened to the more satirical and dramatizing Blake of earlier years. There are touches of wit, and some good dramatic moments, in *Jerusalem*, but the work as a whole is not pitched to an audience that would have had such qualities prominently among its concerns. Blake's shift from the powerful antinomianism of *The Marriage of Heaven and Hell* had initiated a new radical practice of his own, offer-ing suggestions of illumination and inspiration that his readers were invited to follow for what they would reveal:

> I give you the end of a golden string,
> Only wind it into a ball,
> It will lead you in at Heaven's gate,
> Built in Jerusalem's wall[18]

It was perhaps a sign of his stubborn truculence that during these years he also decided to reissue the set of designs entitled 'The Gates of Paradise'. Now he would no longer address his audience as children, with admonitions concerning the life that awaited them under the law and the preferable pleasure of transcending it, but as adults – using the fruits of his later thinking to reinforce his doctrine of forgiveness: his motto now was

> Mutual forgiveness of each Vice
> Such are the Gates of Paradise

In presenting the collection afresh, he introduced a verse passage supplementing the brief epigraphs on each page into a résumé of his mythological account of humanity, which reworked the account of Adam and Eve in Eden. According to this, each individual looks back to the lost eternal Man within, who has set in 'the darkness of his repose'. In the course of this lapse the Female has taken over and enticed the human being (in line with the Book of Genesis) with 'Serpent Reasonings' that have misled it concerning matters such as Good and Evil. This has nothing to do with the gender of such individuals, however; *that* is given them at birth – after which all in either sex must suffer the human experiences represented in the visual designs regardless of their gender: killing the winged delights of joy instead of delighting in them – until even parricide counts for nothing – nursing impossible desires as if trying to build a ladder to the moon, drowning in the depths of human ignorance and cutting the wings of others till they have lost the power of joy involved in being able to perceive the infinite in all things. This in turn induces human beings to tolerate the imposition of imprisonment – including religious incarceration. The only hope in such a situation is furnished by experiences such as Blake's claim to have seen his brother rising at the moment of death. Given such assurance of immortality, the despairing human being can accept the fact of death and even greet unabashed the prospect of being consumed in the grave by worms, who now lose their horror to become emblematic of a whole process by which human beings adorn themselves with the emotions expressed in their human garments (made in some cases by the industry of silkworms) rather than allowing themselves to be eaten alive by destructive passions that turn into the deathly constrictiveness of winding sheets.

In working towards this final, longer version he begins with a statement that looks back to work of some years before. Night the Eighth of Edward Young's *Night Thoughts* ends with the assertion to Lorenzo, the young worldling who is being addressed, that 'Thy wisdom all can do, but – make thee wise', followed by the (somewhat limited) reassurance:

> Nor think this censure is severe on thee;
> Satan, thy master, I dare call a dunce.

Taking it for granted, perhaps, that his reader would be steeped in Young, Blake began his Epilogue:

> Truly my Satan thou art but a Dunce
> And dost not know the Garment from the Man
> Every Harlot was a Virgin once
> Nor canst thou ever change Kate into Nan

(Blake's illustration to Young's page shows a Satan figure bowing down before Jesus with a stone and a loaf of bread – suggesting presumably that his biblical demand for the one to be changed into the other expressed his inability to appreciate the essential difference between what is living and what is dead.[19]) The last two lines of the stanza resemble the line from *Jerusalem*: 'Every Harlot was once a Virgin, every Criminal an Infant Love'.

Even presented as a message for adults, *The Gates of Paradise* can hardly have had many comprehending readers. Cast, as is Blake's frequent custom, in a series of riddles, it depends on acceptance of his convictions (or at the very least an understanding and empathetic view of them) for its effect to be achieved. Without that, he must remain an essentially solitary artist, determinedly believing in his own visionary experiences but unable to expect widespread communication at any level beyond simple admiration of his artistic prowess – an admiration which was, in any case, by no means universal in his time.

His various concerns, religious, intellectual and poetic, came together more directly and availably in the series of verses in his notebook which were later collected under the title 'The Everlasting Gospel'. In this he was able to justify his long stand against the dominant philosophy of the day by disowning ideas such as the assertion that Christians ought to cultivate humility, and invoking instead a model of Jesus as one whom he regarded as having known how to exercise both pride and humility in a proper balance.

> I was standing by when Jesus died;
> What I call'd Humility, they call'd Pride

As he pursued this point he was able to draw on the sense of paradox that he had come to see as endemic in human affairs, showing how it could interpret the Gospel also. In his later lines for *The Gates of Paradise* he had dwelt on the condition of human beings who tried to make sense of the world through reason:

> Two-horn'd Reasoning, cloven fiction,
> In doubt, which is self-contradiction,
> A dark Hermaphrodite we stood –
> Rational truth, root of evil and good.

By this time he had become confirmed in his belief that the moralizing lore of good and evil by which human beings were taught to live was essentially mistaken. To quote his words again,

> Do what you will, this Life's a Fiction
> And is made up of Contradiction.

Once one accepted that this sense of contradiction was the end to which all reasonings must come, the way lay open for a fuller exploration of the senses of paradox, which was the best guide to the Gospel. Above all, in his eyes, it was necessary to recognize that Jesus had been all too ready to subvert moral rules. The assertion had already been made by the Devil in *The Marriage of Heaven and Hell*:

> ... if Jesus Christ is the greatest man, you ought to love him in the greatest degree; now hear how he has given his sanction to the law of ten commandments: did he not mock at the sabbath, and so mock the sabbaths God? murder those who were murderd because of him? turn away the law from the woman taken in adultery? steal

the labor of others to support him? bear false witness when he omitted making a defence before Pilate? covet when he pray'd for his disciples, and when he bid them shake off the dust of their feet against such as refused to lodge them? I tell you, no virtue can exist without breaking these ten commandments: Jesus was all virtue, and acted from impulse: not from rules.

Now, in 'The Everlasting Gospel', the point is repeated slightly less aggressively but no less pointedly, in a series of questions about the behaviour of Jesus:

> Was Jesus Chaste or did he
> Give any Lessons of Chastity
> The morning blushd fiery red:
> Mary was found in Adulterous bed;
> Earth groand beneath & Heaven above
> Trembled at discovery of Love
> Jesus was sitting in Moses Chair,
> They brought the trembling Woman There
> Moses commands she be stoned to death,
> What was the sound of Jesus' breath
> He laid his hand on Moses Law
> The Ancient Heavens in Silent Awe
> Writ with Curses from Pole to Pole
> All away began to roll ...
>
> And she heard the breath of God
> As she heard by Edens flood:
> Good & Evil are no more
> Sinais trumpets, cease to roar!
> Cease, finger of God to write!
> The heavens are not clean in thy Sight.

The Jesus revealed in this poem is someone who does not adhere slavishly to the law but who interprets experience in a more humane manner, understanding that the adulterous woman has at least the virtue of living by love. Other passages show him failing to fulfil any suggestions that he showed humility – or even gentility – so far as relations with his fellows were concerned.

Stress is also laid now on his refusal to be a thinker after the order of figures fashionable in Blake's time. To have been so would have been akin to bowing down before Caesar: It would have been to deny the very knowledge by which he lived:

> He had soon been bloody Caesar's Elf
> And at last he would have been Caesar himself
> Like dr. Priestly & Bacon & Newton-
> Poor Spiritual Knowledge is not worth a button

The invitation extended by Jesus in the poem is for a restoration of the 'spiritual knowledge' slighted by Priestley, Bacon and Newton, which will restore to man his proper dignity in recognition of the divine element they contain:

> If thou humblest thyself, thou humblest me
> Thou also dwellst in Eternity
> Thou art a Man God is no more
> Thy own humanity learn to adore
> For that is my Spirit of Life

In the end, that is, the truth is to be sought in paradox – the paradox by which Blake recognizes the difference between his own vision and that by which the rest of the world seems to be guided:

> The Vision of Christ that thou dost see
> Is my Visions Greatest Enemy
> Thine has a great hook nose like thine
> Mine has a snub nose like to mine[20]*
> Thine is the Friend of All Mankind
> Mine speaks in parables to the Blind ...

It is a final forsaking of the bland Jesus created in the image of eighteenth-century benevolence, in favour of the uncompromising visionary whom he feels he can understand and with whom he instinctively allies himself – though recognizing, a shade more tolerantly, perhaps, by now, that even while he must always stand firmly by his own vision of things disagreements will still be regarded by others as a matter of alternative interpretation and that this must be accepted:

> Both read the Bible day & night
> But thou readst black where I read white

The existence of such alternative interpretations means, however, that it is sometimes difficult to trace a self-consistent attitude in Blake himself.

Morton Paley, who has conducted a searching examination of this text, has drawn attention to the difficulty of reconciling all the statements with each other and with those in other works. This is equally true of a work that he did etch and publish: *The Ghost of Abel*. This late work may have taken some colouring from his visits to the theatre, which he attended from time to time with John Linnell in the early 1820s; it also evidently owed much to the book very popular in earlier years, Salomon Gessner's *The Death of Abel*. But the immediate stimulus for its writing, as he himself made clear in the text, was the appearance of Byron's *Cain* in 1821, and his recognition that Byron was revealing himself there as a fellow-prophet. Blake's view of the divinity had developed over the years, so that he no longer called the God of the Old Testament simply Jehovah, but as far as the creation of the natural world was concerned preferred the name 'Elohim'. Exactly how the two were discriminated is not clear, but it is evident from *The Ghost of Abel* that the Ghost there belongs to the Elohim. When Crabb Robinson retorted to Blake that the Bible was the work of God, and that the statement that God had created the Heaven and the Earth could be found there, 'I gained nothing by this for I was triumphantly told that this God was not Jehovah but the Elohim.'[21] Robinson felt that he was not sufficiently familiar with the Gnostic doctrine involved to continue arguing, but the anecdote suggests that Blake was responding to the fact that the Hebrew name for God in Genesis was Elohim, and employing this fact for his own purposes in pressing his case against regarding Nature as a divinity, so that when the ghost of Abel urges that the earth should not cover his blood, but that it should be avenged, he is revealing his falseness and his allegiance to the Elohim; Adam and Eve, meanwhile, prove the superiority of their faith by rejecting this false ghost, opting instead for the 'spiritual vision' which reveals to them the 'Form Divine, Father of Mercies', in which vision Abel is not dead. The ghost of Abel, continuing to call for his blood not to be covered, turns into Satan, rising in a warlike shape corresponding to the figure of Fire in 'The Gates of Paradise', but is superseded by a figure entitled 'Elohim Jehovah' who proclaims the forgiveness of sins, once again establishing this king-pin of Blake's final message. As Paley points out, this acceptance of atonement seems to contradict Blake's rejection of that doctrine elsewhere, though Blake might have replied that the kind of atonement he was against was that which required human sacrifice, even if it was that of the Son himself – true redemption, he could have claimed, was to be found not in the Son's sacrifice of himself on the cross but in his words of forgiveness there.

19 'The Wise and Foolish Virgins', Fitzwilliam Museum, Cambridge

Blake's interpretation of the Bible, explicit in such texts, was also to be implicit in some of his designs of the time. The need to cultivate vision, increasingly his theme, was responsible for some of his finest conceptions, as in the painting 'The Wise and Foolish Virgins' (Figure 19), where the oil which the latter have neglected to have ready for the bridegroom's coming is interpreted in precisely this way, the energies of the foolish virgins, beautiful as they themselves are, being seen as thrown into confusion by the sounding of the angel's trumpet above their heads, with indications that they have become too attached to the non-visionary aspects of the world. Their visionary counterparts, by contrast, hold their lighted lamps confidently and expectantly.

A more intricate example of this symbolism is to be found in the painting discovered a few years ago at Arlington Court in Devon which has sometimes been called 'The Sea of Time and Space', but which I identified some years ago as a design to illustrate the final chapters of the Book of Revelation. Once interpreted in terms of the motifs of Vision and of Energy as in the present discussion, it turns out to fit surprising closely with the text 'The Spirit and the Bride say Come', with its accompanying invitation to drink of the waters of life freely and other verses at that point.[22*] The design consists on one side of a seascape to the left which evidently corresponds to the mortal world, and over which a male figure in red stretches out his hands, while behind him a beautiful female figure, recalling representations of Blake's 'Jerusalem', points upward with her left hand to a scene of visionary potentiality above and downward with her right (admonishingly?) to what is shown below. On the other side of the design is a more paradisal scene, in which spirits pass and re-pass one another bearing shuttles aloft (reminiscent of the Wise Virgins with their lamps at their side) on a slope leading up to a level where further figures stand, gazing out at what is presented on and above the sea. In the foreground a woman, marked as a denizen of the natural world by the scales on her dress and on her pail, presents herself at the entrance to the paradisal scene, to be greeted by a woman who is presumably greeting and interrogating her. Bearing a pail which is covered with mortal scales she is showing herself to be in the same condition as one of the Foolish Virgins in Blake's design, which suggests that, like them, she lacks the necessary credentials for acceptance.

The male figures in the left-hand part of the design, behind her and in the roots of the tree, can be seen as figures caught up in misuse of human energies, the readiness of one to cut the thread of life suggesting murder, while the action of another in grasping a 'huge phallic coil of

20 The Arlington Court picture: 'The Spirit and the Bride say "Come"', Courtesy of the National Trust

rope shaped like a distaff'[23] indicates, equally, sexual vice. These and the others can thus be equated, respectively, with the 'dogs, and sorcerers, and whoremongers, and murderers, and idolaters, and whosoever loveth and maketh a lie' who in this passage from Revelation are explicitly excluded from the tree of life and the gates of the city. A female figure who appears on the sea beyond to the left with four horses plunging side by side would appear to represent the revelation of natural beauty in the physical world, since a wreath of cloud connects her to a scene above – hidden from all the other figures below, apart from the beautiful woman, who is pointing to it – where a visionary chariot is revealed, with four horses harnessed to it being restrained and groomed by women: in this the charioteer, surrounded by an aureole of glory, lies asleep. These conjoined scenes can be read as Blake's rendering of the major supporting sentences in Revelation XXI: 'I Jesus have sent mine angel to testify unto you these things in the churches' (the revelation on the waters) and 'I am the root and offspring of David, and the bright and morning star' (the sleeping charioteer).

The scene as a whole, on this interpretation, should be seen as one of immanent, ever-impending, apocalypse. Once the charioteer awakens, the whole universe will be transformed into the visionary state that at present is glimpsed only by passing through the fires of energy to reach the paradisal state of the right-hand figures. For the moment, the key to that vision can only be the combined activities of the prophetic Spirit of Man, working away at the creation of beautiful forms, and what is revealed by his Emanation, the bride Jerusalem. In this beautiful cameo Blake has encapsulated the essence of his artistic vision, rendering the philosophy of a human life that makes sense only when seen in terms of impending glory: hidden from it during the time of mortal life but – for Blake – the true reality. That is for him what is meant by Revelation.

So powerful had his sense of the importance of Vision become that in these years Blake could still be mercilessly satirical and teasing when in the company of devotees of rationalism – a fact which should give one pause before labelling any of his reported statements too readily as 'mad' – but he was equally noted for his kindness and consideration to the young. Although the writing of further poetry was spasmodic, he occupied himself with further illustrations, including the well-known *Job* designs. In these he was able to draw once again on his own idiosyncratic reading of the Bible to present Job not simply as the 'perfect and upright' figure of the Old Testament whom God allowed Satan to try through a series of personal disasters, but as a man who was himself already in danger through his failure to cultivate Vision. Accordingly, he was shown initially in a state of prosperity but against a setting sun and under a tree on which hung neglected musical instruments, while in the foreground could be seen somnolent sheep and a dog and in the background a Gothic church. Job and his wife had books on their laps, while the central inscription beneath read 'The Letter Killeth the Spirit giveth Life It is Spiritually Discerned'.[24*] In later illustrations the Gothic church disappeared, to be replaced by stone trilitha, which in turn became largely ruins. In these subsequent plates Job is presented under a God who resembles himself, so that the whole design resembles a psychomachia of his own state in which he must recover his spiritual self through his own sustained vision. In the final plate the sun is now rising. Job sits under the same tree, but with the instruments no longer hanging unused; instead, they have been taken down and are being played by his family (serpentine coils being prominent), while sheep and dog are fully awake. There is now no religious building of any kind – presumably because there is no need. Instead of the family's previous reliance on books a daughter sings from a light scroll.

Blake's final work was a series of watercolours to illustrate Dante's *Divine Comedy*. These were intended in due course, as with *Job*, to be etched in addition, but in this case only a few of the finished works were made. To see these is to appreciate (not for the first time) a point that needs to be stressed in dealing with Blake's visual art. It is common to look at the fact that he worked for the whole of his life as an engraver and to find in this the key to his visual art – his love of strong outlines and dislike of oil painting, for instance. Yet it should not be forgotten that a large number of his designs were executed not with a graver but with pen or pencil – to be followed by watercolour perhaps, and only then engraved. In point of fact, some of his most interesting effects can be discovered by comparing the first rendering with the finished engraving. Pencil and watercolour can be the best vehicle for a first visionary effect, while the act of engraving gives him a fuller scope for expression of his energy. The viewer who empathizes with what he is doing is likely to be caught in similar stages of imaginative delight and respect for Blake's immediacy of vision and his reliance on the force of line to express it; the illustrations to Dante afford an unusual number of instances of his dual nature as stubborn human and radiant visionary.

They also display once again the complexity of his views. At first sight they may seem as if they embody a total submission to Dante's view of the world, but detailed examination of the individual designs reveals that this was not so. In 1825, indeed, talking to Henry Crabb

Robinson, he went so far as to insist that Dante was an atheist:

> ' – a mere politician busied ab^t this world as Milton was till in his old
> age he returned back to God whom he had had in his childhood – '
> I tried to get out from B: that he meant this charge only in a higher
> sense. And not using the word Atheism in its popular meaning But he
> would not allow this –[25]

Whatever Blake intended by this charge, he clearly did not think of
Dante as an orthodox figure. Nor was Beatrice, in turn, presented as
an ideal spiritual woman but as a human figure like himself: when she
participates in the design showing 'The Queen of Heaven in her Glory'
the supreme position is occupied by the Virgin Mary, clad in a thin
transparent garment, holding a fleur-de-lys sceptre in one hand and a
looking glass in the other – evidently a devotee of the goddess Nature.
One or two of the inscriptions accompanying his designs for other
plates illustrate the point, as when he writes:

> Every thing in Dantes Comedia shows that for Tyrannical Purposes
> he has made This World the Foundation of All & the Goddess Nature &
> not the Holy Ghost as Poor Churchill said Nature thou art my
> Goddess ...
>   The Goddess Nature <Memory> <is his Inspirer> & not
> Imagination the Holy Ghost.[26]

As he proceeded, his annotations showed the degree to which his forth-
rightness had survived, as when a design illustrating 'The Goddess
Fortune' was inscribed:

> The hole of a Shit-house

followed by the words:

> The Goddess Fortune is the devil's servant, ready to Kiss any one's Arse.[27]

Despite his reservations about Dante's religious and human attitudes,
however, the designs he produced to illustrate his poetry were some of
the most beautiful he ever made. And in spite of their visionary nature
the man who designed them was still also, as his inscriptions show, the
energetic and radical critic. In his last year, while he was still working on
Dante, he annotated a recently published volume, Dr Thornton's

The Lord's Prayer, Newly Translated. His comments show that he was scornful of its pretensions, regarding it as a 'Tory Translation' and set out what he saw as its real sense – 'Father' really meaning 'Our Father Augustus Caesar', 'daily bread' 'our Taxed Bread', and the purport of the whole being 'lead us not to read the Bible but let our Bible be Virgil & Shakespeare'. The unexpected inclusion of Shakespeare suggests that for the time being at least he was impressed by the warlike quality of some of the plays. The God whom the prayers of people like Thornton addressed, was, he felt, 'the Goddess Nature', who 'Creates nothing but what can be Touchd & weighed & Taxed & Measured'.[28]

If all this seems at times self-contradictory it may correspond to a feature already noted in the man himself: Morton Paley draws attention to a reported remark of his to the Swedenborgian C. A. Tulk, whom he told that he had 'two different states, one in which he liked Swedenborg's writings and one in which he disliked them', the second being 'a state of pride in himself', while the first was 'a state of humility, in which he received and accepted Swedenborg'.[29] How far this report, not published until sixty years after Blake's death, gives an accurate account of his attitudes is by no means clear, but the acknowledgement of alternating attitudes rings true of the man whose statements set up so many puzzles for a reader seeking consistency.

When, after more than a decade, Henry Crabb Robinson, who provided valuable addition to knowledge of his later views not only on Dante but on many subjects, actually met the subject of his 1811 article, he recorded a number of his more enigmatic statements. One of the most extended of their several conversations took place on 10 December 1825, when he began by describing his appearance:

> He is now old – pale with a Socratic countenance and an expression of great sweetness but bordering on weakness – except when his features are animated by expression And then he has an air of inspiration about him ...

Robinson interrogated him on one particular feature of his discourse:

> ... he said – repeatedly the 'Spirit told me' –
> I took occasion to say – 'You use the same word as Socrates used – What resemblance do you suppose is there between your Spirit & the Spirit of Socrates?'
> 'The same as between our countenances – '
> He paused & added – 'I was Socrates.'

And then as if correcting himself 'A sort of brother – I must have had conversations with him – So I had with Jesus Christ – I have an obscure recollection of having been with both of them –'

It was before this, that I had suggested on very obvious philosophical grounds the impossibility of supposing an immortal being created – An eternity a parte post – with^t an eternity a parte ante – ...

His eye brightened on my saying this And he eagerly concurred – To be sure it is impossible – We are all coexistent with God – Members of the Divine body – We are all partakers of the divine nature –

... on my asking in what light he viewed the great question concerning the Divinity of Jesus Christ He said – He is the only God – But then he added – And so am I and so are you –[30]

His views on art tended to be more straightforward. Palmer, another friend, wrote to Gilchrist about some of them:

Among spurious old pictures, he had met with many 'Claudes,' but spoke of a few which he had seen really untouched and unscrubbed, with the greatest delight; and mentioned, as a peculiar charm, that in these, when minutely examined, there were, upon the focal lights of the foliage, small specks of pure white which made them appear to be glittering with dew which the morning sun had not yet dried up. ... His description of these genuine Claudes, I shall never forget. He warmed with his subject, and it continued through an evening walk. The sun was set; but Blake's Claudes made sunshine in that shady place.[31]

In view of the remarks made earlier concerning the strength of his feeling for 'outline', his comment on Dürer was even more revealing:

... he remarked that his most finished woodcuts, when closely examined 'seemed to consist principally of outline; that they were "everything, and yet nothing"...'

In addition, Palmer wrote to Gilchrist about a visit in May 1824 to the Royal Academy, with 'Blake in his plain black suit and rather broad-rimmed, but not quakerish hat, standing so quietly among all the dressed-up, rustling, swelling people, and myself thinking "How little you know who is among you!" '[32] This reminiscence may be set in contiguity with one a few months later describing how he found Blake at work on his Dante drawings: 'He said he began them with fear and trembling. I said "O! I have enough of fear and trembling.' " "Then," said he, "you'll do." '[33]

Whether he was opening himself to the beauties of the world about him or working in the realm of energy that stretched from his states of fear and trembling to those of ecstatic freedom, Blake retained his sturdy independence to the last. One of his final letters showed him facing death with equanimity and with a sense that he was about to be released at last from the body's cage. The images of the prison that haunted his early work may gradually have been exorcised, but Blake still looks forward to death for a final release:

> Flaxman is Gone & we must All soon follow, every one to his Own Eternal House Leaving the Delusive Goddess Nature & her Laws to get into Freedom from all Law of the Members into The Mind in which every one is King & Priest in his own House   God send it so on Earth as it is in Heaven.[34]

Earlier in the letter he inveighs against his fellow countrymen who, since the French Revolution, he says,

> are all Intermeasurable by One Another Certainly a happy state of Agreement to which I for One do not Agree. God keep me from the Divinity of Yes & No too The Yea Nay Creeping Jesus from supposing Up & Down to be the same Thing as all Experimentalists must suppose.

The alternation between vision and vehemence that could be displayed in these alternating modes of his artistic work remained also a feature of his human relationships: among other things, it can be discerned from the memories of people who met him at this time. One, a lady, was taken to him as a young girl:

> He looked at her very kindly for a long while without speaking, and then stroking her head and long ringlets said 'May God make this world to you, my child, as beautiful as it has been to me.' She thought it strange at the time, she said, that such a poor old man, dressed in such shabby clothes, could imagine the world had ever been so beautiful to him as it must be to her, nursed in all the elegancies and luxury of wealth; but in after years she understood well enough what he meant ...[35]

During these years he would also call on some of his disciples at their houses in the environs of London. In September 1825, for instance, there was a visit to Samuel Palmer's house at Shoreham in Kent, which included a visit to a nearby haunted house where the one apparently paranormal event turned out to be after all simply a snail moving up the window. On the following evening, however, Blake gave what seemed an interesting demonstration of such powers on his part when he declared that Palmer, whom they had seen off on the London coach, was walking up the road to the house. Shortly after Palmer came through the wicket gate, the coach having broken down on its way.

The next month he was visiting the Linnells in their Hampstead cottage, as he did regularly on Sundays during this period. Mrs Linnell has left a warm appreciation of how his presence particularly delighted the children, who could look for him as he came over the hill and made his private signal to them. He startled her on one occasion by responding to her mild opinion that Hampstead was a healthy place with the asseveration: 'It is a lie! It is no such thing!' but he modified his opinion in 1826 by conceding that this did not apply in the morning:

> I am again laid up by a cold in my stomach   the Hampstead Air as it always did. so I fear it always will do this Except it be the Morning Air & That; in my Cousins time I found I could bear with safety & perhaps benefit. I believe my Constitution to be a good one but it has many peculiarities that no one but myself can know. When I was young Hampstead Highgate Hornsea Muswell Hill & even Islington & all places North of London always laid me up the day after & sometimes two or three days with precisely the same Complaint & the same torment of the Stomach. Easily removed but excruciating while it lasts & enfeebling for some time after.[36]

Accounts of his ills became more frequent in the months following, as he drew towards death;[37*] meanwhile, the ambiguities that have been explored in these pages showed themselves again, sometimes vividly. Was his religion closer to that of the dissenting tradition or to that of the Anglican Church into which he had been baptized? It might perhaps be true to say that the vehement and rebellious side of his nature allied him naturally with the religious dissenters but that his literary sense (and possibly some residual Anglicanism) made the Book of Common Prayer more congenial, at least so far as the words of its liturgy were concerned That is the conclusion to be drawn from his response to a request concerning his own funeral arrangements:

> Some short time before his death, Mrs. Blake asked him where he
> should like to be buried, and whether he would have the Dissenting
> Minister, or the Clergyman of the Church of England, to read the
> service: his answers were, that as far as his own feelings were
> concerned they might bury him where she pleased, adding, that as
> his father, mother, aunt, and brother, were buried in Bunhill-row,
> perhaps it would be better to lie there, but as to service, he should
> wish for that of the Church of England.

According to Tatham's account of this final period,

> He thought he was better, and as he was sure to do, asked to look at
> the Work over which he was occupied when seized with his last
> attack: it was a coloured print of the Ancient of Days, striking the first
> circle of the Earth, done expressly by commission for the writer of
> this. After he had worked upon it he exclaimed 'There I have done all
> I can it is the best I have ever finished I hope Mr Tatham will like it.
> He threw it suddenly down & said Kate you have been a good Wife, I
> will draw your portrait. She sat near his Bed & he made a Drawing,
> which though not a likeness is finely touched & expressed. He then
> threw that down, after having drawn for an hour & began to sing
> Hallelujahs & songs of joy & Triumph which Mrs Blake described as
> being truly sublime in music & in Verse ... After having answered a
> few questions concerning his Wifes means of living after his decease,
> & after having spoken of the writer of this, as a likely person to
> become the manager of her affairs, his spirit departed like the sighing
> of a gentle breeze, & he slept in company with the mighty ancestors
> he had formerly depicted. He passed from Death to an Immortal life
> on the 12th of August 1827 being in his 69th Year. Such was the
> Entertainment of the last hour of his life His bursts of gladness made
> the room peal again. The Walls rang & resounded with the beatific
> Symphony. It was a prelude to the Hymns of Saints. It was an
> overture to the Choir of Heaven. It was a chaunt for the response of
> Angels.[38]

Reading such accounts we recognize once again the depth to which *The
Pilgrim's Progress* had penetrated the English consciousness. In general,
the profundity of Bunyan's influence had been of a kind that was not
readily expressed in direct verbal debts. Yet as soon as one thinks of

Bunyan's Giant Despair and the Doubting Castle into which he threw his victims the parallel with Blake's attitude to Despair or Doubt is striking. His ability to run together biblical text and literary allusion, equally, had been at its most evident in his adoption of Bunyan's 'Beulah' for one of his blessed states.[39] Meanwhile, the allegory of his predecessor could sometimes come effortlessly to mind, as when, in writing to Hayley questioning the wisdom of employing both Flaxman and himself, on the grounds that it would be 'like putting John Milton with John Bunyan', he continued, commenting on his own newly regained unity of mind, 'I shall travel on in the Strength of the Lord God as Poor Pilgrim says'[40] – recalling the exact words of Christian's assertion in the Valley of the Shadow of Death. A short while after, Bunyan's language was renewed in him as he mourned the death of his advocate Samuel Rose: 'Farewell Sweet Rose thou hast got before me into the Celestial City. I also have but a few more Mountains to pass. for I hear the bells ring & the trumpets sound to welcome thy arrival among Cowpers Glorified Band of Spirits of just Men made Perfect.'[41] George Richmond's account of his death many years later (presumably also derived from Mrs Blake) was cast in a similar vein:

> He said he was going to that Country he had all his life wished to see & expressed Himself Happy hoping for Salvation through Jesus Christ – Just before he died His Countenance became fair – His eyes brighten'd and he burst out in Singing of the things he Saw in Heaven ...[42]

When, in *The Pilgrim's Progress*, the pilgrims reached the Celestial Country 'their ears' were 'filled with heavenly voices'; Mr Despondency's daughter 'went through the river singing, but no one could understand what she said'; on Mr Standfast's knowing that he had been sent for, 'his countenance changed'. To recall such phrases is to be reminded yet again of visionary themes that the two writers shared.

Yet the source of his deepest engagement was always with Milton. The assertion of his resemblance to Dante, quoted earlier,[43] suggests that he regarded him, also, as having become too much bound up with politics in his middle life for his own spiritual good; comments throughout his career suggest, however, that he never gave up regarding Milton's poetic achievements as those against which his own must be measured.

In the heady days of the early 1790s it had been possible to enlist Milton on the side of poetic genius to the extent of ascribing to him a true vision of things which he had not been able properly to understand through his submission to the promptings of Urizen:

> Those who restrain desire, do so because theirs is weak enough to be restrained; and the restrainer or reason usurps its place & governs the unwilling.
> And being restraind it by degrees becomes passive till it is only the shadow of desire.
> The history of this is written in Paradise Lost. & the Governor or Reason is call'd Messiah.
> And the original Archangel or possessor of the command of the heavenly host, is calld the Devil or Satan and his children are call'd Sin & Death

This account was filled out further a few lines later by another well-known assertion:

> … in Milton; the Father is Destiny, the Son, a Ratio of the five senses. & the Holy-ghost, Vacuum!
> Note. The reason Milton wrote in fetters when he wrote of Angels & God, and at liberty when of Devils & Hell, is because he was a true Poet and of the Devils party without knowing it

As the years passed and the revolutionary dream faded, however, he came to accept a view of his predecessor that was more traditional. His belief in poetic inspiration did not flag, but energy was now seen to be an ambiguous endowment, so that, as we have seen above, the Milton behind the poem of his name was notable not for his devotion, conscious or otherwise, to the Supreme Power, but a figure who would inspire his successors as much by his example of self-giving. It is a Milton whom Wordsworth would no doubt have found highly acceptable.

The Milton he could respond to most readily, nevertheless, was the poet of the early poems, whose visionary aspirations seemed most closely to mirror his own. In subsequent years, therefore, this visionary element became the subject of several series of designs, among which the most notable instances in terms of the use of symbolism were those for the poem 'Il Penseroso'. Here the apparent aim was to illustrate the various kinds of vision that had haunted Milton during his career, with the young poet entranced by the moon and then drawn to a reading of Plato, whose spirit reveals to him the nature of human destiny, while as an old man he sits in a hermit's cell contemplating the heavens, where his cultivation of the Zodiac causes everything in the heavens to be viewed in humanized form, and studying herbs and flowers in a manner that again, as in the *Milton* passage,[44] emphasizes their human and visionary relevance.

With his attempts to contact famous people of the past, further detailed comments on Milton could be made, such as the ones to Crabb Robinson in 1825:

> I saw Milton in Imagination And he told me to beware of being misled by his Paradise Lost In particular he wished me to shew the falsehood of his doctrine that the pleasures of sex arose from the fall – The fall could not produce any pleasure I answerd the fall produced a state of evil in which there was a mixture of good or pleasure ... But he replied that the fall produced only generation & death[45]

There is a reminiscence behind this, perhaps, of the poet as he appeared in the poem of his own name when he

> Descended down a Paved work of all kinds of precious stones
> Out from the eastern sky: descending down into my Cottage
> Garden: clothed in black, severe & silent he descended.[46]

In other words, Milton needed to be redeemed from the severer aspects of his Puritanism and to recover the sense of sensuous pleasure that need not be forbidden by its exercise. In this attempt to restore the delights of a puritan art, Blake was once more tuning his back on a version that was little more than nay-saying and looking forward to the robust sexual affirmations of a future puritan such as D. H. Lawrence.

It was for such reasons that he would become iconic for writers to come in the twentieth century and beyond, as he straddled the divide between the rule-bound writing of the previous century and a liberated art of the future – even if that might in turn threaten to become anarchical. As he sat on this perilous perch between the old and new he was in fact creating a legacy that future writers and artists would draw on with pleasure.

21   Head of Blake as the Plowman: detail from 'Chaucer's Canterbury Pilgrims',
Yale Center for British Art, Paul Mellon Collection

22   'The Traveller hasteth in the Evening' From *The Gates of Paradise*

13
Prophetic Afterlife

Exploring the life of Blake leaves the biographer with unanswered questions – more than in the case of most writers. As with Shakespeare, the surviving evidence is sparse and patchy. Were many further designs and illustrations (including, perhaps, more erotic drawings than have survived) among those supposedly destroyed by Tatham after he became a zealous follower of Irving and was persuaded by some of his coreligionists that he had been 'inspired – but by the devil'?[1*] And did such a holocaust include other writing, some of which might have thrown more light on his thought and mythologizing?

Equally important is the exiguousness of the records of his conversation. Had it not been for the pertinacity of Henry Crabb Robinson, indeed, we would know still less. Even Robinson's detailed record was not made until the end of Blake's life, however, and so it is not clear how representative it was. If we had fuller reports from his whole life, would we be faced with an inexhaustible series of brilliant insights, or would we rather echo Robinson's occasional complaints at repetition? Might we, indeed, be made impatient by increasing awareness of self-contradictions? The only hint we have is provided by Robinson's own comment that on some occasions he thought that record-keeping would be pointless because of repetition. On 10 December he set down a most extensive and interesting record of what he had heard; on the 17th he called again, but this time was afraid that he would make no progress in 'ascertaining his opinions & feelings', the reason being the lack of 'system or connection in his mind'. By the 24th he was somewhat apprehensive concerning 'the same half crazy crotchet abo^t the two worlds – the eternal repetition of which must in time become tiresome' and on 6 January he noted that he felt it hardly worthwhile to write down the conversation since it was 'so much a repetition of his former talk'; on 18 February, again, he found himself listening to 'the same round of extravag^t & mad doctrines'; he was evidently at one and the same time both impatient and fascinated. It is evident that his prosaic and systematizing mind found it hard to know what to make of such a man – who in June he found 'as wild as ever with no great novelty', and who shocked him with his assertion that wives should be held in common. In the end it was hard for him to get past the judgment of him that he had expressed as early as 1811:

> ... a man in whom all the elements of greatness are unquestionably to be found, even though those elements are disproportionately mingled.[2]

How that disproportion is to be assessed is of course the question that must preoccupy any student of the man. The lack of a single stable identity is paradoxically balanced by the sense of a consistent personality shining through the whole, with the sense of a strong visionary capacity dominating both.

Even more valuable, perhaps, is the testimony of those who were themselves Romantic writers. Wordsworth, for instance, considered Blake to have the elements of poetry 'a thousand times more than either Byron or Scott';[3] he also copied out poems by Blake from Malkin's account,[4] and 'read and read again' the *Songs of Innocence*,[5] commenting, 'There is no doubt this poor man was mad, but there is something in the madness of this man that interests me more than the Sanity of Lord Byron and Sir Walter Scott.'[6] Blake in turn was equally fascinated by a man whose Immortality Ode expressed so many of his own thoughts, yet who seemed so totally given over to the worship of Nature. One effect was that he expressed his puzzled admiration to Crabb Robinson, who in turn corresponded with Dorothy Wordsworth; had ill health not intervened, a new chapter of intercourse might have opened between all three.

Coleridge, meanwhile, was already captivated, describing Blake as 'a man of Genius – and I apprehend, a Swedenborgian – certainly, a mystic emphatically ... . I am in the very mire of common-place common-sense compared with Mr Blake, apo- or rather ana-calyptic Poet and Painter!'[7] This was in 1818, when Tulk had just lent him a copy of the *Songs*; a week later he provided him with a full range of comments, graded from those that gave him pleasure 'in the highest degree' to those 'in the lowest.' – though the placing of a poem in the latter category he explained to be a sign of perplexity rather than of outright censure. He thought, nevertheless, that 'A little Girl Lost' would be better omitted, 'not for the want of innocence in the poem, but from the too probable want of it in many readers'. Interestingly, the poems in the *Songs of Innocence* gained his approbation more consistently than those in *Experience*.[8] A few years later, as the two men met at parties arranged by Elizabeth and Charles Aders at their house in Euston Square,[9] a contemporary recorded his impression that 'Blake and Coleridge, when in company, seemed like congenial beings of another sphere, breathing for a while on our earth'.[10] Charles Lamb, meanwhile, described Blake as a 'mad Wordsworth' – a judgement, as often with Lamb, more perceptive than it might seem at first sight.[11] A longer response came in an enthusiastic letter to Bernard Barton in 1824:

Blake is a real name, I assure you, and a most extraordinary man, if he be still living. He is the Robert Blake, whose wild designs accompany a splendid folio edition of the Night Thoughts. ... He paints in water colours, marvellous strange pictures, visions of his brain which he asserts that he has seen. They have great merit. He has seen the old welch bards on Snowdon – he has seen the Beautifullest, the Strongest, & the Ugliest Man, left alone from the Massacre of the Britons by the Romans, & has painted them from memory (I have seen his paintings) and asserts them to be as good as the figures of Raphael & Angelo, but not better, as they had precisely the same retro-visions & prophetic visions with himself. ... His Pictures, one in particular the Canterbury Pilgrims (far above Stothard's) have great merit, but hard, dry, yet with grace. He has written a Catalogue of them, with a most spirited criticism on Chaucer, but mystical and full of Vision. His poems have been sold hitherto only in Manuscript. I never read them, but a friend at my desire procured the Sweep Song. There is one to a Tiger, which I have heard recited, beginning

> Tiger Tiger burning bright
> Thro' the deserts of the night –

which is glorious. But alas! I have not the Book, for the man is flown, whither I know not, to Hades or a Mad House – but I must look on him as one of the most extraordinary persons of the age.[12]*

The power he manifested could result in a proneness to states of enthusiasm and fear: later, his assertion that the great events of his time (particularly the American and French Revolutions) took the form for him of visions so powerful that he felt he could hardly 'subsist on the

Earth'.[13] It could also prompt thoughts, like Lamb's, that he might end in a madhouse. Fuseli's 1796 comment that Blake had something of madness about him was quoted earlier;[14] a decade later Hayley spoke of his 'dangerously acute sensibility', which reminded him of Cowper. Even an admirer, Michael Rossetti, could say, many years later, that 'there was something in his mind not exactly sane'.[15] To those who knew only his works, the impression of madness could be even stronger; his more intimate acquaintances, on the other hand, denied the implication indignantly. As early as 1806 B. H. Malkin argued that the imputation came from people who were incapable of appreciating his 'enthusiastic and high-flown notions'.[16] 'I saw nothing but sanity,' said Edward Calvert.[17] 'He was not mad, but perverse and wilful; he reasoned correctly from arbitrary, and often false premises,' said Francis Oliver Finch.[18] Linnell, who confessed that he was 'somewhat taken aback by the boldness of some of his assertions', maintained, nevertheless:

> I never saw anything the least like madness for I never opposed him spitefully as many did but being really anxious to fathom if possible the amount of truth which might be in his most startling assertions I generally met with a sufficiently rational explanation in the most really friendly & conciliatory tone.[19]

Another friend declared that his extravagance was 'only the struggle of an ardent mind to deliver itself of the bigness and sublimity of its own conceptions'.[20] One effect was that his mind could make leaps too fast for the hearer to see the connections, a failure which may sometimes be exacerbated by the reader's lack of the traditional knowledge on which he drew – particularly if it was biblical. A good example is to be found in his reaction to Wordsworth's statement in his preface to *The Excursion* that he could pass Jehovah and his thunder & his 'shouting angels' 'unalarmed':

> Solomon when he Married Pharohs daughter & became a Convert to the Heathen Mythology Talked exactly in this way ...[21]

The immediate reaction of many readers coming across such a statement may well be that of encountering a confused madness. If they are reasonably well read in the Bible, they may be led to suspect that Blake is muddling texts, since it is Moses, rather than Solomon, who is normally associated with 'Pharaoh's daughter'. Yet if they care to look into the matter they will find their suspicions ungrounded, since according to the First Book of Kings Solomon did indeed marry Pharaoh's daughter and made a house for her.[22] Blake's mind has evidently leapt to make a connection between that and Solomon's taking of foreign wives generally and to a suggestion that all this is to be linked with his decline from the sublimer vision of his forebears and a cultivation of the natural rather than the spiritual; in this he could therefore be seen as a forerunner of all who have failed to be true to their higher consciousness: a perception leading to his comment on Wordsworth's assertion that nature and the human mind are 'exquisitely fitted' the one to the other: 'You shall not bring me down to believe such fitting & fitted I know better & Please your Lordship' – an excellent example of his ability to combine an appeal to traditional language with a mischievous touch of radical insubordination.

A desire to raise his contemporaries to acknowledge similar aspirations can be traced throughout his work, being particularly characteristic of the later prophetic books. In terms of the visual arts, for instance, his concern to re-establish a sense of the glorious sublime in Gothic architecture can even help to redeem a line so absurd-seeming as

Go thou to Skofield: ask him if he is Bath or if he is Canterbury.[23]

It is also the case that the impression he sometimes gave of madness was strongest during the middle years of his life. Southey, for instance, who met him in 1811, later told Caroline Bowles: 'Much as he is to be admired, he was at that time so evidently insane, that the predominant feeling in conversing with him, or even looking at him, could only be sorrow and compassion. ... And there are always crazy people enough in the world to feed and foster such craziness as his.'[24] Gilchrist, who evidently felt himself bound to devote some time to the question, entitled a whole chapter in his biography 'Mad or Not Mad?' In addition to retailing some of the opinions just quoted he declared roundly concerning the assertion of 'madness':

To Blake's surviving friends – all who knew more of his character than a few casual interviews could supply – the proposition is (I find) simply unintelligible: thinking of him, as they do, under the strong influence of happy, fruitful, personal intercourse remembered in the past; swayed by the general tenor of his life, rather than by isolated extravagances of speech, or wild passages in his writings. All are unanimous on the point.[25]

Such contemporary evidence is obviously important, but a critic trying to understand the position from a standpoint two centuries later may still find it confusing. There are passages, particularly among the Notebook entries, for example, which are redolent of paranoia. One thinks of his lines 'On H-----y's Friendship', which end:

> And when he could not act upon my wife
> Hired a Villain to bereave my life[26]

The fact that the last line is a direct quotation from his early ballad 'Fair Elenor'[27] simply makes the position even more puzzling. It begins to seem as if Blake may simply be making a spiritual charge, not a physical one at all.

Faced with such confusion it is best to make an attempt at establishing the range of possibilities. At one extreme lies the word that Blake himself uses from time to time to describe the guiding force of his nature: 'enthusiasm'. One must also bear in mind (a point that Gilchrist makes) a sense of mischief, which seems sometimes to have prompted him to offer outrageous propositions in the hope of seeing how the orthodox might react. Samuel Palmer put a similar point:

> He had great powers of argument, and on general subjects was a very patient and good-natured disputant; but materialism was his abhorrence: and if some unhappy man called in question the world of spirits, he would answer him 'according to his folly', by putting forth his own views in their most extravagant and startling aspect. This might amuse those who were in the secret, but it left his opponent angry and bewildered.[28]

True to his views, Palmer was at first hostile to the terminology used in 1836 by Crabb Robinson, who had to satisfy him that

> in calling B *insane* I was not repeating the commonplace declamation against him. He at length yielded to my statem[t] – Tho' he at first tried to maintain that in asserting the actuality of spirits he was but giving personality to ideas as Plato had done before –[29]

It seems also that Blake had mastered the art of setting himself in a mode of composition in which he switched off as far as possible any inhibitions concerning usage and orthodox expectation that might operate for other writers and opened himself to whatever might spring from his own unconscious springs. In this way he could write, concerning *Milton*: 'I have written this poem from immediate Dictation twelve or sometimes twenty or thirty lines at a time without Premeditation & even against my Will' and 'I may praise it, since I dare not pretend to be any other than the Secretary; the Authors are in Eternity'.[30] For a more extreme version of this claim we can turn to Crabb Robinson's 1826 account:

'I write' he says 'when commanded by the spirits and the moment I have written I see the words fly abo^t the room in all directions – it is then published and the Spirits can read – ...'[31]

One of the modes in which he could negotiate the border between the discourse of enquiry and the certainty to be associated with statements based on assurance was furnished by his occasional habit of simply allowing the two to be elided – which might be the result of an occasional surrender to his capacity for enthusiasm. Thus in a letter of self-examination already quoted he could write:

Perhaps the simplicity of myself is the origin of all offences committed against me. If I have found this I shall have learned a most valuable thing well worth three years perseverance. I have found it! It is certain! that a too passive manner inconsistent with my active physiognomy had done me much mischief[32]

A similar use of the mode is to be found in one of the *Jerusalem* prefaces:

Jerusalem the Emanation of the Giant Albion! Can it be? Is it a Truth that the Learned have explored? Was Britain the Primitive Seat of the Patriarchal Religion? If it is true: my title-page is also True, that Jerusalem was & is the Emanation of the Giant Albion. It is True, and cannot be controverted.[33]

Within the space of a few lines, Blake has contrived the leap from enquiry to assertion; and the appearance, two or three lines later of the exclamations 'Amen! Huzzah! Selah!' reinforces the sense that 'enthusiasm' is the driving power carrying him through the ellipsis. R. A. Knox's study of the subject shows how this kind of 'certainty' flourished among religious believers, transporting them into a region in which they would find themselves clear from the probing queries of rational enquiry. We need only turn to the account of the Shaker settlement that Dwight visited in 1783 – 'They believed themselves to be under the immediate guidance of the Spirit'[34] – to recognize a kind of language that is sometimes found in the Prophetic Books and that Blake himself was likely to have encountered during his childhood years in the enthusiasm of the Moravians.

What was the difference between the language of such certainty and that of similar assertions by the mad? Blake was evidently himself interested in some of the questions involved, as is shown by his reading of Spurzheim's *Observations on Insanity*, published in 1817. Spurzheim argues, for instance, that

> Religion is a fertile cause of insanity. Mr. Haslam, though he declares it sinful to consider religion as a cause of insanity, adds, however, that he would be ungrateful, did he not avow his obligation to Methodism for its supply of numerous cases. Hence the primitive feelings of religion may be misled and produce insanity; that is what I would contend for, and in that sense religion often leads to insanity.

Picking up this mention of Methodism, Blake commented:

> Cowper came to me & said. O that I were insane always I will never rest. Can you not make me truly insane. I will never rest till I am so. O that in the bosom of God I was hid. You retain health & yet are as mad as any of us all – over us all – mad as a refuge from unbelief – from Bacon Newton & Locke[35]

The last point was expanded in two assertions to Crabb Robinson: '*Bacon, Locke & Newton* are the three great teachers of Atheism or of Satan's doctrine' – further expounded as 'Every thing is *Atheism* which assumes the reality of the natural & unspiritual world.'[36]

As we have seen, the period during which Blake himself came closest to letting his enthusiasm pass over into something like a mild paranoia was in the first decade of the nineteenth century, when he was most deeply at odds with those around him. More often, however, what is to be witnessed is a vehement energy that refuses to be bound by the demands of convention. In *The Marriage of Heaven and Hell* he spoke of himself as 'walking among the fires of hell, delighted with the enjoyments of Genius, which to Angels look like torment and insanity'. His own writing, taken as a whole, is so unlike that of some other well-known writers who suffered from insanity as to give one pause, moreover, before licensing such a diagnosis. Finch's adjectives 'perverse and wilful' may be better guides – along with renewed attention to the concept of enthusiasm.

As has sometimes been noticed, Blake's very individualist nature, lead-ing among other things to his insistence on private publication, ensured that his reputation would remain obscure for many years after his death. Despite the existence of a number of short memoirs, the key event in establishing his eminence was the publication of Alexander Gilchrist's *Life of William Blake, 'Pictor Ignotus'* in 1863; this led to a much revived interest, the flames of which were fanned by writers such as Dante Gabriel Rossetti and then W. B. Yeats, who made an early attempt to elucidate Blake's mythology and who with E. J. Ellis produced the first collected edition of the *Works* in 1893. Yeats was impressed enough to take over elements of Blake's imagery into his own, a good example being the quatrain into which at one and the same time he condensed the failure of the Eternal Man in the Garden at the heart of *The Four Zoas*, the malign effect of Locke's philosophy as a harbinger of Enlightenment philosophy, and the connection between that and the Industrial Revolution:

> Locke sank into a swoon;
> The Garden died
> God took the spinning-jenny
> Out of his side.[37*]

Yeats was evidently struck by the gnomic possibilities of what Blake had achieved in his poetry and carried them into his own explorations. As the twentieth century opened, the example of Blake as a writer and artist came to appeal even more to young writers hoping to make their mark, who could see in him a hero to be emulated. D. H. Lawrence, during his early love for Jessie Chambers, spoke to her of his admiration for a man who was

> quite poor … how he made pictures and wrote poems that were inter-dependent, and did the printing and engraving himself, in fact producing the book entirely by his own hands. He told me that Blake's wife was a poor girl whom he taught to read, and also to print and engrave, and what a marvellous helpmate she was to him … For a little time we lived with Blake and his wife.[38]

At about the same period James Joyce, in Dublin, was equally impressed. Lecturing in Trieste in 1912 on Defoe and Blake as the two men most representative of Englishness, he laid emphasis, according to Richard Ellman, on

> Blake's marriage to an uneducated woman, paralleled by his own quasi-marriage, Blake's sympathy for the poor, similar to his own socialism, Blake's feeling for children, an important claim of his own, and Blake's understanding, in 'The Crystal Cabinet', of gestation, a process so important in both *A Portrait* and *Ulysses*.[39]

Other writers whose own cast of mind might be quite different still confessed a fascination. In his essay on Blake, T. S. Eliot remarked:

> We have the same respect for Blake's philosophy ... that we have for an ingenious piece of home-made furniture: we admire the man who has put it together out of the odds and ends about the house.[40]

The comment is, of course, congruent with Eliot's larger agenda and involves placing Blake on the distant outskirts of European culture. It would be as easy to express a similar respect for Eliot's own ability to construct, out of a mélange of echoes from Laforgue, Baudelaire, Jacobean drama and Dickens, a substitute for the lost tradition of grand European writing that he valued. If one once accepts that Blake's concerns were not cultural and European so much as human, and that it was his aim to set himself in a situation where he could judge them primarily in terms of those features which one had in common with all human beings of every race or culture, the situation shifts dramatically. In this context he had indeed tried to evolve a mythology which might transcend those of the world's main religions.

It was a heroic venture, but – as Eliot also saw – one desperately difficult to achieve. Eliot diagnosed a 'certain meanness of culture',[41] but this was no more than to point to the lack of a common cultural discourse. In the event Blake was constantly going to existing mythologies for their most vivid and accessible images and incidents; yet he shrank from taking them over on any extended scale. As has already pointed out, his ventures into anything resembling an 'antinonomian tradition' involved accepting the paradoxical rider that it must be essentially *anti*-traditional.

Eliot's attempt to rule him out of court could also be regarded as a failure to recognize how Blake was, as described by a contemporary, 'a new kind of man'.[42] For the first time, in other words, a breed of men was emerging who were largely indifferent to the claims of tradition, and who felt that they must live and work outside it. It must also be borne in mind, nevertheless, that Eliot was equally impressed by Blake's extraordinary directness, which was the bright side of his refusal to conform. By that very fact of standing outside his culture for which Eliot was from his general theory criticizing him, he must also be acknowledged to be in a peculiarly privileged position:

> He was naked, and saw man naked, and from the centre of his own crystal. ... He approached everything with a mind unclouded by current opinions. There was nothing of the superior person about him. This makes him terrifying.[43]

This sense of Blake made him for Eliot not only alarming but energizing, since while he recognized in him a man who ignored all the normal rules of traditional and civilized discourse, he could not ignore his own pressing intuition that when it came to poetry he had the heart of the matter in him.

Other writers have been able to latch on to a particular element in Blake's thought or a particular saying to develop in their own work: one thinks of Lawrence Durrell, who noticed to his pleasure that his own initials, LGD, were the same as those of the Lineaments of Gratified Desire and so felt licensed to give the character corresponding to himself in the *Alexandria Quartet* the nickname 'Lineaments'; also of Aldous Huxley, who discovered on taking mescalin that he immediately understood Blake's saying in *The Marriage of Heaven and Hell*, 'If the doors of perception were cleansed every thing would appear to man as it is, infinite' and wrote a small treatise with the title *The Doors of Perception* to elaborate on what he had come to understand.

For certain writers, sayings like this in Blake's writing were so important that they could serve as a kind of touchstone for values that they wanted to indicate – even if only in passing. Sometimes, indeed, they might be so striking and memorable that they needed simply to be cited, without further elaboration, to make the point.

Among poets who have confessed an important debt, Theodore Roethke is prominent: He admired Blake's writing about children for the manner in which he felt that it combined directness of approach with a readiness to ignore normal barriers between different kinds of sense-perception. It was a notion that he was prepared to pick up and run with, as when he developed Blake's inscription 'I want! I want!' from *The Gates of Paradise* into the title of his poem 'I need, I need', which begins with

the extraordinarily basic perceptions of a child experiencing the alienating
separation from its mother in the very moments of tasting its food:

> A deep dish. Lumps in it,
> I can't taste my mother.
> Hoo. I know the spoon.
> Sit in my mouth.[44]

He also admired the achievement in 'Vala', where he found that the
emphasis on psychic division corresponded to fissures in mental life
recognizable from his own experiences of stress and breakdown.[45]

The most notable exponent of such a response was Joyce Cary. In his
1944 novel *The Horse's Mouth*, accounts of the thoughts and speeches of
the hero, Gulley Jimson, are punctuated from time to time by lines or
extracts from Blake's verse – without ever being dwelt on in detail. At
one point, where Gulley is thinking at length about his earlier life, stanzas from 'The Mental Traveller' are used in this way to give a sense of his
relationships with the women in his life. After he has spent time in jail
reading Blake even more obsessively, extracts from *Milton* and *Jerusalem*
are used to particular effect. There is little or no sign that Cary ever puzzled at length over the meaning of the Prophetic Books; for him, it
seems, their gnomic quality was enough. And indeed, his usage brings
out the benefits for the reader when Blake's verse is quoted selectively,
and in short bursts. For the purposes of his novel, at least, Cary is
particularly interested when Jimson's hero is enacting the role of the
committed artist and in those statements which bring out his antinomianism. In some respects he gets closer than any other critic has done to
showing what it would be like to live a life as close to Blake's in ignoring
the call of the material and abandoning everything in the cause of continuing creation. In this respect it is as if Los has been re-embodied as a
shrewd Cockney operator who takes his next sustenance from whoever
offers it, while always keeping an eye open for the next blank wall or
canvas and the next supply of artist's materials which he can use to
paint or adorn it. Yet it must also be noted that the novel ignores Blake's
equally essential adherence to some normal codes of society – particularly
where respect for property is concerned – along with his high view
of art and the potentialities of the human imagination. Jimson's exclusive concern with the right use of colour and form makes him blind to
that other side of Blake's aim which was always religious in a loftier
manner, seeking to find an adequate substitute for the Christianity

which he felt had become perverted, and restore to his fellow human beings a higher sense of their calling.

Looking further at such effects on later writers it seems as if British writers are more likely to be drawn to those elements in his work that are lyrical and visionary, Americans to those that express his delight in energy. In her novel *The Time of the Angels* Iris Murdoch conveys the consciousness of the autodidact servant Pattie O'Driscoll as she comes to terms with her life in a London rectory:

> A train passes beneath and jolts everything in the house a millimetre or two and jolts Pattie's heart with a little reminder of death. She murmurs the poetry which takes the place of the prayer which took the place of the poor defeated magic of her childhood. Turn away no more. Why wilt thou turn away? The starry floor, the watery floor is given thee till the break of day.
>
> She goes into the kitchen where the strawberry blond is waiting to take her to see his father.[46]

In Saul Bellow's *Herzog*, the hero recalls the train journeys that began his summer holidays in childhood:

> ... he had not forgotten his mother's saliva on the handkerchief that summer morning in the squat hollow Canadian station, the black iron and the sublime brass. All children have cheeks and all mothers to wipe them tenderly. These things either matter or they do not matter. It depends upon the universe, what it is. These acute memories are probably symptoms of disorder To him perpetual thought of death was a sin. Drive your cart and your plow over the bones of the dead.[47]

For both writers, interestingly, Blakean reminiscence is associated with mortality.

Lawrence's admiration for Blake, meanwhile, turned out not to be in the end short-lived. More than any of the writers considered here, he can be regarded as having penetrated to the core of the ideas, understanding the terror that had caused Blake to see in the universe an eternal struggle between the abstract, formalizing power of Urizen and the flame of energy which was pent in every form of life, waiting to emerge in destruction if it was not allowed its own free play.

As with Blake's absorption of Bunyan and his revisionary view of Milton, the manner in which Blake's views could be seen as prophetic of

Lawrence's most central concerns is yet another reminder of what he owed to the dissenting tradition in which he had been brought up. Attempts to claim Blake for the radical tradition in English thought have been both rewarding and ultimately thwarted. If it is as a great Dissenter that he deserves above all to be celebrated, however, he is best viewed not through the perspective of any single Nonconformist tradition; instead one must take bearings from the other writers that have been looked at in this chapter: each throws an important light, none captures the man himself into full focus.

What then are we to make of his enduring gifts to the age that was to come? His creation of Urizen – probably the most original of his conceptions – may now be thought to have involved an exaggerated view of the future. Since his time, after all, the mathematical and scientific developments by which he seemed to be limited have taken place in the hands of practitioners who have been concerned to utilize them for humane ends. Can one contemplate the growth of medical discovery and view it as simply sinister? Yet if, equally, one thinks of the officials who ran the Nazi concentration camps while showing a loving concern to record accurately all the items of their victims' belongings and apparel, what name are we to assign to the deity they were ultimately serving if not that of Blake's rational deity? Only people who had contrived to cut off the activities of the head from those of the whole body could be capable of such separation.

It is in the further ramifications of his schema, when he becomes more vulnerable, that he is also at his most characteristic. Just as his visual conceptions might reach out towards infinity yet still remain firmly within the quadrilateral of the conventional picture-frame, so he could imagine the immense range of the human faculties yet confine them firmly within a similar durance, that of the Zoas to define three separate spheres, belonging to the head, heart and genitals respectively. This could be said to correspond to a knowable and testable reality; but with the further move to a fourth Zoa, to be defined by the creativity of the hands and feet, the thinking became hostage to its own neatness. The problem makes his subsequent readers most conscious of the struggle that was always continuing in his mind between the imaginative projections that reached out and into infinity and the organizing power which felt most secure when he could bound his living conceptions within foursquare designs.

Because he had remained so firmly independent of his fellows, he had cut himself off from some of the resources of communication that would have facilitated reception of his work. To this day a full appreciation of it calls for unusual efforts – not simply a sympathy with Blake's various states of vision, but a willingness to enter into the strenuous dialectic of mind involved. It is necessary to understand both the moods when he could remain passive to the visitations of imaginative experience and those where he committed himself to the harmonies and energies of creative work. Yet in all his works there are taproots to the vividness of the works to which the general reader responds first of all. As one penetrates them further, moreover, one comes to see that his firm independence, baffling at first sight to the aspiring reader, was really the defence for his identity as a visionary, finding its best nature in his cultivation of the bounding line of freedom and in a capacity for illumination that he believed to be the inner condition of all human beings, if they could only find their way back to it. Stubborn and self-assertive he might be at one pole of his humanity, but at the other he forever believed himself to be serving the cause of true human freedom.

23 Autograph entry in the Album of William Upcott, Henry W. and Albert A. Berg Collection of English and American Literature, The New York Public Library, Astor, Lenox and Tilden Foundations

Notes

Where note signals are followed by an asterisk (*) this indicates the existence of information supplementary to a single reference.

Chapter 1

1 Boswell's record of his conversation, 12 June 1784.
2 *A Portrait of the Artist as a Young Man* (1916) end.
3 'Elegy to the Memory of an Unfortunate Lady', Lines 17–18: *Poems*, ed. J. Butt (1963) p. 262.
4 'There is a House not Made with Hands': Isaac Watts, *Hymns and Spiritual Songs* (1755) p. 103.
5 'My First Acquaintance with Poets': *HW*. xvii, 107.
6 Statement to Richmond: see *BR* 294, citing A. H. Palmer, *Life and Letters of Samuel Palmer* (1892) p. 24 fn.
7 Nancy Bogen, 'The Problem of William Blake's Early Religion', *The Personalist* 1968, XLIX, 509–22.
8* See Margaret Ruth Lowery, *Windows of the Morning: A Critical Study of William Blake's Poetical Sketches, 1783* (New Haven, Conn., 1940). Margaret Lowery was one of the first to discuss William Muir's statement that Blake's parents had worshipped at Fetter Lane.
9 Transcribed by A. P. K. Davies in his unpublished PhD thesis, 'William Blake in Contexts', University of Surrey, 2003, p. 297, and in his article (published with M. K. Schuchard), 'Recovering the Lost Moravian history of William Blake's Family', *BQ* (2004) XXXVIII, 36–43.
10 E 449; K 44.
11* In the above thesis Davies takes issue (pp. 50–1) with the supposition that James Blake had radical leanings, since such evidence as there is from voting records points the other way.
12* Crabb Robinson is the authority for saying that the family were dissenters (*BSP* 7n). For the evidence of Blake's father's having been a Baptist worshipper in the relevant years, see *BR* 8 and n.
13 E 707; K 807.
14 Letter of 11 August 1800: *BSP* 8n.
15 See below, p. 14.
16 E 708; K 799.
17 Ibid.
18* Watts himself was associated with the Independents, but when the words were thought suitable his hymns seem to have been sung across chapels of different persuasions.
19 See below, p. 61.
20 'Divine Wrath and Mercy': Watts, *Hymns and Spiritual Songs*, 37.
21 'Divine Judgments': Isaac Watts, *Horae Lyricae* (1779) p. 5.

22   E 57; K 203.
23   'God's Eternity': Watts, *Hymns and Spiritual Songs*, 166.
24   'The Faithfulness of God in the Promises': Watts, *Hymns and Spiritual Songs*, 220.
25   *The First Book of Urizen*, E 72; K 224.
26   The early terror was reported in Crabb Robinson's presence by Mrs Blake: *BR* 543. For Ugolino, see my essay, 'Influence and Independence in Blake' in *Interpreting Blake*, ed. M. Phillips (Cambridge 1978) pp. 204–11.
27   E 554; K 604.
28   Cf Revelation XXI. 21 and the conclusion of Part First in *The Pilgrim's Progress*.
29   G (1942) p. 6.
30   Ibid., 5.
31   E 171–2; K 649–50.
32   *Blake* (1995) p. 33.
33   E 775; K 870–1. He thought that at Hampstead he could face 'with safety & perhaps benefit' only the 'Morning air'.
34   E 143–4; K 534.
35   E 222; K 706.
36   E 159; K 636.
37   E 242; K 728.
38   E 655–6; K 783.
39   *Milton* 22. 55, 61: E 118; K 506.
40   J. T. Smith, *Nollekens and his Times* (1828), reproduced *BR* 457.
41   Ibid.
42   *W Prel* (1805) VII 706–20, 722–3.
43   Boswell's record of his conversation, 20 September 1777.
42   *LL* (Marrs) I 267.
45   *BR* 18.

Chapter 2

1   *BR* 510–11.
2   E 628; *BR* 17.
3   See Mrs [A. E.] Bray, *Life of Thomas Stothard, R.A.* (1851). 'Blake's First Arrest, at Upnor Castle,' *BQ* XXXI (1997–8) 82–4 and *BSP* 59–60, where it is accompanied by a plate (27) showing Stothard's design recording the event.
4   Illustration to p. 146 of Gray's *Poems* (1790) in the Yale Collection of British Art.
5   E 625; K 445.
6   E 691; K 815.
7   'To the Muses,' E 417; K 10–11.
8   E 416–7; K 9–10.
9   E 412–13; K6.
10   *TWB* 58; *BSP* 8, citing *Songs of Experience*: E 26–7; K 216.
11   E 615; K 389.
12   *The History of Modern Enthusiasm* (1757), quoted *TWB* 54.
13   See above, p. 199.

14* *TWB* 28–9, etc. His pointing out that Blake's mother's name, as entered in the marriage registry of her wedding, was 'Hermitage', a noted Muggletonian surname (and not as in *Blake Records* 'Harmitage'), was undermined by the discovery that her legal name (from her first marriage) was in fact 'Armitage': see Keri Davies, 'William Blake's mother: a new identification', *Blake: An Illustrated Quarterly* (1999) XXXIII 28, 39, 41 and *BSP*. The rates on her first husband's property, 28 Broad Street, were paid from 1748 to 1752 by '– Armitage' (*BR* 551–2), but in 1753 were taken over by James Blake; on the other hand, the name of 'Thomas Hermitage, hosier of Broad Street' appeared among the voters in the 1749 Westminster election. Laura Wright, an expert on London pronunciation and writing, finds no puzzle in the discrepancy, in view of the known variations in pronunciation and spelling at the time. The Westminster vote may have been recorded by an officer who heard the name as what was the more common form in the south of England.

15 See above, p. 6.

16 The Song of Los' 3: 23–4. E 67; K 246.

17 William George Meredith, Taylor's patron, writing on 30 December 1829 (*BRS* 94–5).

18 Annotation to Reynolds, E 658; K 473.

19 Annotation to Berkeley, E 664; K 774.

20 E 274; K 776.

21 See Morton Paley, *The Traveller in the Evening* (Oxford 2003) pp. 6–7; Andrew Welburn, *The Truth of Imagination* (1989) pp. 18–19 et passim.

22 Sources of this story, from Gilcrhist and, apparently, Linnell, are given in *BR* 32.

23 E 490; K 431.

24 See entry in the *Columbia Encyclopaedia* (New York, 2001–4).

25* When, in his letter to Trusler of 23 August 1799 (K 794; E 677) he said that his visions had been particularly elucidated by them, he is more likely to have been thinking of those illuminated books where the direct appeal of colour served to reinforce whatever imaginative appeal they found in the designs.

Chapter 3

1 For the latter two see *The Marriage of Heaven and Hell* 21 and his letter to Flaxman of September 1800: E 43, 680; K 158, 799.

2 E 463; K 60.

3 E 463–4; K 60.

4 E 465; K 62–3.

5 *BR* 35–7.

6 F. W. Bateson, *Selected Poems of William Blake* (1957). Cf. Kathleen Raine, *Blake and Tradition* (1969) I 20.

7 E 49; K 157.

8 Rev. XIX, 6. See Heather Glen, *Vision and Disenchantment: Blake's Songs and Wordsworth's Lyrical Ballads*, (Cambridge, 1983), p. 124.

9 Andrew Baxter, *An Enquiry into the Nature of the Human Soul* (1745) I 296.

10 *An Essay Concerning Human understanding*, II xi 17 (1788) I 150.

11 Edward Larrissy, *Blake* (1985) p. 80, quoting from Cassirer *The Philosophy of the Enlightenment*, p. 73.
12 See e.g. the accounts gathered in Judith Plotz, *Romanticism and the Vocation of Childhood* (2001) pp. 91–106.

Chapter 4

1 See Tatham's ms 'Life', *BR* 20–1.
2 *BR* 517–18.
3 A story, according to Bentley, almost certainly heard from Tatham.
4 *BR* 30.
5 *BR* 521, 31.
6 Malkin in *BR* 422.
7 Tatham, transcribed in *BR* 524–5.
8 Ibid., 523–4.
9 Ibid., 28.
10 E 680, 37–8; K 799, 153. Cf. Peter Ackroyd, *William Blake* (1995) p. 159.
11 E 49; K 194.
12 E 47–8; K 193.
13 The probable source is Swinburne: see his *William Blake: A Critical Essay* (1906) p. 16. Blake seems to have been prone to express unusual views on the question, however: in June 1826, he shocked Crabb Robinson by saying that 'he had learned from the Bible that wives should be in common': *BR* 332, 548.
14 *BR* 106.
15 E 696; K 440–1.
16 E 597; K 82.
17 *Paradise Lost* iv 299.
18 *BR* 316–17.
19 Isaiah LXII 4 and margin.
20* John Bunyan, *The Pilgrims Progress* (Cambridge 1862) pp. 174–5. Bunyan relates Pilgrim's sickness specifically to the 'love-sickness' in the Song of Solomon.
21 E 470; K 179.
22 E 63; K 241.
23 Tristanne J. Connolly, *William Blake and the Body* (2002).
24* In May 1802, Hayley reported that both he and his wife had spent a week in bed with a severe fever (*BR* 95) and Catherine suffered particularly from 'Agues & Rheumatisms', while they were at Felpham (Letters of 10 January and 30 January 1803: E 707,725; K 811, 819) – though by December 1804, as a result of 'Mr Birch's Electrical Magic', which she had been able to discontinue after three months, she was well again (Letter of 18 December 1804: E 759; K 854). (It may well be, of course, that this benefit had been brought about less by the effects of Mr Birch's treatment than by their withdrawal from a damp cottage.)
25 Plates 36:31 and 42:28.
26 Page 84, lines 5–6: E 359 (= lines 271–2 in K 327).
27 Gilchrist in *BR* 237.

Chapter 5

1 E 708; K 799.
2* His engraving 'Glad Day' was inscribed 'WB inv 1780', together with the words 'Albion rose from where he labourd at the Mill with Slaves | Giving himself for the Nations he danc'd the dance of Eternal Death'. Unless the words were added later they must be seen simply as a fortuitous invocation of *Samson Agonistes* 41; but it is unlikely that the pertinence of the London mill's name would have been lost on him.
3 Inscriptions in the 'Vala' MS: K 380, reading 'An' for 'All' (E 697).
4 K 172–3 (E 794).
5* E 24; K 214. Blake seems to have remained uneasy about this effect and in a late copy altered '& what' to 'formd thy' – given as 'forged thy' in B. H. Malkin's *A Father's Memoirs of his Child* (1806). See E 794 again. Most readers are likely to prefer the more gnomic published version.
6 K 164 (E 470–1, 853).
7 E 27; K 217.
8 For the rise of this motif in Romantic and later literature, see Geoffrey Grigson's article 'The Upas Tree', in his *The Harp of Aeolus and other Essays* (1947) pp. 56–65.
9 *Concerning the Earths in Our Solar System* (1787) sect. 79; Raine *Blake and Tradition*, I 25–6.
10 See the citation of Enid Porter's collection in her *Vision and Disenchantment* ... (Cambridge, 1983) p. 99 and note.
11 *The Poetical Works of Gray and Collins*, ed. Austin Lane Poole (1917) p. 21.
12 *Lear* IV, i, 38–9.
13 E 23–4, 794; K 183–4, 213.
14 E 38; K 152.
15 E 26–7; K 216.
16 See V, de Sola Pinto's essay in his collection *The Divine Vision* (1957) pp. 79–81.
17 'Praise for Mercies Spiritual and Temporal': Song iv in *Divine Songs attempted in Easy Language for the Use of CHILDREN* (1715) p. 6.
18 E 26–7; K 216.
19* See Glen, *Vision and Disenchantment*, 210–12 for further discussion of 'mark'. I am not sure how far the discussion can be pressed, given the common use of the word in Shakespeare and poetic usage following him, but her invocation of the appearance of the word in Revelation is telling, given Blake's fondness for that Biblical book.
20 *The Rights of Man* (1791–2), cited by Thompson, *TWB* 179. Paine's further discussion at this point repays attention.
21 See my *Blake's Humanism* (Manchester 1968) pp. 76–9.
22 See Larrissy, *Blake* (1985) ch. 4, pp. 70–95. Anne Mellor has also discussed the paradox involved, in *Blake's Human Form Divine* (Berkeley and Los Angeles, 1974) pp. xv–xvii, etc.
23 '[Experiment]': E 469–70; K 168.
24 Verse fragments: E 474; K 168 and E 474; K 178.
25 E 467–8; K 163.

Chapter 6

1 Mona Wilson, *Life of William Blake* (1948) p. 310.
2 E 507; K 551.
3 A. Blunt, *The Art of William Blake* (1959) p. 41.
4 Mellor, *Blake's Human Form Divine*, 126.
5 'To Nobodaddy' E 471; K 171.
6 'Let the Brothels of Paris be opened ...' E 499, 861; K 185.
7 E 37–8; K 153.
8 'The Dethe of Charles Bawdin': see Harold Bloom, *Blake's Apocalypse* (1963) p. 83.
9 See e.g. the sentence from *The Marriage of Heaven and Hell* discussed above, p. 59.
10 Annotation to J.C. Lavater's *Aphorisms on Man*, E 590; K 74.
11 *Lectures on the Sacred Poetry of the Hebrews* (1787) II 168; Mee, *Dangerous Enthusiasm*, p. 27.
12 E 702; K 793.
13 Annotation to Richard Watson's *Apology for the Bible*, E 617; K 392.
14 E 294; K 142.
15 *Paradise Lost* vii 225–7.

Chapter 7

1 *BL* (CC) I 17.
2* The number for October 1791 includes a mention of the name 'Bne Seraphim', which has not been traced elsewhere. There are also mentions of 'Zazel', 'Adonai' and 'Tiriel', the last of which Blake is normally assumed to have found in Cornelius Agrippa.
3 See above, p. 32.
4 See, for instance, the motif of the serpent as explored in Mary Jackson's article, 'Blake and Zoroastrianism': *BQ* XI, 72–85.
5 See his inscription on the epitome of Hervey's *Meditations among the Tombs* in the Tate Gallery, London, recorded in Erdman's *Blake Concordance* (Ithaca, NY, 1967) II, 2315.
6 *The Poetical Works of Gray and Collins*, ed. Austin Lane Poole (1917) p. 78.
7 'A Vision of the Last Judgment', E 565; K 617.
8 'Auguries of Innocence', E 491; K 432.
9 See above, p. 76.
10 See Plate 14.
11 *Jerusalem* 5:21–2. E 147; K 623.
12 'On Virgil' E 270; K 778.
13 E 671.
14 See e.g. the reproduction constituting endpapers to *William Blake's Engravings*, edited with an introduction by Geoffrey Keynes (1950).
15 See E 144; K 620; Northrop Frye, 'Notes for a Commentary on *Milton*', *The Divine Vision*. ed. Vivian De Sola Pinto (1957) p. 131.
16 Plates 6 and 70 respectively.
17 See illustrations V–VII (followed by more elaborated forms in VIII and XII): Andrew Wright, *Blake's Job: A Commentary* (Oxford, 1972).

18   E 543; K 578.7.
19   *Jerusalem* 27: E 171; K 649.
20   See e.g. *Prel* (1805) xii, 337–53
21   See *Milton* Plate 6A, (E 99–100; K 485–6).
22   See his letter to Roger Gale, quoted in Hutchinson's *History of Cumberland* (1794) I, 241–2, and in my *Coleridge the Visionary* (1959), p. 69.
23   William Stukeley, *Stonehenge: a Temple Restored to the British Druids* (1740) p. 54.

Chapter 8

1   John Barrell's article 'Imagining the King's Death', *History Workshop* 37 (1994) 1–32, gives a sense of the current anxieties.
2   *CL* I 397.
3*   For more light on Watson, see Morton Paley's discussion of him in *BQ* XXXII, pp. 32–42. He had aroused the anger and scorn of radicals by his 1793 publication 'The Wisdom and Goodness of God in Having Made Both Rich and Poor'.
4   E 611; K 383.
5   *TWB*, 60–1.
6   E 614–15; K 387–8.
7   Letter of 23 August 1799: E 702–3; K 793–4.
8*   In my *Blake's Humanism* (Manchester, 1968) p. 254 I suggested that Blake might have found a hint towards the idea of 'LOS' as a reversal of 'SOL' in Dürer's presentation of 'APOLO', inscribed backwards, in his design 'Apollo and Diana', where Apollo is carrying both sceptre and inscribed sun in a most Blakean manner. See Figure 42 in my book and the cognate illustrations there.
9   Night the Ninth, 709, 364–5: E 403, 395; K 376, 366.
10   Night the Fourth, 135: E 334; K 301.
11   Night the Third. 162–5: E 330; K 296.
12   Night the Second, 266–86: E 322; K 287.
13   Night the Second, 397–418: E 325; K 290–1.
14* Some years ago it was observed that the second page of the Fourth Night contained a faint impression of printing, traceable to a proof of one of Hayley's *Ballads*. The dating of this suggests strongly that the page was still being worked on after May 1802. See G. E. Bentley, Jr., 'The Date of Blake's *Vala*': *Modern Language Notes* (November 1956) LXXI, 487–92.
15   E 706; K 798.
16   E 708; K 799.

Chapter 9

1   See Robert N. Essick and Morton D. Paley. 'Dear Generous Cumberland: A Newly Discovered Poem and Letter by William Blake' (reporting a new letter of 1 September 1800), *BQ* XXXII 4 on, and E 708; K 800.
2   E 710; K 802.
3   E 711; K 803.
4   Ibid.

5 E 712–13; K 804–5.
6 E711; K 803.
7 [Richard Dally], in *The Bognor, Arundel and Littlehampton Guide* (Chichester, 1828) 55, reported by Bentley: *BSP* 214.
8 Letter to Butts of 11 September 1801: E 716; K 809–10.
9 Letter of 30 January 1803: see above, p. 132.
10 E 721; K 817.
11 E 722; K 818.
12 See his comment to Crabb Robinson in E. J.Morley's *Henry Crabb Robinson on Books and their Writers* (1938) I 327; quoted in my *Blake's Visionary Universe* (Manchester 1969) p. 29.
13 See above, p. 48.
14 E 722; K 818.
15 E 720; K 816.
16 See e.g. above, p. 135.
17 See above, p. 46.
18 Quoted Morchard Bishop [Oliver Stonor], *Blake's Hayley* (1951) pp. 278–9.
19 E 729; K 556.
20 *The Feast of the Poets* (1814) p. 49.
21 Byron, 'English Bards and Scotch Reviewers': *Complete Poetical Works*, ed. J. J. McGann (Oxford 1980) I 238.
22 Southey, *Letters*, ed. M. H. Fitzgerald, 1912, p. 57. Quoted Morchard Bishop, *Blake's Hayley*, 20.
23 Letter to Butts, 10 January 1803: E 725; K 812–13; for the new dating of this letter see article in *BQ* XIII 148–51. The 2 line quotation reproduces 4 lines from Thomas Tickell's 'Lucy and Colin' (also in Percy's *Reliques* (1765) III 308).
24 E 725–7; K 821.
25 E 730–1; K 825–6.
26 E 728; K 823.
27 E 732–3; K 826–8.
28 *TWB* 127n.
29 E 733; K 828.
30 Letter of 25 November, *BR* 135.
31 Ibid., 163.
32 E 733; K 828–9.
33 E 733; K 828–9.
34* On a visit there some years ago I was struck by the curious and sometimes grotesque misericords which Blake could have seen in the choir stalls and found myself wondering whether he had not also seen them and gained some fertile ideas for subsequent designs. More recently, I noticed that Anne Mellor was also struck by this thought and reproduced some of the designs in question for her book *Blake's Human Form Divine* (Berkeley and Los Angeles, 1974): see pp. 167–9, 171, 173–6 and plates 46–8.

Chapter 10

1 See especially Robert W. Rix, 'Healing the Spirit: William Blake and Magnetic Religion', *Romanticism on the Net 25* (February 2002) and M. K. Schuchard, 'Blake's Healing Trio: Magnetism, Medicine and Mania', *BQ* XXIII, 20–32.

2   E 43; K 157.
3   loc.cit., para. 17.
4* Rix points out that Hayley took a keen interest in Animal Magnetism, purchasing an 'electrical machine', which functioned as a healing 'shower bath' (Bishop, *Blake's Hayley*, 95–6). He thinks that Hayley would therefore have understood the connection Blake makes between poetry and electrical phenomena in a letter: 'My fingers Emit sparks of fire with Expectation of my future labours' (Letter to Hayley. 16 September 1800, E 709; K 801). He also casts *Jerusalem* in a framework steeped in magnetic-spiritualist metaphors. On the frontispiece of that work, we see a type of nightwatchman entering a portal carrying in his right hand a spherical disc of concentric circles emitting a radiant light. What at first seems to be a solid lamp or lantern is not solid at all, as the figure's thumb and fingers are visible through it. Albert Boime has persuasively argued that the ball-shaped lantern is an 'image of a rotating glass globe used to generate electricity in contemporary electrical experiments', of which several illustrations were reproduced in Joseph Priestley's *History and Present State of Electricity* (1767) pp. 351–2. Boime could also have mentioned that Blake is likely to have seen such apparatuses with his own eyes when Dr. Birch cured his wife Catherine (Rix, op. cit.).
5   Letter to Hayley. 6 May 1800, E 705; K 797.
6   Letter to Butts. 25 April 1803 E 728; K 822.
7   Letter to Butts. 6 July 1803 E 730; K 825.
8* Letter to Hayley, 18 December 1804: E 759; K 854. 'Dr John Birch was a surgeon of St Thomas's Hospital in London (where de Mainauduc had been a student in 1789), where he established a department for treating patients with medical electricity. Birch describes his methods and machines in *Essay on the Mechanical Application of Electricity*, which was published and sold in 1802 by Joseph Johnson (Paley, *Apocalypse and the Millennium* (1999), 82). In his letters, Blake several times refers to Birch in favourable terms (Letters to Butts. 11 September 1801, E 717; K 810 and 25 April 1803, E 728; K 822). It appears from the correspondence that Birch was a mutual friend of both the Butts family and the Blakes' (Rix, op. cit.).
9* E 505; K 545. 'Of "Frazer" we know little, but he has been identified as a student of de Mainauduc's (Schuchard, *BQ* XXIII, 21). Cosway set himself up as a popular magnetic entrepreneur. Blake's patron George Cumberland wrote on the verso of a broadsheet entitled 'A Syllabus of Dr. de MAINADUC's INSTRUCTIONS,' a memorandum criticizing Cosway for his commercial opportunism. He denounces him as part of a "Sect" headed by de Loutherbourg, "who I suspect have a Scheme to empty the pockets of all the credulous christians they can find – the price of Initiation is £25 Guis and 4 must enter at a time" (Bentley, 'Mainauduc, Magic and Madness': *Queries* (1991) p. 295). 36. George Baldwin, also, ventured into the commercialism of magnetic healing, and upon his return from Egypt, set up a magnetic salon in London. In Mr Baldwin's *Legacy to his Daughter, or the Divinity of Truth* ... (1811), he refers to the Bible as an authority to prove that divine Vision is an essential part of spiritual life. However, he also admits his hesitation in committing himself to Spiritualism in public, which has delayed the publication of his book, out of the fear 'that I shall be called a Visionary' (iii)' (Rix, op. cit.).
10 E 109; K 496.
11 E 96; K 481.

12 E 114; K 502.
13 E 145; K 621.
14 E 756–7; K 851–2.
15 E 728–9; K 823.
16 E 136; K 526.
17 *W Prel* (1805) xi, 257–9.
18 E 127; K 516.
19 E 216–17; K 699–700: plate 65: 12–36. Part of these passages was taken over with additions from 'Vala', Night VIIb, lines 170–90.
20 E 147; K 623.
21 Isaiah LII 14, LIII 11.
22 Genesis XXX 14–17.
23 E 145–6; K 621.
24 E 157; K 633: plate 13 34–6.
25 E 180; K 665, plate 38 [34] 29.
26 Gilchrist *Life* (1862) ch. vii.
27* In 1815 the hospital moved from Moorfields to Southwark – not far from Blake's old residence in Lambeth, as it happens – but there the statues were moved inside as being too alarming. (Information from J. Michael Phillips, the senior archivist.)
28* This motif in Blake has also been noticed by Jenijoy LaBelle, who made it the subject of an article ('Blake's Bald Nudes', *BQ* XXIV, 52–7), in which she reproduced both a contemporary engraving based on the Cibber statues and the striking portrayal of a bald madman in plate 8 of Hogarth's *The Rake's Progress*, as well as several of the relevant designs from Blake.
29 *Jerusalem* 91.27: E 251; K 738 and 22.22: E 167; K 645.
30 E 223; K 707.
31 E 121; K 509: plate 24, 68–73.
32 *Milton* 31: E130–1; K 520–1
33 Ibid., plate 29 4–26: E 127; K 516.
34 Ibid., lines 12–13.
35 *Excursion.*, 128, app. crit.: *WPW* V 290.
36 E 297; K 264, assigned as a cry of Tharmas to Enion.
37 E 475; K 415.

Chapter 11

1   E 707; K 799.
2   *BR* 52.
3   E 704; K 795.
4   E 724; K 812.
5   See above, p. 125. See also above, pp. 130–1 and note, p. 229.
6   E 738; K 831.
7   E 505; K 538.
8   E 631; K 452.
9   E 768–9; K 864.
10 See above, p. 149.
11 Letter to Hayley of spring 1805: E 764; K 859.

12 Gilchrist, quoted in *BR* 238.
13 E 624; K 401.
14 See the article by Robert W. Rix, 'Blake Bacon and the Devil's Arse': *BQ* XXXVII 137–44.
15 E 501; K 187.
16 E 530–1; K 565–6.
17 *Blake: Prophet against Empire* (1954) p. 416.
18 E 580; K 600.
19 *Annual Review* (1805) IV (1806) 575.
20 E 147; K 623.
21 See e.g. *BSP* 214–15.
22 *BR* 430n.
23 *BR* 323.
24 Annotation to Lavater 612: E 599; K 86.
25 Record by Cunningham: *BR* 481.
26* *BR* 275–6. Tatham mentions that Catherine, however, 'always kept a guinea or sovereign for any Emergency, of which Blake never knew, even to the day of his Death. This she did for years ...' (*BR* 525).
27 E 722; K 818.
28 Paley *PTE* 98, citing E 771 and 784 (K 867 and 878–9).
29 Letter to Dawson Turner, 9 June 1818. E 771, K 867.
30* *BSP* 278, citing Allan Cunningham, *Poems and Songs* (1847) p. xix n. For a more favourable view of Cromek and his activities see Aileen Ward: 'Canterbury Revisited: the Blake–Cromek Controversy' *BQ* XXII, 80–92.
31 E 509; K 540.
32 E 505, 506; K 556, 539.
33 E 508; K 540.
34 E 506; K 545.
35 E 102; K 489.
36 E 106; K 493.
37 E 642; K 452.
38 'The Caverns of the Grave Ive Seen,': E 480–1; K 558.
39 E 477–8; K 418.
40 E 488–9; K 429–30.
41 E 483–6; K 424–7.
42 Lines 7–8 echo Psalm CXXVI, 5–6.
43 See above, p. 137.
44* E 487–8; K 428–9. The poem has been associated with Mary Wollstonecraft, but on flimsy grounds.
45 See above, p. 27.

Chapter 12

1 G (1863) 298–9 (*BR* 294).
2 C. R. Leslie, *Memoirs of the Life of John Constable, Esq. R.A.* (1843) p. 123 (*BR* 258).
3* *BSP* 349–50. In his response to commiseration from other artists Blake was robust: 'They pity me, but 'tis they are the just objects of pity: I possess my

visions and peace. They have bartered their birthright for a mess of pottage.' G (1942) 308.

4   A. T. Storey, *The Life of John Linnell* (1892) I 168.
5   These are conveniently relayed in full in *BSP* 368–79.
6   Journal of 18 February 1826 (*BR* 321).
7   From his MS 'Autobiography' (*BR* 257).
8   See above, p. 16.
9   Letter of February 1827, *BSP* 387 (citing '*BR* [2]').
10*   *BR* 566, which also includes his assertion that there were not many pictures in the work-room but a good number in his dark show-room, along with Blake's description of the Thames, seen from the window, as 'like a bar of gold'.
11   G (1942) 313–14 (*BR* 280–1). Blake's glasses are preserved in the Fitzwilliam Museum, Cambridge.
12   BM Add. MS 36520D, quoted *BR* 232.
13   BM Add. MS 36505, quoted *BR* 235.
14   *BR* 294.
15   G (1942) chapter xxxiv.
16   Ibid., chapter xxxiii near end.
17   E 520; K 750.
18   Preface to the last section of *Jerusalem*: E 231; K 716 (previously written as an entry in the Notebook, p. 46: E 812; K 551).
19   See *William Blake's Designs for Edward Young's* Night Thoughts (ed. Erdman, Grant, Rose and Tolley), Oxford, 2 vols., 1980. Cf. Matt IV. 3, Luke IV. 3.
20*   'I always thought that Jesus Christ was a Snubby,' he once wrote, 'or I should not have worshipd him if I had thought he had been one of those long spindle nosed rascals.': E 695; K 555.
21   *BR* 545.
22*   My interpretation has been questioned in detail by John Grant in *BQ* IV, 12–25. Grant makes a commendable demand for precise accuracy in examining detailed evidence but seems less happy with the broader sweep of Blake's vision – as shown in his querying my term 'idiosyncratic' to describe it. I would be surprised if readers of the 'Descriptive Catalogue' and 'Public Address' did not find the word justified, and I maintain my positions.
23   Sir Geoffrey Keynes's description.
24*   Whereas most texts in the margins of the series are from the Book of Job this one is a compound of II Corinthians III 6 and I Corinthians II 14. The texts are identified and tabulated in Andrew Wright's *Blake's Job: A Commentary* (Oxford 1972) pp. 53–64.
25   *BR* 316.
26   On Design no 7, illustrating Canto 4 (E 689; cf. K 785).
27   On Design no. 16: E 668; K 785. For the scabrous language see also above, p. 161.
28   E 668–70; K 786–9.
29   *BR* 38, cited Paley, *PTE* 219.
30   Robinson's diary for 10 December 1825 (*BR* 310).
31   See *BR* 315 and n for an account of the MS.
32   G (1942), chapter xxxiv.
33   A. H. Palmer, *The Life and Letters of Samuel Palmer* (1892) pp. 9–10 (*BR* 291).
34   Letter to George Cumberland, 12 April 1827: E 783–4; K 878–9.

35 From a MS letter of Thomas Woolner to D. G. Rossetti, reproduced *variatim* by Gilchrist. (*BR* 274–5).
36 Letter to Linnell, 1 February 1826. E 775; K 870–1.
37* Recent work has suggested that the exact cause of his death was biliary cirrhosis, perhaps caused by the amount of copper dust he had been forced to inhale: see Lane Robson and Joseph Viscomi, 'Blake's Death': *BQ* XXX 36–48.
38 Frederick Tatham, MS 'Life', c.1832 (*BR* 527–8).
39 See above, pp. 48 and 126.
40 E 758; K 935.
41 E 759; K 854.
42 George Richmond, letter to Samuel Palmer, 15 August 1827, quoted from MS (*BR* 347).
43 See above, p. 196.
44 See above, pp. 155–61.
45 *BR* 316–17.
46 E 138; K 529.

Chapter 13

1* See *BR* 417–18 and nn for the evidence that in spite of pleadings by Edward Calvert 'blocks, plates drawings, and MSS' perished. It is at the same time noticeable how many pieces have survived and passed into later collections.
2 Essay in *Vaterländisches Museum*, January 1811: *BR* 432–455. See also above, p. 225, note 13.
3 HCR's diary for 24 May 1812: *BR* 231.
4 *BSP* 286n.
5 *BSP* 342.
6 *BR* 536, quoting HCR' s 1852 Reminiscences.
7 Letter to Cary, 6 February 1818 *CL* IV 833–4.
8 Ibid., 836–8.
9 See *BSP* 410 and n.
10 'Anon.' (C. A. Tulk?) 'The Inventions of William Blake, Painter and Poet', *London University Magazine* (March 1830).
11 Henry Crabb Robinson, letter of 10 August 1848 (*BRS* 68).
12* MS letter in Huntington Library quoted *BR* 184–5, where it is also noted that Lamb's main source of information was Crabb Robinson, who took him and Mary to see Blake's pictures in 1810 (p. 226) and sometimes recited 'The Tyger' in company (p. 286).
13 E 708; K 779.
14 Diary of 24 June: *BR* 52.
15 Morchard Bishop, *Blake's Hayley* (1951) p. 280.
16 *BR* 424.
17 G (1863) 323–4; *BR* 268.
18 Ibid.
19 Autobiography: *BR* 257.
20 Possibly Tatham: see *BR* 268.
21 E 666; K 784.
22 I Kings VII 8.

23   E 162; K 640 (plate 17.59).
24   Letter of 1830, *BSP* 341.
25   G (1942) 120.
26   E 506; K 644.
27   E 412; K 6.
28   G (1942), ch. xxxiii end. Cf. Proverbs XXVI. 4.
29   *BR* 363.
30   Letters of 25 April: E 728–9; K 823; 6 July 1803: E 730; K 825.
31   Henry Crabb Robinson, Diary, 18 February, 1826: *BSP* 419 (*BR* 322).
32   See above p. 137.
33   E 171; K 649.
34   See his *Enthusiasm* (1950) p. 564, together with the references there and else-
     where
35   E 663; K 772.
36   *BR* 313.
37* W. B. Yeats, *Collected Poems* (1950) p. 240. Although Yeats continues in the
     second part of the poem to muse over the poem's origins, 'a medium', 'noth-
     ing', 'the forest loam', 'dark night where lay I The crowns of Nineveh', it is
     clear that his reading of Blake was paramount.
38   'E. T.' (Jessie Chambers), *D. H. Lawrence A Personal Record* (1935) pp. 62–3.
39   Richard Ellman, *James Joyce* (1986 edn) p. 330, citing *Joyce's Critical Writings*,
     ed. Mason and Ellman (1959) p. 218.
40   T. S. Eliot, *Selected Essays* (1934) p. 321.
41   Ibid.
42   Francis Finch. G (1942) 300 (*BR* 294).
43   T. S. Eliot, *Selected Essays* 1–2.
44   Roethke, *Collected Poems* (1968) p. 74.
45   For a fuller discussion of these points, see Jennijoy LaBelle, *The Echoing Wood
     of Theodore Roethke* (Princeton, NJ, 1976) pp. 54–66, 92–100.
46   *The Time of the Angels* (1966), chapter 1. Cf. E 18; K 210.
47   Saul Bellow, *Herzog* (NY 1964) p. 33. Cf. E 35; K 150.

Select Bibliography

The List of Abbreviations above (p. xiii) acts as a guide to the best texts and guides to Blake's biographical records. *Blake: An Illutrated Quarterly* (formerly the *Blake Newsletter*) publishes many short pieces, particularly of research. Among volumes of essays may be mentioned Geoffrey Keynes's *Blake Studies* (1949), Morton Paley and Michael Phillips's *William Blake: Essays in honour of Sir Geoffrey Keynes* (1973), Phillips's *Interpreting Blake* (Cambridge, 1978), David Erdman and John Grant's *Blake's Visionary Forms Dramatic* (Princeton, NJ, 1970;) Robert Essick and Donald Pearce's *Blake in his Time* (Indiana, 1978) and two by Steve Clark and David Worrall: *Historicizing Blake* (1994) and *Blake in the Nineties* (1999).

Among the many studies of Blake the following offer particularly distinctive views:

Biographies

G. E. Bentley Jr, *The Stranger from Paradise: A Biography of William Blake*, New Haven, Conn., 2001.
A. Gilchrist, *Life of William Blake, 'Pictor Ignotus'* 1863 and 1880; new edn. by Ruthven Todd, 1942.
Mona Wilson, *Life of William Blake* 1927, revised edn. by Geoffrey Keynes, 1948.

General and critical studies

Peter Ackroyd, *Blake*, 1995.
John Beer, *Blake's Humanism*, Manchester, 1968.
John Beer, *Blake's Visionary Universe*, Manchester, 1969.
David Bindman, *Blake as an Artist*, 1977.
Bernard Blackstone, *English Blake*, Cambridge, 1949.
Harold Bloom, *Blake's Apocalypse*, 1963.
Jacob Bronowski, *William Blake: A Man without a Mask*, 1944.
Tristanne Connolly, *William Blake and the Body*, 2003.
Leopold Damrosch, Jr., *Symbol and Truth in Blake's Myth*, Princeton, NJ, 1980.
J. G. Davies, *The Theology of William Blake*, Oxford, 1948.
David Erdman, *Blake, Prophet against Empire* 1969.
Thomas Frosch, *The Awakening of Albion*, Ithaca, NY, 1974.
Northrop Frye, *Fearful Symmetry: A Study of William Blake*, Princeton, NJ, 1947.
Heather Glen, *Vision and Disenchantment: Blake's* Songs *and Wordsworth's* Lyrical Ballads, Cambridge, 1983.

Nelson Hilton, *Literal Imagination: Blake's Vision of Words*, Berkeley, CA, 1983.

Desirée Hirst, *Hidden Riches: Traditional Symbolism from the Renaissance to Blake*, 1964.

Zachary Leader, *Reading Blake's* Songs, 1981.

M. R. Lowery, *Windows of the Morning: A Critical Study of William Blake's 'Poetical Sketches' 1783*, New Haven, Conn., 1940.

Jon Mee, *Dangerous Enthusiasm: William Blake and the Culture of Radicalism in the 1790s*, Oxford, 1992.

Jon Mee, *Romanticism, Enthusiasm, and Regulation: Poetics and the Policing of Culture in the Romantic Period*, Oxford, 2003.

W. J. T. Mitchell, *Blake's Composite Art: A Study of the Illuminated Poetry*, Princeton, NJ, 1978.

Anne Kostelanetz Mellor, *Blake's Human Form Divine*, Berkeley and Los Angeles, 1974.

Peter Otto, *Blake's Critique of Transcendence: Love, Jealousy and the Sublime in* The Four Zoas, Oxford, 2000.

Morton D. Paley, *Energy and the Imagination*, Oxford, 1970.

Morton D. Paley, *The Traveller in the Evening: The Last Works of William Blake*, Oxford, 2003.

M. O. Percival, *Blake's Circle of Destiny*, New York, 1938.

Michael Phillips, *William Blake: The Creation of the* Songs, 2000.

E. P. Thompson, *Witness against the Beast: William Blake and the Moral Law*, New York, 1993.

Joseph Viscomi, *Blake and the Idea of the Book*, Princeton, NJ, 1993.

Index